RONALDO!
KING OF THE WORLD

Wensley Clarkson

RONALDO!
KING OF THE WORLD

BLAKE

Published by Blake Publishing Ltd,
3 Bramber Court, 2 Bramber Road,
London W14 9PB, England

First published in hardback in 2002

ISBN 1 85782 595 0

British Library Cataloguing-in-Publication Data: A catalogue record for this book is available from the British Library.

Design by Envy

Printed and bound in Great Britain by CPD

1 3 5 7 9 10 8 6 4 2

Papers used by Blake Publishing Ltd are natural, recyclable products made from wood grown in sustainable forests. The manufacturing processes conform to the environmental regulations of the country of origin.

GLOSSARY

Atriz -	Actress
Avião -	Airplane
Batucada -	Fans
CBF -	Brazilian Football Federation
Campo -	Pitch
Casa -	House
Chopp -	Draft Beer
Dinheiro -	Money
Drogas -	Drugs
Favela -	Slum
Gringo -	European
Pagode -	Salsa type dance
Puta -	Prostitute
Macumba -	Black Magic
Maria Thuatiras -	Girl soccer groupies
Matar o jogo -	Killing the ball
Morena -	Brunette
Novela das oito -	Soap opera
Pelada -	Street Football
Urubu -	Vulture

A DICTIONARY DEFINITION

CARIOCA (kah-rree-'aw-kah) native of,
pertaining to, Rio de Janeiro.
Nickname given by the Indians
to the first white men
who came to live in Rio de Janeiro.

CONTENTS

INTRODUCTION

In the path of a genius

Reader beware. This is a book about a footballing icon whose life has never been fully exposed before. It may not reveal all of Ronaldo's most secret or outrageous thoughts, but it is the most fascinating account of his life and that bizarre World Cup Final in Korea you are ever likely to read.

Who is the man behind the public face of the world's premier soccer player? Whence comes his love of life's luxuries, his apocalyptic drive? How is it possible for someone from such a humble beginning to cope with being a multi-millionaire while still in his teens?

I first noticed Ronaldo when he sat on the substitutes' bench throughout the World Cup Finals of 1994. As Brazil progressed through the tournament towards their hard-won victory against Italy, there was a very real sense of disappointment that the youngster didn't get a chance properly to show off his tremendous skills. No one knew for sure if he really was that good, but most knew it would only be a matter of time before Ronaldo became a soccer force to be reckoned with.

I later encountered Ronaldo at the nightclub he opened in the Leblon district of Rio just five weeks after those ninety angst-ridden minutes in the final of France '98. I got a feeling for my subject by watching the way he reacted to the enormous crowds. He looked awkward, shy and uncomfortable but there was a steely expression on his face that seemed to be saying, 'Let's get back to business.' Close by, his army of bodyguards, agents, relatives and supposed friends watched his every move.

I consulted many in Rio who knew Ronaldo well. One of them, the world-famous physio, Filé, declared, 'He's at a crossroads. The roller-coaster ride has only just begun.'

For the sake of this book, many agreed to open up old wounds and disclose their true feelings about Ronaldo. I spent many hours interviewing those people, finding out about Ronaldo's strange habits as a child and the truth about his relationship with his troubled parents. Those who helped me expressed a genuine desire to ensure that this book was going to be the only truthful and balanced account of Ronaldo's life and the ups and downs of France '98. They were all convinced that Ronaldo would appreciate that my intentions were to 'get it all right'. Their decision to sanction my efforts above all other coverage of the Ronaldo story deserves my heartfelt thanks. I sincerely hope this book reflects the courage and determination of those individuals who dared to speak out.

Ronaldo's brilliant performances on football fields across the globe were another vital source. They tell so much of his life that they provided the thread I needed to sew the narrative together. Ronaldo's life is his football and his football gives us a glimpse of his life.

When we briefly met in August 1998, Ronaldo carefully chose his words, answering my questions in a calm, collected manner despite the crowds hemming us in. I greatly appreciate that neither he or his two main agents,

Alexandre and Reinaldo, tried to block my efforts to write this book. Although he never came on board officially, he never stood in the way of any of his friends when they agreed to help me. I think the book is better as a result. With their generous contributions, a picture with words has emerged that fully conveys the unique stature of the man. All of it is here — the abject poverty, the escape from the slums, the rise to superstardom, and the mystery of those heartbreaking ninety minutes that changed the face of world soccer.

* * *

Ronaldo is not the first football star in sports history to be treated like an icon. But he is the first to be owned lock, stock and barrel by the sportswear giants, sponsors and — during the past two years — two of the richest football clubs on earth. Screaming adolescent girls and boys mob him everywhere. The Sixties and early Seventies had Pelé; the Eighties had Maradona; the mid-to-late Nineties, apparently, have Ronaldo. Even the Pope blessed Ronaldo before France '98.

The celebrated goal he scored for Barcelona against Compostela on 12 October 1996 was one of his trademarks. For lovers of football, it is one of those moments that will stay in the memory for ever. It was a goal comparable to George Weah's for AC Milan against Verona, or to Maradona's second goal against England in 1986. Ronaldo's goal involved three elements that refuse to submit to existing logic and knowledge of the possibilities of foot and ball. Even after ten replays it's hard to understand exactly what happened.

Having received the ball, Ronaldo broke free of a huddle of players, shrugged off challenges which would have brought down lesser men, and danced his way round five opposition players. Finally, with two defenders flanking him, and apparently losing his footing, he effortlessly caressed the ball past the oncoming keeper and into the net.

That single flash of brilliance lasted just 14 seconds, but it reflects everything that makes Ronaldo special. When he is challenged in a body-check he doesn't drop melodramatically, but simply bumps back. Like a pinball he shoots through the enemy lines. A Brazilian with the granite physique of a German.

That goal was shown thousands of times on TV screens across the globe. So-called experts discussed its merits over and over again. Yet no one ever said they were bored of seeing it. It was virtually a work of art.

There is no simple way to explain this worldwide mania. Perhaps as with all geniuses, the question is best explored from different points of view.

In the past only a handful of players have generated so much attention. Maradona is undoubtedly top of that list. Some have even suggested that Ronaldo is another Maradona. Both were brilliant strikers who worked their way up from the slums; both were discovered, packaged and sold almost like slaves at a frighteningly young age. But there all the similarities end. Maradona had a disturbing self-destruct button both on and off the field. Ronaldo had not, until the final at France '98, seemed to put a foot wrong. But other factors must surely be involved in the Ronaldo appeal.

In general, the surest way for a football player to achieve adulation and visibility beyond the limits of their chosen discipline is to have extraordinary sexual charisma. Youth and an air of danger will, if that artist is lucky, invite comparisons with rock stars or actors. Yet Ronaldo was almost an ugly duckling. He had to be virtually re-built as a teenager so as to become the self-assured, handsome individual he is today. Youth is certainly part of his attraction — he was only 17 when he made his début for Brazil — but there is far more to it than that.

Unlike Shearer, Bergkamp, Del Piero and Vieri, Ronaldo

has achieved his amazing success in a frighteningly short time. In many ways, the disasters of France '98 may well help strengthen his grip on world football because it could yet prove to be a powerful character-building exercise that no amount of training or success can equal.

Yet Ronaldo is the sort of person who, until his skills began to be spotted, would have gone unnoticed in any gathering of more than two people. That is part of his appeal. Ronaldo may be God to tens of millions of soccer fans across the world, but he is also Everyman.

Young fans, in particular, lap up everything he has to offer. Many of them would, no doubt, like to be able to play like him.

Most matches involving Ronaldo are instantly sold out. His performances on video tapes have been bought by millions of people worldwide, even though soccer videos usually only sell to ardent soccer fans and would-be players.

His astonishing success may be at least slightly due to his name. Ronaldo is easy to remember and it sounds inoffensive. Yet, however much Ronaldo may sound like a brand name, his skills definitely have a style all of their own. Michael Owen is probably the only other contemporary whose skills on the field are so instantly recognisable. Despite what his detractors say, there is a great deal more to Ronaldo than diligence, a solid grounding in soccer and a knack for exploiting the wooden legs of opposing defenders. His use of physical strength is actually the most commonly misunderstood aspect of Ronaldo's skills. His average body count is, in fact, no worse than the Shearers and Bergkamps of this world. More importantly, his approach to on-the-field violence is extremely controlled and mature.

His skill lies in coaxing the opposition into thinking they should come and get him. It's almost like the suggestion of gruesome violence in a movie without it actually happening on screen. A true attacking genius, his control of defenders' reactions often conjures up infinitely more terrible scenes of soccer carnage than anything that will actually occur.

Ronaldo's work on and off the ball is all cut — or rather, hacked — from the same cloth. Combining the offbeat, unpredictable skills with an awesome inner strength is the trademark that has helped raise his profile so far so fast.

Then there is the fact that Ronaldo — more so than any other so-called soccer legend — has always had two trusted agents on hand to offer advice and guidance. This gives his career development an added dimension because every transfer is calculated down to the last dollar. Ronaldo has been convinced that moving from club to club is healthy for his career and his bank balance, which is now believed to top the $40 million mark. However, the danger of spending too much time in off-the-field discussions will be examined in depth in this book.

Ronaldo's story in many ways is like the reworking of the storyline from a television drama. The plots and characters are familiar, but the structure of Ronaldo's life and dialogue transcend category. His style is rooted firmly in a world of Nineties business tycoonery that has never truly existed before in world football.

Although this story possesses a distinct blend of comedy, tragedy and violence which hopefully will appeal to both his fans and critics, it is undoubtedly his footballing skills which continue to account for Ronaldo's status as a youth icon. There is a sense of danger in his play. His performances could even be likened to the hit of a banned substance. The highs and lows generate surges of adrenalin in soccer fans and provoke intense debate.

This dangerous element is a crucial part of the Ronaldo myth. What troubles so-called football experts about his skills — his ability to burst into life for just a few minutes of an entire match — is precisely what appeals most to his young fans.

Although, in person, Ronaldo may seem harmless enough, it is the blank-eyed determination of his attacking runs, their callous disregard for defenders, that has rated him the best player in the world. Yet he has tried to remain approachable and exudes the focused charm of one completely aware of his status. It's as if he's saying, 'If I can do it, so can you ...'

'Football reflects the nationality,
it mirrors the nation. Without football,
we Brazilians do not exist –
just as one would not conceive of Spain
without the bullfight ...'

Betty Milan

PROLOGUE

30 June 2002, World Cup Final, Yokohama, Japan

Brazil's World Cup final showdown with Germany was certainly no walk over. It took Ronaldo and his so-called Samba Boys more than an hour to break down Rudi Voller's storm troopers. For the opening half hour it even looked like the unthinkable might happen. Germany, in the shape of Liverpool's Dietmar Hamman and the brilliant Bernd Schneider seemed to have a vice-like grip on midfield and the highly suspect Brazilian defence had to draw a line in the sand to stem the tide.

But everyone in the 63,000 crowd in Yokohama knew that Ronaldo and his team-mates were always capable of unlocking the door at the other end of the pitch in one brilliant instant. After 19 minutes, the redoubtable Ronaldinho, back in the side after his semi-final suspension, sent a defence splitting pass into Ronaldo's path and it seemed as if the reborn maestro couldn't miss. But he managed to push it wide with the outside of his left foot to the stunned astonishment of the crowd.

Then on the half-hour, Ronaldinho flicked the ball over the defence and Ronaldo was in again. This time his control was poor and he got only the faintest of touches which allowed keeper Oliver Kahn to manage an easy save.

The next time a chance came Brazil's way, Ronaldinho made a perfect pass to Kleberson, who dragged his shot wide of the left post. A few minutes later Kleberson hit the bar from 20 yards before Ronaldo spurned another opening.

This time Roberto Carlos drilled a superb cross into the box which struck Ronaldo, came off Germany's Metzelder and arrived back at the superstar's feet. Ronaldo turned and smacked the left-foot shot but it was too straight and Kahn saved superbly with his legs.

On 49 minutes at the other end of the pitch, Brazil's keeper Marcos pulled off an incredible save to keep Brazil level when he pawed a 35-yard freekick by Oliver Neuville onto a post.

Then Ronaldo proved that his comeback was complete. Man mountain German keeper Kahn - who had conceded only one goal in six games - handed Ronaldo a gift that the maestro could not refuse. Ronaldo had made his own luck by hassling Hammann, then winning the ball and setting up Rivaldo to fire in a shot from 20 yards.

Kahn was perfectly in line but as he fell forward to grasp the ball, it span out of his hands and Ronaldo pounced to slot home the goal.

Now Brazil had broken through it seemed that it would be impossible for the big Germans to pull one back. With eleven minutes left, Kleberson went down the right flank, played a low ball in and Rivaldo knew exactly what to do. With Thomas Linke coming in for the challenge, Rivaldo showed the presence of mind to step over the ball knowing that Ronaldo was behind him.

One deft touch with his right foot took Ronaldo away from German sub Gerard Asamoah and the net was within his sights. Kahn had no chance as Ronaldo curled the ball beyond his left hand.

Game, set and match to Ronaldo. Now he truly was back on top of the world.

ACT I

Voodoo Child

'If in your childhood or adolescence
you didn't have a very good life,
I think it makes you fight for your goals
with more determination than a person
who has been born in a golden cradle.'

Clodoaldo, Brazilian 1970 World Cup winner

CHAPTER 1

A Tale of Two Birthdays

18 Sept 1976, Bento Ribeiro, Rio de Janeiro, Brazil

Sonia Barata Nazario De Lima, a pretty, young mother-of-two, hurried out into the humid heat from her tiny one-bedroom shack on the edge of the hillside *favela* to a relative's rusting wreck of a VW Beetle. She was extremely worried. The pains in her stomach indicated that her pregnancy might end prematurely. She wanted to have her baby like all the others she had given birth to. But life never seemed to go smoothly for Sonia. Here she was, pregnant at 25 and feeling deeply insecure about the role her wayward husband Nelio might continue to play in her life. She fully expected him to jump ship at any moment because he seemed incapable of resisting the lure of drink and drugs.

But Sonia was determined to make sure this child was born healthy. She had never forgotten how a local witch doctor invited into the family shack by a relative had predicted that her third child would be a boy who would possess incredible skills that would help Sonia and her loved ones escape the slums for ever. She insists today that he said, 'One day, a boy will come and illuminate your life and make you a millionaire.' At the time she had been dismissive of the black magic session but as she was driven along a bumpy, rocky dirt-track towards the local medical centre, she began once more to hear the witch doctor's words ringing in her ears. It was preferable to the other reminders of her disastrous marriage to handsome Nelio.

To Sonia — ever the daydreamer — the marriage had at first seemed to offer a well-used route to happiness for a woman who had then felt her destiny was to remain permanently on the poverty line.

'I truly fell in love with Nelio. But it was blind love. I was so young I didn't notice the cracks that were there for everyone to see,' says Sonia now. She pauses then adds, 'I guess I should have known better.'

Sonia and Nelio's marriage five years earlier had actually provided nothing more than a brief respite from the drudgery and poverty of life in a slum where electricity for a TV set was considered a higher priority than running water and a plumbing system. Sonia's family saw the marriage as an ideal way to get her off their hands. In their eyes, she was a maternal young girl who had struggled at what little schooling she received. Marriage was the only answer for her survival in the *favela*. In Sonia's eyes, she was a child who always played second fiddle to a bottle of booze or a wrap of dope.

But, as usual, Sonia's happiness was short-lived. Nelio drifted from job to job. Once he even left the family home for six months while trying to get manual work in the Amazon state in the north of Brazil where the wood choppers had gained a vice-like grip on the rainforest regions.

So Sonia worked as a cleaner in a pizza parlour, working gruelling double shifts to try to feed her family. Then both she and Nelio had got a job each at the local telephone company, but she was told she would have to give it up when she became pregnant for a third time. Now the strain of life was threatening to turn that third pregnancy into a disaster.

The day before Sonia went into labour, she cleaned their home from top to bottom. In many ways it had helped her avoid thinking about her desperate situation — often alone, and about to become a mother for the third time when she could barely afford to feed one child on the $30 a week Nelio sometimes provided from his salary.

Her pride had prevented her from asking for money from relatives. In any case, most of them were in just as desperate straits. But nothing was going to faze Sonia. She had already decided she would make it with or without Nelio's help.

As her relative's rusting VW Beetle charged through the crowded streets of Bento Ribeiro, Sonia felt no fear. But then she had no choice.

The São Francisco Javier Medical Centre was only marginally more hygienic than her shack of a home. As she was helped through to the maternity ward, the sheer numbers of other women about to give birth seemed overwhelming. Many of them were screaming and some of them were actually giving birth in the open ward as dozens of others looked on.

Half-an-hour later, Sonia was the one giving birth.

'It's a boy,' announced the doctor, holding up the tiny infant with his mop of black hair. 'What are you going to call him?'

Sonia looked up bleary-eyed, and forced a smile as she looked in the direction of the doctor who had overseen the birth. 'Thank you, doctor. What is your name?'

'Ronaldo,' came the reply.

'Then we will call him Ronaldo in celebration of your skills,' replied Sonia.

The truth was that Sonia had not given the name much thought. She had felt it a bad omen to do so just in case there had been complications.

But, as Sonia lay there recovering from the birth of her son who had weighed in at 3.3 kilograms, she found herself feeling incredibly detached from everything that had just occurred. It was as if those dramatic events had happened to someone else. She was worried about the welfare of her daughter Ione and other son Nelinho (little Nelio) back at their tumble-down home. Would Nelio stay there with them or go out on his frequent drink and dope sessions?

Sonia was determined to raise Ronaldo and the others herself if Nelio continued to let her down. She knew he would never be a really good father.

Nelio had been born in an even poorer slum called Erja and lived there with his family until he married Sonia in 1971. But in the years following the birth of his two older children, Nelio had become increasingly distracted by excessive amounts of alcohol and drugs. At his favourite bar in Bento, called Julio's, they still remember his marathon boozing sessions.

Barman Ronadaldo Pires recalled, 'When Nelio had a few drinks he was the life and soul of the party.' When Nelio was really drunk he'd buy everyone else in the bar a drink and then spend the following few weeks trying to avoid paying the barman what he owed.

When Nelio eventually visited his wife at the medical centre he told her he could not afford to register the birth of Ronaldo even though he was obliged by law to do so immediately. He even paid the doctor's medical fees with coins that he later said he borrowed from friends and relatives. It wasn't until four days later that Nelio scraped together the $10 birth registration fee and, because he wanted to avoid being fined for failing to register it earlier, he declared that his son had been born on 22 September.

But there was nothing unusual about this. More than one million births every year in Brazil are not registered at all.

Ever since, Ronaldo has celebrated two birthdays every year. As far as his family are concerned, it's on

18 September. Officially, it's 22 September.

But back in 1976, Sonia had no time for post-natal depression. She breastfed Ronaldo for many months because it was the natural, cost-effective way. By the time she had left hospital, with the tiny Ronaldo wrapped in a blanket in her arms, she had already worked out a game plan. The child was going to be her inspiration. He would be a success. That witch doctor and his crazy predictions might just turn out to be true.

Soon after the birth, Sonia got another job serving behind the counter of a luncheonette, sometimes working 12-hour shifts for no more than $10 a day. She would leave little Ronaldo in the care of her sister who lived in the same street, Rua General Cesar Obino. Sonia had reluctantly decided that she had to make work her priority if they were to survive financially. She would drop her baby son at her sister's even more dilapidated shack across the dusty pathway from hers, then take the bus into work every morning. Ronaldo would not see his mother again until the early evening.

Not surprisingly, Sonia felt enormous guilt over having to leave her children with relatives while she went out to work. However, she steadfastly refused to rely on husband Nelio for support.

On her return to the family home each evening, Sonia would change nappies, cook supper and then flop in front of the television. She had no spare cash to go out with so she would lap up the corny dialogue and appalling story lines of the Rio soap operas — the *novelas das oito* — that dominate evening viewing.

'It was not a real existence,' explains Sonia today. 'I had few friends. Nelio was out a lot of the time. My life was wrapped around the children and work when I should have been out having a good time with my husband.'

Sonia's addiction to the Rio soap shows was her only release. She would sit and watch them for hours on end. The men seemed so handsome and honourable. Why couldn't she find a man who was the perfect embodiment of these TV characters?

'Ronaldo and his brother Nelio and sister Ione and I all grew up together in a way, perhaps more than most mothers and their children. TV was an escape. I didn't have much else in those days,' says Sonia.

Sonia was engrossed by the Rio soaps because in real life she felt let down by her husband and the world in general. The heroes of cheesy television shows and the countless women's magazines she would constantly flick through provided a welcome escape from the grim reality of life in the *favela*.

Sonia often thought back to the witch doctor who had made those bold predictions about her third child. Maybe the answer to her problems lay in that infant? Certainly when she looked at his beaming face he gave her a feeling of optimism and she believed he might be the key to her happiness.

CHAPTER 2

Sweat and Fear in Bento Ribeiro

Rua General Cesar Obino was like many of the dusty, rock-covered streets of the Rio *favelas*. It had a bar, a primary school and an evangelical church, as well as dozens of rusting, burnt-out old cars. The older women tended to sit in the sun on the steps outside their shanty homes. Children would be constantly kicking footballs around.

The *favelas* sprang up because a fifth of Brazil's population of 160 million people live in what local homeless charities call 'absolute poverty'. In a country where the minimum wage even now is still only $120 a month and the cost of renting an apartment in Rio is $450 a month, it is no surprise that a large percentage of the population ends up in self-built properties about the size of a large garden shed in Britain.

Many of the *favelas* like the one on the edge of Bento Ribeiro were built on to hillsides because, with non-existent plumbing, it allowed waste water to drain away. Many of the kids played football in the *favelas* during the day because there was nothing else they could afford to do. Some didn't even learn to read or write. Their only currency was their footballing skills.

Ronaldo's family would often find themselves looking across to the better parts of Rio and its sprawling suburbs, dreaming of what life must be like with such luxuries as carpet, sanitary systems, cars and, most important of all, money.

Sixteen of Ronaldo's relatives lived at one time or another in or near to the place his family called home. It was a messy plot of land, home to three small shacks. Written in black paint across a strip of wood was the number 114. A paper sign taped to the stone gatepost announced: 'Kites For Sale'.

And when strangers appeared, the boys playing street football would stop kicking and gather round them in the hope of scrounging a coin.

For the first few years of his life, Ronaldo shared a bed with his mother and father. Ronaldo was scared of the dark and would start crying unless the light was left on in the shack's only bedroom. His mother and father would wait until he was fast asleep before climbing in next to him. It wasn't until he reached the age of five that Ronaldo slept on the sofa in the living area with his older brother Nelio.

Meanwhile, father Nelio was just managing to hold on to his job at the local telephone company. It didn't pay much but it was steady and as long as he had it, Sonia believed there was a chance her husband might eventually settle down.

The De Lima home was extremely simply furnished. There was no telephone despite Nelio's employer. No fridge to keep essential foodstuffs, just a cold store and two Calor gas rings. There was only makeshift plumbing, and two electric sockets for a light and a TV set.

When you're born into poverty any toy can provide a vital

means of escape from reality. In the shack where Ronaldo spent his childhood years, he had a teddy bear and little else until his father gave him a plastic football for Christmas. He was four years old when this football bounced into his life and he took to it like a bee to honey.

'I had a poor childhood and I am not ashamed to say it,' said Ronaldo many years later. 'That first football gave me and the other kids the freedom to go off and play on our own. We soon found the space ... and I began to fall in love with the game.'

The space consisted of a rough piece of hillside adjacent to the *favela*. The football never replaced his beloved teddy bear in his bed but it became a comforter in the daytime.

Ronaldo was an awkward, slightly tubby child. His teeth were so prominent that it was often difficult to understand him. He also gave the impression to the other kids that he was a bit slow.

During daylight hours, Ronaldo would frequently kick that plastic ball about on the kids' makeshift pitch on the outskirts of Bento Ribeiro. As the ball bounced awkwardly on the scorched earth amongst the stones and rubble, the young Ronaldo learned his first skills. At first, the other boys hardly ever offered the ball to the heavy-footed four-year-old. He would have to go in and win it through sheer strength. It was that physical aspect of his play that was to make him such a force to be reckoned with in later years.

Soon Ronaldo was rushing off to the pitch at every available moment and drawing a cross on the ground with chalk before challenging other kids to see who could keep the ball up the longest.

According to his mother, Ronaldo became so rapidly immersed in playing football that he often used to talk in his sleep at night, shouting, 'Pass it, pass it, let me score!' and then kicking his legs in the air, much to the amusement of the rest of his family.

Ronaldo's biggest weakness at the time was a fondness for sweets. As Sonia recalls, 'I don't know where he got them from or who gave them to him, but every time he came home he'd have a cake or lollipop in his hand.'

Ronaldo's cousins and his older brother Nelio were an important influence on his life. They often defended him when he was taunted by other kids. He was already nicknamed 'Dadado' from when he was a baby and his sister Ione had difficulty pronouncing his name. Often, Ronaldo would be the last player to be picked for any makeshift soccer side because he looked so uncompromising. Even at that young age, Ronaldo seemed determined to prove them wrong and would race around the field the moment a game started, chasing everything that moved.

* * *

Many years later, Ronaldo became the idol to millions of people worldwide, including many in Britain. Yet it was Britain who had introduced the beautiful game to South America. Seamen had come ashore in ports such as Rio, Buenos Aires and Montevideo, in the late nineteenth century, and kicked a football around in their spare time while unloading ships.

The game rapidly became immensely popular in South America because it required nothing more than a ball. A hundred years later, that was still the reason why football remained the most popular sport in the slums of Bento Ribeiro.

On a typical weekend day, Ronaldo, his cousins and their friends would march over to the barren hillside, pick sides and play for often five or six hours at a time. Before kicking off, they'd clear away the countless shrines and pagan ritual sites that had been left there by the *favela* residents the previous evening. Football for the kids and black magic for the adults seemed the only means of escape from the deprivation.

Like so many of Rio's shanty towns, Bento Ribeiro had a

reputation as a dangerous breeding ground for criminals and drug dealers. Some even reckoned an assassin could be hired for $250 in one of the town's many bars without much effort.

The harsh reality was that the residents of the *favela* didn't care about yesterday because it was irrelevant and they certainly didn't worry about tomorrow because it might never come. Many were drawn to crime or quick thrills like drugs, sex or alcohol. It was a lethal combination.

Even the police, overworked and undermanned, would at best stand by helpless in many instances. Sometimes they even joined in, taking bribes and kick-backs or venting their macho spleens by using street kids, just like Ronaldo and his pals, for target practice.

That Ronaldo did not sink immediately into criminality like so many other young boys in the *favela* was largely thanks to his mother. Sonia was an honest, hard-working woman and it was an unwritten rule in the De Lima household that while no one volunteered to pay any taxes, you should never rob one of your own.

At first Sonia was slow to acknowledge that her son's skills with a football might hold the key to their escape from the slums. She dreamed of a full school education followed by university and a safe, responsible well-paid job for Ronaldo. She believed that the witch doctor's prophecy must have referred to that kind of success.

There was also another reason, as she explained many years later: 'It wasn't that I didn't like football, but I felt it could be a trap. A brother of mine, Pipico, played for Fluminense [a Rio football club] and later in Venezuela and Colombia. Now he can barely keep his head above water.'

Ronaldo's father regularly rowed with his wife about where their son's footballing talents came from. Nelio insisted it was his side of the family, not Sonia's brother, who had provided the inspiration.

'I could have been a pro myself. Bangu, Madureira,

Portuguesa, they all wanted me. But I preferred to play with my friends. And still I play every Saturday,' he recalled many years later.

But Ronaldo had already caught the football bug. At every available moment he would be out in the dusty back yard dribbling, balancing and juggling with the lightweight plastic football. Even his cousins and brother Nelio were starting to realise that Ronaldo's growing obsession with football might actually lead to something.

By the age of five he was no longer the last player to be picked for their makeshift sides. He was so in demand that fights would break out between the kids if they couldn't have Ronaldo on their side. The unlikely-looking kid was also proving to be a brilliant secret weapon against other kids' teams from different neighbourhoods who didn't realise how good Ronaldo was.

At weekends, Ronaldo and his friends began jumping a train into Rio and heading for Copacabana Beach. Thousands of kids regularly made the same trip to play soccer on the sand. The beach always had hundreds of makeshift pitches with games being played. They often played a soccer version of volleyball using the same net.

As Ronaldo's childhood hero, Brazilian star Zico, explained, 'Many of the kids don't have computer games and videos to go home to, so they play football, develop their skills and dream that one day they can escape the poverty and become a famous footballer. For many Brazilians, it's the only way out.'

Rio's beaches had been a breeding ground for young footballers as long as anyone could remember. The uncertainty of the sand meant that players had to learn quickly how to control the ball, both in the air and on the ground. It proved a superb way for the young Ronaldo to improve his skills.

So it was that Ronaldo and his young friends headed, dribbled, volleyed, shot and learned to appreciate the game for all it was worth. Ronaldo also soon realised that he was only ever happy when he had the ball and that meant he needed to get himself into a position to make himself available to receive it again quickly.

In 1982, Ronaldo watched his first World Cup on a tiny black-and-white television in the front room of the family home in Bento Ribeiro. He was just five years old and sobbed when Paolo Rossi scored a hat-trick for Italy which knocked Brazil out of the competition.

Even as a young child, football was *that* important to Ronaldo.

CHAPTER 3

Macumba

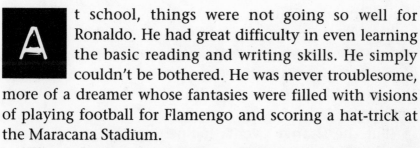

At school, things were not going so well for Ronaldo. He had great difficulty in even learning the basic reading and writing skills. He simply couldn't be bothered. He was never troublesome, more of a dreamer whose fantasies were filled with visions of playing football for Flamengo and scoring a hat-trick at the Maracana Stadium.

Those dreams drove him straight back to the craggy hillside and a game with kids of any age immediately after school. Sometimes he'd even skip school for entire afternoons to join older kids for kick-arounds.

As Sonia later recalled, 'I didn't even want Ronaldo to play football. I tried to stop him but it was his great passion. I couldn't accept the fact that my son thought only of a ball.

'What future could he have? When I started finding him playing *pelada* (street football) when he was supposed to be at school, I knew then I had lost my battle.'

But off the football field, Ronaldo did not exactly cut an impressive figure. His cousin Fabio Shine explains, 'Ronaldo was timid and reserved. He was almost frightened. It sometimes seemed as if the only way he could express himself was when he played football.'

* * *

Black magic — or *macumba* as it is known in Brazil — plays an important part in the lives of many of Rio's poorer residents. Some see it as a means of escape from the appalling poverty while others consider the bizarre world of witch doctors and the occult as an essential religious practice.

In the case of Ronaldo's family, *macumba* wasn't a round-the-clock preoccupation but it definitely played a part in all their lives. Sonia was an extremely superstitious person and, although she was a committed Catholic, her relatives and friends in Bento Ribeiro often involved her in their spiritual activities.

Ronaldo's childhood friend Calango recalled, '*Macumba* was just part of everyday life. There was nothing unusual about it. Superstition is always a preoccupation amongst the poor. They find solace in it. It gives them something of importance in life.'

But the strange events happening inside the family home greatly concerned some of his friends and cousins. Fabio Shine, Ronaldo's cousin, explained, 'Ronaldo's family believed in *macumbo* and stuff like that and they would hold seances and sometimes black magic ceremonies.'

On one occasion, Ronaldo came running out of the family home after 'being completely freaked out' by an occult ceremony being held in the house. There was even talk of chickens being sacrificed. Cousin Fabio added, 'Ronaldo was scared by what he saw but as he grew older he came to accept that his mother and other relatives found it completely normal to believe in witches and stuff like that.

Ronaldo seemed to want and need the protection of his mother all the time. His dad wasn't around that much and he sought out his mum constantly.'

On another occasion, Sonia was seriously burned in an accident at a restaurant where she worked. Her burns were so severe she had to have skin grafts. On her arrival home, some of her relatives asked round a witch doctor to rid the house of the evil spirits which they believed had caused the accident.

Ronaldo was actually known as a bit of a cry-baby by some of his cousins and pals, something that team-mates to this day have witnessed themselves. 'Ronaldo would burst into tears very easily if he didn't get his way or if he was scared,' added Fabio. 'But when he was playing football he seemed to change character and become a real man.'

And football provided the perfect diversion from some of the awful crimes being committed within a stone's throw of that same *favela*.

On one occasion, armed police decided to raid the street where Ronaldo lived. They dragged a bunch of alleged drug dealers into the dusty track and beat them with rifle butts. Then, according to locals, a 16-year-old dealer was dragged away by three officers and taken to the back of a nearby police station where a vat of acid was kept. The officers then took bets on how quickly the teenager would dissolve.

Being a *favela* kid also made you the subject of appalling humiliation. At the nearest McDonald's to Bento Ribeiro, rich kids in expensive cars liked to drive slowly round the car park tossing French fries out of the window and watching the street children scratch and claw each other in a battle to grab the tiny morsels of food.

* * *

Ronaldo doesn't actually remember the scoreline of the first competitive football match he was taken to by his father — but he never forgot the atmosphere because it was at the Maracana Stadium in Rio, which, to this day, still holds the world record attendance of 199,584 people at a match.

Ronaldo and Nelio were there to watch what promised to be a ferocious local derby between home side Flamengo and Vasco. Father and son struggled through the congested Rio streets after taking a train and then two buses to reach the largest soccer stadium in the world.

It might have been huge but it was more like a dilapidated dinosaur than a 1980s sports complex. The first thing that struck the young Ronaldo was that it was such a rusting mess; just a huge expanse of concrete with a roof on it. In fact, it had seemed far more impressive from a distance; the scale provided by the surrounding buildings and dockyards placed it in its correct jaw-dropping perspective. Then there were the foot-long hotdogs for sale at dozens of rusty sidewalk stands.

The Maracana was built for the 1950 World Cup and from that moment on it was plagued with unfortunate mishaps. In only the second game at the stadium, a Yugoslav player called Mitic slipped and cut his head on an exposed girder.

The infamous 199,584 attendance was claimed for the 1950 World Cup Final between Brazil and Uruguay. In 1969, 183,341 turned out to watch Brazil play Paraguay in a World Cup preliminary match.

The young Ronaldo never forgot some of the bizarre features of the stadium, like the twin tunnels (one for each team) and a dry moat deep enough to stop any foolhardy pitch invader.

Nelio even allowed Ronaldo to take along a drum that he beat incessantly throughout the match. His father swigged from a bottle of *chopp* (beer) as they both shouted insults that ranged from disparaging remarks about the referee's mother to the ability of the opposition's goalkeeper. Throughout all this, father and son chanted

Flamengo's name at the tops of their voices.

That match at the Maracana also marked the beginning of Ronaldo's obsession with the man who was then hailed as the finest player in the world — Zico. Father and son watched Zico lead Flamengo to victory over Vasco da Gama. Years later, Ronaldo said, 'Zico was incredible. Magic. He was that good.'

As he recalled, 'All kids have their heroes and Zico was mine. For me, he is still the greatest. Everything that he did I've tried to copy. Everything he did on the field was incredible.

'He had so much ability. Of course, I looked at parts of his game and tried to copy them. But I came to realise I could only be myself.'

When the 1986 World Cup Finals were played in Mexico, Ronaldo was once again glued to the TV set throughout. Unfortunately Zico missed a penalty against France that cost Brazil their challenge for the World Cup. Ronaldo replays that scene over and over to this very day. He remains convinced that Zico was the greatest player ever to wear a Brazilian shirt but he can also still picture every moment of that heartbreaking penalty miss.

The World Cup represented a welcome diversion from the misery and deprivation of life in Bento Ribeiro. For a few weeks, the only thing that mattered was the glory of the nation's footballers.

In 1986, the then nine-year-old Ronaldo shed buckets of tears when his childhood hero Zico missed that penalty. As Ronaldo later explained, 'In 1986, we had the best team again but we lost on penalties to France. I cried with an intensity I have only experienced since with the death of Ayrton Senna.'

Shortly after the 1986 World Cup Finals, Ronaldo joined Valqueire, a local boys' team. He was nine years old, with protruding teeth and painfully shy on a conversational level, but dazzling once he got on a football pitch. Ronaldo and his friends from the *favela* decided they would all apply together for the Valqueire under-10s team. But he left home too late and only arrived when the club trial was almost finished. They would only agree to use him as the team goalkeeper, a position no *favela* kid would ever seriously consider.

But Ronaldo didn't mind just so long as he got to play football. It had already become his religion. It meant everything to him. In spite of the poverty and struggles that he experienced with his family, football made him happy and content. Even Sonia started to listen to her other son Nelio's prophecy that Ronaldo would one day be a footballing star.

Ronaldo's coach at Valqueire, Fernando dos Santos, moved him out of goal after an injury crisis. He did so well as a striker he never played in goal again.

However, at school Ronaldo was starting to play truant so much that Sonia was having to walk him to school and wait by the gates for at least an hour each morning to make sure her wayward son did not try to leave the premises.

Ronaldo simply changed tactics; he waited until the first school break and then he would disappear, usually to the nearest makeshift football pitch. On a number of occasions, he'd even spot his mother and dash through a back gate to avoid being caught.

And when Ronaldo actually did attend classes, he continued to daydream about playing for the one of the big professional clubs, and drew pictures of footballers. He genuinely felt a sense of predestiny about his life. He said later, 'I felt that football was my natural profession, my role in life: to play football and entertain others.'

(Many years later, Ronaldo was asked if that comment stood comparison with the classic Roberto Baggio remark when he compared himself to Michelangelo and Leonardo da Vinci. Ronaldo replied, 'With who? I never heard of them.')

Like many of his friends, Ronaldo's physical

development started at an incredibly early age. At ten he had strong muscular legs from the many hours of football practice he had put in each week. He also had a powerful torso for one so young. It not only helped him score goals during matches but also made him appear older than his age. But as a shy, awkward, ordinary-looking child it was quite a surprise that Ronaldo kissed his first girl at such an early age. As he said many years later with almost no regard for the implications, 'I didn't use my tongue or anything. It was just a mouth-to-mouth kind of thing. But it was definitely a real kiss.'

Much more worryingly, drugs were already being used by some of ten-year-old Ronaldo's friends and acquaintances. Crack was the drug of choice amongst the young in the *favelas* and that often led to children offering their bodies in exchange for narcotics. Football really was the only healthy alternative.

In 1988, at the age of 11, Ronaldo joined another local team, the Social Ramos Club, which only played indoor football. The club coach Alirio Jose de Carvalho insists he was 'just an average player'. But he did concede, 'What was special about Ronaldo was his attitude. It was as if he came from the moon. Nothing bothered him, nobody could impress him.'

Ronaldo soon led the city youth league in scoring and in one memorable game against Clube Municipal scored 11 of his team's 12 goals. In all, he scored 166 goals that season.

Football also provided an escape from Ronaldo's problems at home. His parents split up when he was 11 years old but he tried his hardest to detach himself from the trauma by throwing himself into playing the beautiful game. But the reality always hit when he got home in the evenings and his father was nowhere to be found.

* * *

Just after his 13th birthday, Ronaldo was asked to attend a trial at the world-famous club, Flamengo. It was a dream come true for Ronaldo because this was the club he wanted to play for more than any other.

Flamengo was the most popular club in the country, and therefore South America. Flamengo's mascot was the *urubu*, a type of scraggy black vulture that could be seen circling over the *favelas* at virtually all times of the day.

As it would take almost an hour each way to travel to Flamengo, Ronaldo's family asked the club to pay his bus fare if he passed the trial. The club refused and Ronaldo was rejected and sent home. He was heartbroken. He later said, 'It was the worst day of my life. I cannot remember ever feeling so upset.'

In many ways, Ronaldo blamed his father for his rejection by Flamengo because he believed that if his parents had stayed together maybe they would have found the money to be able to afford the bus fare.

Sonia recalled years later how the teenager had rushed home in tears. 'The problem was money. We just couldn't afford to pay the bus fare. He was so sad.'

And even Ronaldo still rates Flamengo's rejection as the biggest disappointment of his entire life, including the World Cup Final at France '98.

But there was another reason for his tears when he eventually got home. As he waited to hop on a bus without paying the fare, two youths approached him and stole his $20 watch before giving him a beating. It really was the worst day of his life.

For a few weeks following his rejection by Flamengo, Ronaldo seriously considered giving up his chosen path. But his continued failure at school combined with his desperation to escape the *favela* drove him to practise his footballing skills with even more fervour.

Shortly afterwards, he went for a trial at the São Cristovão club which was much closer to home. He'd been recommended by Social Ramos coach Alirio and some of

Ronaldo's friends — Alexandre Calango, Ze Carlos and Alirio's own son Leonardo. They all remembered Ronaldo because his football boots had holes in them.

The following World Cup in 1990 in Italy proved just as stressful for the then 13-year-old Ronaldo. He was still living in Bento Ribeiro and, as usual, the entire nation was gripped by football fever. Even the *favelas* were festooned with yellow and green flags.

Ronaldo, his cousin and a handful of friends chose the house in the street with the biggest TV set to watch Brazil's decisive match against arch-rivals Argentina. They bought in sodas and a vast supply of French fries.

Brazil were strongly favoured to win that year but despite dominating the game, they failed dismally to win. Ronaldo burst into tears as the final whistle was blown and the boys wandered home in a depressed daze. In Brazilian terms, it was a national disaster.

Around this time, Ronaldo's father Nelio tried to re-ignite his relationship with his estranged son. He had woken up to the fact that Ronaldo was on the verge of immense footballing success. With small, thin legs it was difficult to imagine them being father and son. Nelio has always, typically, attributed this to the fact that 'Ronaldo had a better childhood than I did.'

But Nelio was a wily, shrewd man despite his drug and drink problems and he tried his hardest to pass those characteristics on to his son.

Today, he insists he taught Ronaldo the importance of mental strength. It was this determination, some say, that made Nelio attach himself to Ronaldo's career even before he reached his 14th birthday in September 1990, for reasons that will become crystal clear.

ACT II

The Good, the Bad and the Ugly

'As a footballer I wasn't even his shadow. At the most, he inherited my passion for soccer. His class? No – that's the divine gift.'

Nelio, father of Ronaldo

CHAPTER 4

Circling Urubus

São Cristovão was a club steeped in tradition which had once threatened the domination of such giants as Flamengo, Vasco da Gama, Fluminense and Botafogo. But that was in 1926 and they hadn't done much since.

In fact, São Cristovão's decline ran in parallel to the downward spiral of the neighbourhood in which it was located. It had become a club of the poor for the poor, kept alive by love and the favours of businessman or small-time sponsors. The entrance still had a classic old plaque bearing the legend, 'São Cristovão Football Club'. Beside it was the club's equally beautiful black-and-white coat of arms.

Graffiti-covered cement stairs led past the canteen up to the trophy room. The entire place had not been given an overhaul since those far off days between the two world wars.

At São Cristovão there was no sauna, bubble bath or fitness room. The showers produced water that consisted of a brown drip. The best-kept object in the changing rooms was the statue of the Virgin Mary.

On 12 August 1990, Ronaldo played his first match for São Cristovão. He scored three times against Tomazinho in a 5-2 victory, but coach Ary Ferreira de Sa was not overly impressed with the 13-year-old.

'He was so wooden, so inelegant. He and the ball stumbled through everything, by luck it seemed. Calango, who was playing next to him up front, pleased me more.'

But Ronaldo kept scoring more and more goals. And Ary pandered to the youngster to keep him happy. He gave him shoes, food, bus tickets, often paid out of his own pocket or from the club till. It soon became clear that Ronaldo's parents were not capable of paying for anything.

Once, Ronaldo literally begged Ary for a pair of Nike boots. The coach shook his head slowly and told his star player, 'Oh shit, Ronaldo. I cannot even get my son a pair.'

But Ronaldo would not give up and for the following month he kept asking the coach if he would get him a free pair of Nikes.

'It was typical of Ronaldo to be pushy about things like boots,' says Ari today. 'At one stage, he even started insisting that I should get one pair for him and one for his friend Calango.'

In the end, one of the club directors bought one pair and the two strikers wore them for alternate matches.

At São Cristovão, Ronaldo also earned himself a new nickname — 'Monica' — after a Brazilian cartoon character with big teeth. 'Monica was a strong little bitch with a cast-iron attitude,' recalls Ary. 'That was Ronaldo down to a tee.'

Unfortunately, Ronaldo soon gained a reputation as a 'bit of a scrounger' amongst the coaching staff at the club.

'He was always asking for something, always rubbing his fingers together. Lunch money, boot money anything,' said one of the club trainers. 'He would ask anyone; other kids, directors, even the supporters. He had no money and he saw it as his duty to scrounge from others.'

During training, Ronaldo would try and pull every trick in the book to avoid any strenuous exercise. One day when the team was at the club training field, Ronaldo hid behind a tree so as to avoid some circuit training.

However, his coaches at the São Cristovão did not appreciate that Ronaldo's reluctance to train was partly caused by extreme breathing problems that had dogged him throughout his life. Unusually, he breathed in and out through his mouth. As one orthopaedic specialist pointed out, 'This is the worst way to breathe. This creates problems of oxygen supplies to the brain and to the muscles. Breathing through the nose means air is filtered and goes in greater quantities to the lungs which will enhance the performance of the body.'

But all Ronaldo's offbeat behaviour was soon forgotten when he got out on the football field. In one juniors game against Flamengo, Ronaldo received the ball by the touchline. He dribbled past six players as he strode infield and then scored the perfect goal from 15 yards. It all happened in nine incredible seconds.

Ronaldo learnt a lot about the footballing facts of life when he played for São Cristovão. For although it might seem that Brazil would be the last place in the world that lacked attacking football, the domestic game at all levels had suffered from negative tactics for years.

The tactic of *matar o jogo* (killing the play), whereby as soon as possession is lost one player commits a foul to allow his team-mates to regroup, was commonplace. Other more sophisticated spoiling approaches included different players on the same team taking it in turns to foul the other team's most dangerous player, thus reducing the risk of a man-marker being sent off.

It was in this kind of atmosphere that Ronaldo thrived. Not to mention the eccentric disciplinary rules that meant if a player accumulated three yellow cards it meant an immediate suspension while a red card required a trip to the disciplinary tribunal which frequently resulted in a let-off or a postponement of the suspension.

* * *

No defender in the world, not even Bobby Moore, succeeded in taming Brazil's 1970 World Cup winner Jairzinho for an entire match. He scored in every single game for Brazil's victorious, legendary 1970 World Cup winners. But many believe that even that statistic failed to do justice to the brilliance of his skills as a provider as well as a predator. So it was hardly surprising that more than 20 years on he'd become a talent spotter searching out the stars of Brazil's footballing future, mainly in Rio's *favelas*.

In many ways, the Jairzinho of yesterday greatly resembled the Ronaldo of today; photographs of a shirtless Jairzinho at Brazil's 1970 training camp reveal a heavily muscled upper body with powerfully built legs to match. In sprinting tests he had been by far the quickest man in the squad over 50 metres.

In 1990, Jairzinho had showed an even faster turn of mind after the then 13-year-old Ronaldo moved from Ramos Social Club to São Cristovão, where Jairzinho occasionally helped out with training some of the junior sides.

Having watched Ronaldo on only two occasions, before the end of the second game Jairzinho was on the phone to two young ex-bankers who were making moves into the world of football as agents. Alexandre Martins and Reinaldo Pitta responded immediately to the veteran's suggestion and went to see the young Ronaldo play at São Cristovão.

The two agents were riveted as they watched the 13-year-old score five goals in his side's 9–1 victory. They might have just quit the Rio money exchange market but didn't need to know much about football to recognise Ronaldo's potential.

'We knew right away that he could be something

different from most other players,' Pitta later recalled.

Martins and Pitta's vision on seeing Ronaldo spelt millions of dollar signs. It was going to be more lucrative than anything they'd ever been involved in before.

Not long afterwards, the two men made an initial approach to Ronaldo through his father Nelio. They proposed purchasing Ronaldo's playing pass for just $7,000 from São Cristovão plus a nominal fee to Nelio. The hard-up club reluctantly sold their most valuable asset for less money than it cost to buy a new car. Nelio was delighted. Agents Pitta and Martins immediately suggested that Ronaldo leave school to concentrate on football full-time. He was just 14 years old.

Martins and Pitta looked like two successful bankers trying to be casual. They wore well-pressed jeans with Armani jackets and only put on their $1,000 suits when they wanted to talk serious business. They immediately signed Ronaldo to a ten-year contract that was virtually unbreakable thanks to a penalty clause worth millions of dollars. In the contract, Ronaldo was obliged to pay the two agents 10 per cent of any contract he signed during that ten-year period even if they had no involvement with the negotiations. The deal also clearly stated that the two agents would add all expenses to their commission on Ronaldo's earnings.

One clause in the contract even specified that the two agents had the right to 'manipulate how they saw fit the public image and private image of Ronaldo, his name and his nickname, to even have a share of any photos of the star or any other means of promoting him'. The contract also guaranteed that Ronaldo would not sign any agreements without first the prior authorisation of the two agents. If he did so, he would face huge fines of many hundreds of thousand of dollars.

'In basic terms, they had just bought the rights to Ronaldo, the man,' explained one sports agent. 'He virtually couldn't breathe without their approval.'

But the most disturbing aspect of this deal was that Ronaldo had to allow his father to sign the contract for him because he was still under the age of legal consent. Neither Ronaldo nor his father had apparently turned to anyone for advice.

Martins and Pitta shrewdly decided not to sell Ronaldo off immediately to the highest bidder as many had presumed. Instead, they sat back and let the young player's skills and transfer value grow as he scored more and more goals.

Their gamble paid off brilliantly when, in February 1993, Ronaldo earned a call-up to Brazil's Under-17 side for the South America Championships in Colombia. Ronaldo was one of the stars of the tournament and finished as leading scorer with eight goals. Word of the so-called phenomenon was spreading fast. Agents Martins and Pitta sat back and watched the meter clock up the dollars. They knew they were sitting on a fortune.

Meanwhile, talent scout Jairzinho was complaining that he'd got nothing for discovering the kid who would go on to become the most famous footballer the world has ever known. In fact, out of $7,000 there wasn't much to spread around and agents Pitta and Martins promised Jairzinho his pay day would come if their master plan for Ronaldo came true.

It seemed that, already, the *urubus* were circling for their piece of the cake.

CHAPTER 5

Escape from the Favela

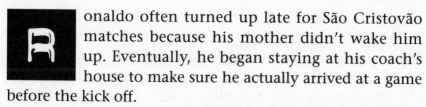

Ronaldo often turned up late for São Cristovão matches because his mother didn't wake him up. Eventually, he began staying at his coach's house to make sure he actually arrived at a game before the kick off.

Coach Ary insists that Ronaldo's father Nelio hardly ever showed up at matches to watch his son, unlike most parents. But what Ronaldo didn't tell his coach at the time was that Nelio and Sonia were going through an extremely acrimonious divorce. Ronaldo was actually relieved his father did not show up at the ground because he wanted to escape from the constant reminders of his troubled family home.

As Ary pointed out, 'His father never showed himself here much. In all the time Ronaldo played for us, I saw his father two, three times. It sounds harsh, but the biggest blessing in his career was his parents' divorce.'

In fact, signing that contract with agents Pitta and Martins had caused more problems between father and son because the rest of Ronaldo's relatives, especially his mother, felt that they were in some way being tricked. That air of suspicion rubbed off on Ronaldo and the relationship between father and son once again became strained. It was only the intervention of Pitta and Martins that helped convince Ronaldo and the rest of his family that everything was above board.

Ronaldo's best friend at São Cristovão was Calango, his childhood buddy from Bento Ribeiro. The two came from very similar backgrounds — even their parents divorced under the same circumstances — and their relationship was sealed when they played as a striking partnership for the lowly second division club.

It was with Calango that Ronaldo first climbed the steps to the giant statue of Christ which looks out over Rio. They made that trip together in the *teleferique* (cable car) to the Sugar Mountain. During such journeys the two teenagers talked about everything from football to their unhappy families.

'We shared many secrets and learned to understand each other very well. It probably even helped on the football field as well as in life,' says Calango today.

At São Cristovão, Ronaldo had quite a reputation as being a lazy player. Leonardo, another team-mate, recalls, 'He would never run to win the ball. He's still like that.'

Coaching staff at the club also never forgot how Ronaldo was always the first player in the queue for second helpings of food. 'When we had breakfast at the club, every player was given half a loaf of bread and cheese. When we asked if anybody wanted seconds Ronaldo was always the first one to stick his hand up; and if there were thirds he'd be straight up for more bread and cheese — I don't know where he used to put it all.'

* * *

But the infamous *urubus* were nowhere to be seen when

Ronaldo and his best friend Calango dived into the deep blue Atlantic ocean to try out two surfboards they'd been lent by some friends. Ronaldo and his friend had made the long journey to Copacabana Beach to meet one of the São Cristovão coaches who'd offered to give them extra training one Saturday morning.

After a gruelling two-hour session they decided to cool off with a swim amid the 12-foot waves that were crashing down on the golden sands.

Within minutes, they got into trouble. Calango takes up the story: 'It was incredibly rough but we still paddled out into the middle of the waves. Suddenly, a huge wave was coming towards us.

'I shouted to Ronaldo to watch out and told him to duck because that was the best way to deal with big waves. But before I could turn it was on us.

'We were both swept under by the wave. I tried desperately to get to the surface but the wave was so big it was impossible to reach.

'I drifted down through the water and then I felt Ronaldo's leg crashing into me. We were being thrown in all directions. I thought we were going to die. It seemed to go on for so long.

'Then I found myself flung up against Ronaldo's body. We clung to each other. Suddenly, we were thrown on to the beach and the wave subsided. It was a terrifying experience. We just lay there on the beach holding on to each other with fear and relief.

'We both agreed that day that God was looking down on us, protecting us. It was truly a miracle.'

As bright, streetwise, if relatively poorly-educated street kids, Ronaldo and his best friend Calango should have been reasonably successful at picking up girls, but Ronaldo definitely suffered because of his very ordinary appearance and natural shyness.

Calango confirmed, 'At parties, he always ended up

talking football. He just couldn't find a girl. They just weren't interested.'

Ronaldo was deeply hurt at his apparent rejection by many girls in the neighbourhood. He might have kissed a girl at ten but not much had happened since in that department. It moulded his attitude towards women in later life, as did the way his father treated his mother.

Calango even recalled that Ronaldo was so hopeless with girls, many of their friends used to tease him about being gay.

He explained, 'Ronaldo was upset at first but then he developed this brilliant routine impersonating homosexuals. I suppose it was his defence mechanism but some of the kids who didn't know him so well started to think he really was gay at one stage. He had this gentle, lispy voice and that made everyone even more convinced.'

* * *

According to Queen Victoria, when losing one's virginity one must close one's eyes and think of England. Attaching a little more lyricism to the act, the great romantics, from Cervantes to Byron, saw virgins as roses and their deflowering as a poem to passions that would saddle lions.

Ronaldo's first real taste of romance — not necessarily an act of overt passion, but certainly an important point in his romantic development — finally came when he encountered a feisty 15-year-old neighbour called Kelly Christina Peres. And, by all accounts, he was the romantic one in the relationship.

Kelly dropped Ronaldo after a handful of dates 'because he was too ugly'. She added, 'We were very good friends but it didn't work out because of his looks.' It was a cruel rebuttal for Ronaldo, one which he would not forget for a very long time.

Ronaldo had wooed Kelly by stealing fruit from the trees of houses neighbouring his home and presenting them in baskets as gifts for the pretty, young, dark-haired schoolgirl. She insists today, 'He wanted to please me in any way. It was very sweet of him but I wasn't so keen when he became much more explicit about what he wanted.'

Kelly says that at one stage Ronaldo promised to buy her a Ford Escort car 'when I make it as a footballer'. She is still waiting for the vehicle to show up.

But Kelly did admit that Ronaldo is now a changed man. 'He's not ugly any more. He is so much more handsome today. He is athletic and he has real style. If only he'd been like that when I knew him.'

But Ronaldo was a very different person back in 1991.

At São Cristovão, Ronaldo continued his remarkable scoring record. But other aspects of his game were still far from perfect.

São Cristovão coach Alfredo Sampaio explained, 'Ronaldo was very popular with his team-mates. He was always chatting and laughing. Even as a kid, he was a natural athlete, but he was never interested in tactics — he was only interested in getting hold of the ball and scoring. His only weakness was heading and his total disinterest in defending. He was obsessed with scoring spectacular goals. I used to say to him, "The tap-ins are as important as the blockbusters."'

Ronaldo scored 36 goals in 54 games for São Cristovão. And coach Sampaio added, 'When things were going badly for the team, I always shouted to my lads to give the ball to Ronaldo. He did the rest.'

As far as the club was concerned, Ronaldo was a good kid from a problem family and they reckoned the $7,000 sellout deal was a fair reflection of what they considered remained a big risk. His mother was still having to work at a snack bar to make ends meet and father Nelio had long since moved out of the marital home.

The club eventually rewarded Ronaldo by moving his mother, brother and sister into a small house nearer the club ground. It was nothing special but a vast improvement on the *favelas*. To Sonia it was a palace and she at last started to realise that if her son's true potential was realised, their lives were on the verge of changing for ever.

Meanwhile, Nelio was claiming that he'd been fired from his job at the telephone company for taking too much time off work to watch his son play football. Sonia countered this by insisting that she would get up at five or six in the morning to make sure her son was up in time to play in an important club fixture.

The following month, First Division side Cruzeiro moved in and signed Ronaldo for $30,000 giving his 'owners' — agents Martins and Pitta — an instant return on their investment since they had bought out Ronaldo for that $7,000 from São Cristovão. Ronaldo was so delighted to be entering the big-time that he told his mother to stop work immediately. He was going to be the main breadwinner from now on.

Ronaldo made his first-team début for Cruzeiro on 25 May 1993, aged 16. Coach Pinheiro was impressed.

'He dribbled with incredible ease, gave inch-perfect passes and he scored goals that only a genius can score.'

But some people at the club accused Pinheiro of playing Ronaldo too soon and therefore risking burning him out at an early age. He ignored their comments on the basis that he desperately needed anyone who could score goals.

And Ronaldo's move to Cruzeiro made him the heart-throb to a lot of the club's extremely young female fans. Soon he'd fallen head over heals in love for the first time, with a 16-year-old brunette called Luciana. She dated Ronaldo for at least six months and tried her hardest to please his mother.

Ronaldo eventually dropped Luciana after Sonia told her son he could do much better. And when Sonia spoke, her son listened. Ronaldo's confidence had grown enormously and he became obsessed with going out with girls. He was always on the lookout and started to become particularly interested in girls with blonde hair.

'They were — and still are — the ultimate status symbol for a young footballer or any guy who escapes the *favelas* for that matter,' explained Ronaldo's old friend Calango. 'A male *Carioca*'s dream woman has blonde hair, small tits and a big ass. It's the personification of white and black combined. The girls know it and the boys want it.'

Ronaldo proved a huge hit for Cruzeiro in the Brazilian National Championships, scoring 49 goals in his first 50 professional games, including a record five in one match. Club coaches were delighted with his form but constantly lived in fear that the well-built youngster might turn to fat because of his continual craving for hamburgers, sweets and ice cream.

As one club coach recalled, 'Ronaldo ate his way to the top, you could say.'

In the autumn of 1993, Ronaldo made the biggest decision of his short life and moved into an apartment on his own in Belo Horizonte. He felt it was time he tried to cope without his mother always watching out for him. Sonia was distraught about her 17-year-old son's decision as she felt he needed the security of a family home to keep his feet on the ground.

It didn't take Ronaldo long to move in as he only had one suitcase! On his first day at the apartment, Ronaldo turned up alone at a local restaurant and complained to one of the waiters that he didn't have any plates or cutlery in the apartment. The restaurant manager took pity on the teenager and gave Ronaldo an entire dinner service.

Ronaldo's eventual total goal tally for Cruzeiro was 58 in 60 games. The Rio press corps had taken him to their hearts and he featured in the sports pages virtually every day. So it was no great surprise when, at the age of just 17, he was called up to the full Brazilian national team squad.

Ronaldo made his début against Argentina on 23 March 1994, aged just seventeen years, six months and one day. He came on for the last ten minutes as a substitute for Bebeto. It was a quiet performance and no one seriously expected him to light up the pitch on his début, but a couple of glancing runs created enough havoc among the Argentinians to give a good indication of what was to come.

On 6 April 1994, Ronaldo sparked even more media attention by scoring a wonder goal for Cruzeiro against Maradona's old club Boca Juniors, when he took the ball all the way from the half-way line and beat an entire defence to score.

Less than a month later, Ronaldo made his second international appearance and turned in a superb performance, including a goal against Iceland, and booked himself a place in Brazil's squad for the 1994 World Cup finals in America. Veteran coach Mario Zagallo, who was on Brazil's backroom staff, liked what he saw. He even told one startled reporter, 'Pay attention to this kid. He's going to be the next Pelé.'

On the personal front, another girl entered and then swiftly exited Ronaldo's life after Sonia stepped in to vet her suitability. Significantly, she was a blonde with all the assets any self-respecting *Carioca* would appreciate. This particular beautiful blonde was called Katia. Unfortunately, her love for Ronaldo led to her letting slip to a Brazilian TV programme during the World Cup '94 that she was Ronaldo's latest squeeze.

Sonia was furious and quickly ended the romance. She proudly explained later, 'This girl was always calling up Ronaldo but I wouldn't let him come to the phone. He didn't even know I was doing this because I didn't tell him she was calling. I don't regret it for a minute.'

Sonia had some very clear ideas as to what qualities a future Mrs Ronaldo should have. She explained, 'Well, for one thing she has got to be with him day in day out. She's got to go with him on all his trips and she must not complain about being lonely.'

Ronaldo tended to stand by and listen to his mother's advice. She would often glance back at him as if to say, 'Please take note ...'

CHAPTER 6

Butch Nike and the Sundance Kid

The 1994 World Cup Finals in the USA proved a complete anti-climax for Ronaldo. In Brazil, he had been hailed as a brilliant, potent force in world football, but coach Carlos Alberto Perreira and his assistant Mario Zagallo decided to keep him on the substitutes' bench throughout the competition because they felt he was too young at 17 to cope with the pressure.

But Ronaldo still attracted a great deal of attention in the USA even though he didn't play. Many questions were asked in the Brazilian media as to why he never the made the first eleven. One report claimed that Ronaldo was so nervous about playing that team coach Perreira felt he wouldn't be able to cope. One Brazilian reporter who attended the finals said, 'Ronaldo was terrified. Here he was, this young kid still aged 17. There were times when he was on the bench and you could see the tears of fear welling up in his eyes. They might have wanted to play him for tactical reasons but the reality was that it would have been a disaster.'

Little Romario proved to be the man of the moment when he secured Brazil's first World Cup victory for 24 years. The rich, flamboyant traditions of the most exciting and entertaining football nation on earth were not exactly in abundance as Brazil re-established their place at the pinnacle of the world game after winning a penalty shoot-out against Italy at the Pasedena Rose Bowl, in California. Many back home in Brazil complained bitterly that they were the dullest Brazilian victors ever.

Ronaldo later claimed he felt he should have got a chance to play, although he fully respected the wisdom of the Brazilian coaching staff on the basis that he would take even greater pleasure from winning the World Cup in France in 1998.

Brazilian TV reporter Pedro Bial covered the tournament and spent many evenings out drinking and eating with the Brazilian squad, including the teenage Ronaldo.

He recalled, 'Ronaldo was extremely childish in those days. My lasting memory is of him eating hamburgers and looking at every pretty girl who walked by.'

Bial particularly remembered that Ronaldo 'enjoyed getting journalists to buy him drinks and food. He never put his hand in his pocket. He was always after something; a cheeseburger here, a beer there.

'Ronaldo had little to say in those days. He was careful with his words, even then. But it was clear that his development was part of a carefully devised master plan by his agents.'

But Ronaldo did fall in love with America. 'He was fascinated by America and the whole idea of fame,' Bial added.

Ronaldo liked the way that Americans never hassled him for autographs because they didn't really have a clue who he was.

At the World Cup Final that year, Ronaldo's agents

made contact with executives from the sportswear giant Nike, who were very anxious to make inroads into the lucrative world football market. They were soon talking about getting Ronaldo a multi-million dollar sponsorship deal. Pitta and Martins also indirectly helped introduce Nike to the Brazilian national team president Ricardo Teixeira.

On his return to Rio, Ronaldo discovered that numerous *Maria Thuatiras* — soccer groupies — were beginning to take a keen interest in him. To a frisky 17-year-old, it must have seemed like a dream come true, especially after years of feeling so insignificant.

Pitta and Martins also took note of the female interest in their client and decided that if they could turn Ronaldo into a sex symbol as well as a world force in football, then they would have a very lucrative combination on their hands.

But Ronaldo's hair was tufty and unkempt and he tended to look untidy and awkward. He had, however, at least stopped wearing cheap watches, despite that experience when he was robbed when he was younger.

Ronaldo's agents decided to encourage Sonia to persuade Ronaldo to have his teeth fixed so they wouldn't stick out so much. They actually committed $5,000 to have his teeth done.

It was a deliberate corporate policy on the part of the agents who knew that Ronaldo's looks were an essential part of him as a marketing package for major corporations who might wish to sponsor him.

After being fitted with a teeth brace, he was encouraged to shave off all his hair and adopt a cooler image. It was just stage one of the agents' attempt to turn Ronaldo into a sex symbol. But there was a lot more to do yet.

Gradually, Ronaldo became a more confident character as a result of these changes. He began to believe in himself and even told his mother one day that he was going to become the best player in the world.

His attempt to sever the umbilical cord with Sonia by living alone hadn't really worked out because she was always popping round to Ronaldo's apartment with food.

And when the girls began flocking around him, his mother stepped in with yet more friendly advice; 'I told him not to encourage too many women. I know he's a sensible boy, although he does like to dance.'

When one beautiful blonde appeared on the scene shortly after the World Cup, Sonia soon came between them.

'The other day Ronaldo met this girl who insisted on starting up a relationship even though he told her he was only interested in football. I feel sorry for that girl because he's not really interested in her. There are many girls in Ronaldo's life. It looks like I'm going to have many daughters-in-law!'

* * *

There was a distance between his eyes, but also pleasure, devotion. A drop of sweat hung from the lobe of his left ear. He was laughing. White spittle clung to the corners of his mouth.

It was just after the '94 World Cup and Ronaldo was about to kick off for Cruziero in a league match. It wasn't a particularly memorable game except for one incident that many in Brazil still talk about to this day.

Just minutes before the match kicked off, Ronaldo sat down on the centre circle and began whistling to himself in that nervous way people do when they are doing something they hope no one else will notice.

He was urinating on the grass in front of him and 10,000 spectators. The entire 'event' was captured in glowing technicolour by a TV crew who were at the ground to film the game.

Rio TV journalist Pedro Bial recalled, 'It was quite

incredible. He thought no one would see what he was doing but it was so obvious. He really was a little boy at heart. He certainly proved it that day.'

Besides being an incredibly childish thing to do, this incident also provided evidence of just how nervous Ronaldo was before any game of football. He actually admitted to Brazilian journalist Pedro Bial that he usually emptied the contents of his stomach and bladder before every single match.

* * *

Back in 1960, when the Italians came in with an incredible $1 million offer to lure Pelé to Europe, the Brazilian congress went into emergency session. The Italians were told in no uncertain terms to go away and Pelé was declared a 'non-exportable national treasure'.

Unfortunately, in 1994 no such attitude existed towards exporting the so-called 'new Pelé' and the result is clear to anyone who realises just how small the Brazilian domestic game of football has become. All the best stars have escaped abroad.

Ironically, many of them were encouraged to do precisely that by the Brazilian national team coaching staff who genuinely believed that the more players who were at European clubs the better because then they would be perfectly acclimatised for France '98.

Ronaldo's instant success at the top level of Brazilian football — 54 goals in 54 games — earmarked him for the big European clubs and by the close season of 1994, Benfica, Juventus, AC Milan, Parma and Ajax were all queuing up in admiration for him.

But it was the less familiar provincial Dutch team of PSV Eindhoven which attracted Ronaldo the most. The club had acted as a clearing-house for some of the most talented performers in modern football — Romario, Ronald Koeman and Ruud Gullit had all demonstrated that a few years at the PSV school of soccer constituted an ideal preparation for the tougher environments of Italy or Spain.

PSV had actually come in with a bid earlier than any of the other clubs because of the wealth of their backers, the electronics giant Philips. It had actually been through one of their scouts based in a factory in Rio that Ronaldo had even come to their notice in the first place.

So it was no surprise when Ronaldo opted to pick PSV as his first European port of call when he departed from Cruzeiro Belo Horizonte shortly after the World Cup in 1994. Ronaldo agreed to the transfer to PSV for a cool $4 million. His agents shared more than $400,000 in commission. Their earlier investment of $7,000 was bringing them extraordinary dividends.

If ever a player had blue blood running through his veins it appeared to be Ronaldo. Back in Brazil, he was being talked about in the same way as world football's royal family — the 1970 Brazilian World Cup winning side. And, of course, it was Jairzinho, the fabled winger in that team, who had discovered Ronaldo at the age of 14.

It seemed amazing to some of his old childhood friends that here was a young man on which the first beard hairs were barely visible, with teeth caught in the steel frame of a brace, who was about to become a multi-millionaire.

At first, Pitta and Martins had been all in favour of cashing in their chips and packing Ronaldo off to Italy in the hope of securing a $10 million windfall. But acting on the advice of PSV old boy Romario, they decided that PSV would provide the perfect springboard. It was probably the only time that Ronaldo's well-being was given priority over the desire to make millions of dollars.

Even Ronaldo admitted at the time, 'Romario told me that PSV Eindhoven is one of the most professional and best organised clubs in Europe. Everything is there; a huge coaching staff, interpreters, professional managers, a superb stadium and a perfect blend of youth and experience in the team.

'Romario said it would be the best set-up to acclimatise in Europe and to learn about European football. I think he is right.'

Unsurprisingly, PSV manager Frank Arnesen believed that Ronaldo would be a prized asset and he could hardly disguise his glee at scooping the teenager ahead of such formidable opposition.

'All the big clubs had their agents on his doorstep holding bags of money,' he gloated. 'Our financial offer was certainly not the best. It just shows how keen Ronaldo is to play for PSV and that he is convinced that the Netherlands is the best platform to start climbing the ladder of top class international football.

'I told Ronaldo myself that he will never regret this decision in his career. Romario is the perfect example of the way we groom our talented players.'

Fellow Brazilian player Ricardo Gomes of Paris St Germain echoed that opinion by telling Ronaldo, 'You're in the right hands at PSV.'

He explained, 'It is already certain that Ronaldo is going to be the most complete striker for a long time. This boy comes very close to the perfect player. Left foot, right foot, it does not matter. He can do magical things with both feet.'

Sometimes Ronaldo had to pinch himself to make sure his move to Europe wasn't just a dream. 'Not long ago I used to dream about people like Romario and Bebeto. I collected their photos in a sticker album. Then, when the World Cup started in America, I was suddenly training with them every day. Now I am following in their footsteps to Europe and I have become a star myself.'

Even back in those heady days, Ronaldo found it embarrassing to be compared to Brazil's all-time footballing hero, Pelé.

'People are constantly talking about me as the new Pelé. They keep saying I am the new star of Brazilian football. But there is only one Pelé. All I can hope and pray is that I will become as good as him or even come close and that people will later say that there is only one Ronaldo.'

To celebrate his new teeth and hair and the fact that he was about to depart for PSV Eindhoven in Holland, Ronaldo held a party for 30 of his closest friends at the Royal Grill, in the up-market suburb of Barra de Tujica. His companions that night were amazed at the transformation following six months of dental work, which included having a permanent brace.

Ronaldo looked tired but happy at the party. He was worried about leaving his friends and family behind, and the cold weather. But Martins and Pitta said it was an essential next step in his bid to become the best — and richest — footballer in the world.

The two agents even gave Ronaldo a good luck charm — a solid gold St Christopher medal. But they insisted luck would play no role in his future.

Naturally, Sonia was extremely worried about losing her little boy. 'We haven't really had time to talk about it. I still can't quite believe he is worth all these millions of dollars.' Sonia had already assured her son she would come out and look after him as soon as she could.

But even she couldn't hide how impressed she was by the life he seemed to be embarking upon. 'He's going to get a detached house and *two* cars,' she gushed to one friend proudly.

Another guest that evening was Jairzinho, the man who had discovered Ronaldo in the first place. Despite his earlier complaint that he had not received a penny from the Ronaldo deal, Jairzinho actually earned a six-figure 'fee' from the Ronaldo transfer to PSV Eindhoven. It was a buy-out by Pitta and Martins to avoid any problems later on in Ronaldo's career.

Ronaldo's girlfriend at that time, Luciana, told everyone at the leaving party that evening that she intended to join Ronaldo in Holland in the New Year. 'I'm going to talk to him every day on the phone.' She did not hear Ronaldo's mother point out that any girl going out with her son had to expect to accompany him all the time otherwise there was little chance of the relationship surviving.

Within days of arriving in Holland, Ronaldo was predictably finding it very lonely. The club had given him a house in a quiet suburb but he rarely went out because he didn't like driving in a strange country.

He'd often spend entire days and evenings watching television, videos of his favourite films, football games and occasionally some of the explicit pornographic videos that were easily available in Holland.

Back in Rio, Sonia was extremely worried about her son's well-being. She spoke to him every day on the phone and could sense that he was feeling very isolated. Within six weeks of arriving in Holland, Sonia asked her son outright why he was so lonely and unhappy. Ronaldo did as he had done a hundred times before and burst into floods of tears. Sonia took the next available plane to Europe.

She later recalled, 'He had enormous problems in Holland so I flew over and found him a much nicer new house. I cooked his favourite dishes and ended up staying eight months with him.'

PSV were delighted that Sonia had moved in with her teenage son because it would help avoid the sort of emotional problems that could so easily have affected his footballing form.

Sonia was so concerned about Ronaldo's welfare in Europe that she told Pitta and Martins that if her son did not find some kind of female companion he was likely to walk out on PSV, and that their lucrative plans for transfers to other, richer European clubs would end up in ruins.

The answer, as it turned out, lay with a beautiful 19-year-old blonde Rio beach girl called Nadia Valdez Franca.

CHAPTER 7

It's in His Kiss

At the new house in Eindhoven, Philips provided Ronaldo with the latest in electronics: laser-disc, telephone, answering machine, fax, TV, video. In fact, apart from a couple of beds, there wasn't much else in the house.

New girlfriend Nadia and mother Sonia spent much of that first year sharing the house with Ronaldo. It wasn't easy for either woman. Sonia tended to pick holes in everything Nadia said or did. In the middle of all this, Ronaldo played computer games. He was particularly embarrassed by his mother's habit of wearing Nike trainers that were as big as clogs. Nadia stuck to three-inch stilettos, red-painted lips and skin-tight miniskirts.

Watching TV and sleeping with Nadia seemed to be Ronaldo's two favourite hobbies. Eurosport regularly showed Brazilian football. For hours on end he would sit in front of the TV, open mouthed with a glassy expression, while Sonia and Nadia clattered about in the ill-equipped kitchen preparing meals.

Sometimes Ronaldo would punch a video of his latest game for PSV into the VCR and watch it, hitting slow-motion every few minutes whenever he had the ball.

When Nadia was away, Ronaldo and his mother did a lot more things together. She later recalled, 'He would do the craziest things to cheer me up — wrestling, chasing me, or he'd buy me a fake toy, a spider or something, and try to frighten me. Or he would suddenly put a big toy bear on the toilet or get his bike out and cycle it through the room singing and shouting, just to distract me.'

If anyone important visited the house, Ronaldo's club-appointed interpreter Koos Boets would show up to help translate. Ronaldo actually got on very well with Boets and the two men enjoyed the sort of playful banter that exists between most teenagers. Ronaldo's favourite greeting to Boets was, 'Hello, you fat turd'. Boets did not seem bothered.

In fact, he was full of nothing but admiration for this strange little Brazilian colony. 'Such sweet, brave people. Strong boy, that Ronaldo, a bit shy. And terribly playful, he just can't concentrate. That's why the Dutch lessons are going so badly.'

Often, Ronaldo would just sag into the cheap sofa and fall asleep in the arms of Nadia. She'd usually follow suit within a few minutes. It wasn't exactly a glamorous existence. Most of the time, Ronaldo was so exhausted from training or playing that he rarely stayed awake past 10.00pm.

The home base did have one advantage. Ronaldo was able to watch videos of many of Brazil's classic performances over the previous 40 years. He was particularly impressed by Garrincha in the 1958 World Cup.

'Garrincha was dribbling when suddenly, with his marker chasing him, he ran away from the ball and let one of his team-mates pick it up. Such a crazy sight, so brilliant,' he'd say.

Sonia tried her hardest to make the house feel like home. She would serve visitors sweet black Brazilian coffee and proudly pull out photo albums of her extremely talented son. With short, well-used phrases, she'd tell anyone who would listen, 'This picture was taken at Valqueire, his first club. He was eight. He and his friends decided to ...' And so it went on.

And Sonia often attended PSV matches to cheer on her beloved son. She did find the tension very difficult to handle, though, especially as she had been suffering from high blood pressure since Ronaldo's birth.

'I have to take a great many pills to control my blood pressure, so watching Ronaldo isn't particularly good for my health. Sometimes, I take a bottle of beer with me and drink that to relax during a match. I shake and cry when he loses and I tend to swear at the referees.'

TV watching, driving lessons, training, Dutch lessons, phone calls, a game of tennis with a PSV team-mate — that was Ronaldo's life in Holland. In many ways, it was adolescent heaven.

Ronaldo kept his latest toy in the garage — a Chrysler Jeep. He was so nervous of damaging the car that he only started to drive it at a snail's pace around the town some months after arriving in Holland. He took curves with painful accuracy and performed every manoeuvre with total concentration.

'He just kept asking "How do I drive? How do I drive?"' said one old friend who visited Ronaldo in Holland.

Then there was the fan mail. There was always an enormous bag filled with airmail envelopes, ready to be sent off to Brazil. In Holland, footballers only ever answer fan mail if a stamp has been enclosed. Ronaldo was completely unaware of this rule. In the first few months of life at PSV, he sent off at least 2,000 letters with signed photographs, including 700 to Brazil. It had cost him at least £500 but that was peanuts compared to his phone bill.

But there was another very childish side to Ronaldo.

When Dutch journalist Frans Oosterwijk visited the house to interview the striker, Ronaldo at one stage surprised his guest by disappearing into a bedroom with Nadia.

At PSV, Ronaldo scored goals with all his usual regularity. His moves were quick and to the point. The Dutch reckoned he had what they call 'the third acceleration'; the sprint within the sprint, with which he could suddenly shake off two or three men.

Ronaldo was particularly enthusiastic about PSV coach Dick Advocaat. 'He is pleased with me, and I am with him.' Ronaldo even agreed to give up Coca-Cola and potatoes for his new father-figure/mentor.

During a rare day off, Ronaldo and his girlfriend Nadia accepted the invitation of an Italian football agent Giovanni Branchini to visit Milan. Branchini had come highly recommended by Ronaldo's 'owners' Pitta and Martins, who recognised that the Italian might play a vital role in any future transfer to the highly lucrative Serie A.

Ronaldo saw the trip as nothing more than a pleasant way of spending a couple of days. He knew it would be interpreted by some as a concrete move and he didn't help quash the rumours by meeting the president of Inter Milan for dinner.

Massimo Moratti got him to agree in principle to give his club first option when Ronaldo decided to move on from PSV. Ronaldo didn't actually look for a house during the visit, but he liked everything that he saw.

Branchini took Ronaldo and Nadia to the cathedral, La Scala and Inter's headquarters at the San Siro Stadium. They also shopped extensively. Nadia proudly showed all her family and friends the photos later — Armani, Moschino, a hotel festooned with chandeliers, and a meal seated next to the very welcoming Senor Branchini and the Inter president.

During that trip Ronaldo and Nadia went back to the hotel at least five times to make love and changed clothes each time. 'They were like lovesick teenagers,' said one friend. 'But then, that's precisely what they were.' It was a memorable trip and Ronaldo knew that one day he'd be back.

As the months in Holland rolled by, Ronaldo seemed to gain in confidence. He began to laugh more easily at his own jokes and those of others.

When friends visited his house in Eindhoven, he always made a point of serving them drinks; he would even lay the meal table with real grace. But he still became embarrassed by his over-protective mother.

When Sonia told one visitor that 'Ronaldo is on earth to score', he admonished her quite coldly.

Back in Brazil, many of his old friends had started complaining that they never heard from him. He took the attitude that that was the past. 'Nadia is my only friend now,' he told one PSV team-mate. He hadn't forgotten people like Calango and Ze Carlos but he didn't want to live in the past.

In Holland, the reality was that he was an alien without a cultural hinterland. In many ways, he had adjusted terrifically well. He seemed to move with ease through life, and his wardrobe grew by the day, as did Nadia's. At home, he'd listen to samba and reggae music. His tennis was improving. But unlike most footballers he never read newspapers.

Not surprisingly, Nadia grew increasingly restless with Ronaldo and it was obvious to everyone around them that they would not be spending the rest of their lives together.

And as the months flew by, the arguments between Ronaldo and Nadia became more serious. During one meal, she yelled at him, 'You're so annoying. Annoying. You can't keep away from me. You're like chewing gum. So why don't you want to marry me?' The other guests, including Sonia, looked away in embarrassment, but Ronaldo's mother made a mental note to bring up the subject later with her son.

Nadia later recalled that Ronaldo was extremely jealous and untidy when they lived together in Holland. 'He would come in from training and throw his socks on the living room table.' It was clear to Nadia that Ronaldo had got so used to his mother always clearing up after him that he did not know any better.

At the end of his first season at PSV, Ronaldo left Eindhoven to travel to Rio before Nadia. She drove him to the airport. Ronaldo looked good. His teeth had straightened out and he had a knew-found confidence. A year in Holland had made him calmer, more business-like.

Within weeks, Nadia and Ronaldo had, unsurprisingly, broken up. Over in Rio, Ronaldo had met another Brazilian blonde called Vivianne who moved in with him when he returned to Holland. By a strange twist of fate the two women had actually known each other before they met Ronaldo.

Vivianne bore a remarkable resemblance to Nadia but this time Ronaldo kept the relationship much more low-key, although he later told friends that Vivianne also made the mistake of presuming that one day the couple would marry.

'But neither Nadia or Vivianne were considered even vaguely suitable according to Sonia,' said one of Ronaldo's oldest friends back in Rio.

Once again, Ronaldo's mother seemed to be a significant factor in her son's romances and she made it clear she felt he could do a lot better.

Less than two months after splitting up with Nadia in August 1995, she contacted Ronaldo and claimed she was pregnant by him. Nadia lost the child and she remains heartbroken about the affair to this day.

'I lost a child because he had left me. I wanted to have a boy who would play football like Ronaldo.'

Both Nadia and Vivianne later recalled that Ronaldo was a 'great lover who kissed very well'.

Vivianne alleged that Ronaldo kept in touch with her

after he started dating other girls. But there was never any substantiation for these claims.

Both women were unsure as to whether Ronaldo was a faithful lover to either of them. Nadia said, 'I don't believe he was faithful to me.'

But, bizarrely, they were both enchanted by Ronaldo's small feet. They also recalled that while he did keep himself clean by taking regular baths 'he was not the type to rub himself down for hours'.

But it was their lasting memory of Ronaldo's almost unhinged jealousy that provides another fresh insight into his character.

Vivianne recalled, 'He wouldn't let me wear short skirts and he hated me coming to soccer practice because he didn't want the other players staring at me.'

Nadia added, 'I sometimes went to the soccer practice but he would get very jealous if he caught me looking at any of the other players.'

It was clear that Ronaldo felt very insecure after his childhood years during which he had witnessed so much unhappiness between his mother and father. Despite his fame and riches he still believed that other men could attract the attention of his partners.

Both Nadia and Vivianne also recalled that another abiding memory of Ronaldo the lover was of a man who liked to seduce women rather than the other way round.

As Nadia said, 'He was very sweet and always slept naked. He called me his little baby and that was nice.'

But what was his best quality?

'Sincerity,' said Vivianne.

'And he kisses really well,' Nadia added.

On 21 December 1994, Ronaldo was called up to play for the Brazilian national side in a home international against Yugoslavia. Nike had just paid out $40 million for the rights to sponsor the national side for the following ten years. It had been controversial as Brazilians interpreted the move as implying that Nike would, in many respects, 'own' the team. Some were convinced that the deal would eventually blow up in the CBF president Ricardo Teixeira's face.

Meanwhile, Ronaldo agreed to numerous requests for interviews in Rio and found himself scuttling between his hotel room, reception and the bar.

He found it so much more relaxing talking to his own countryman that he didn't carefully weigh up every word he uttered as his agents, Martins and Pitta, had told him to do countless times since they had signed him up four years earlier.

The army of Brazilian journalists on hand to record his every thought and deed were surprised by the earring stud that Ronaldo had acquired in his left ear since going to play in Holland. Ronaldo simply replied that 'in Holland, everyone wears them'.

In the middle of one interview, a beautiful girl approached Ronaldo seemingly from nowhere. Ronaldo's eyes lit up and he dissolved into a silly grin as he watched her every movement, but he was too shy to ask her name and she disappeared without saying a word. But his response did not go unnoticed.

During the same trip, Ronaldo ended up joining three pretty girls for a drink one evening in a hotel bar after accepting a rose from one of them. He later gave the rose to yet another, older woman. He told one friend that he was enjoying being young, free and single once again after his trials and tribulations with girls.

Before, during and after the Yugoslavia game, Ronaldo formed a true bond of friendship with the Brazilian captain, Dunga. He was one of the few players in the squad with a high school education. His father was even a civil servant with the provincial government in Rio del Sul.

Dunga knew that Ronaldo was going to experience a great deal of problems because he was so young. 'Everyone expects him to play brilliantly in every match,' he told one journalist. 'He sees me, Branco, Romario and Bebeto as big brothers, and himself as a little boy who has it all to learn. But he is convinced that he has a great career ahead of him. There will come a day when he is as important to the others in the teams as the others are to him.'

Ronaldo's other guardian angel in the Brazilian side at that time was granite-like defender Marcio Santos. And there was a saying in the side: 'If you hurt Ronaldo, you hurt Santos.'

Intriguingly, during the team practice session before the Yugoslavia game, Ronaldo experienced immense problems with a relatively simple exercise. He had to throw the ball from beneath his legs and over his back, and then, when the ball landed in front of his nose, start a short dribble. No matter how hard he tried he could not get the hang of it. The ball would bounce off his backside or end up somewhere behind him. Ronaldo looked embarrassed at the end of it all. Jeering, the other players imitated his incompetence. Ronaldo looked mortified but said nothing.

Then, during a closing kick-around later that same day, he took his revenge by performing with such speed and power that some of the other players just sat back and watched in admiration, powerless to stop his surging runs.

During that visit to Brazil, Ronaldo agreed to be filmed for a TV documentary that was being made on one of the golden beaches near the main route to São Paulo.

Ronaldo was asked to show off his ball juggling skills and occasionally go into the sea to retrieve the ball as part of the set-up. But after three hours of repeating the same tricks over and over again and with teeth chattering from the cold sea, Ronaldo let his diplomatic mask fall momentarily. Angrily, he complained to the director, whom he described afterwards as a 'fatso ... the organisation was shit'. It was an all-too-rare outburst and afterwards Ronaldo seemed much happier simply to have spoken his mind.

Back in Holland, Nike followed up their contract with the entire Brazilian national side by negotiating with PSV to take over sponsorship of their team from arch-rivals

Adidas. They also continued complex talks with Ronaldo's agents about 'owning' the player themselves. It seemed as if they were trying to acquire the entire footballing world.

PSV Eindhoven knew they had a special talent on their books. At 18, Ronaldo had the body of a 25-year-old. He seldom committed fouls and never protested to referees. He was cool, calm and collected.

The only thing that irritated PSV was his obvious lack of interest in training. It was a quality he shared with many of the world's top footballers. At PSV, Ronaldo was the only player who never did weight training.

He seemed unconcerned by the coaches and players who tried to force him into a structure that didn't suit him. He never talked back, never argued — he just laughed, shook his head and went off and did precisely what he wanted to do.

Ronaldo's favourite musical group at this time was a Brazilian rap outfit called Gabriel O Pensador. He even appeared on a promotional video accompanying one of their songs called '*Nada Especial*' (nothing special). It described a ride through Rio on a 175 bus; Ronaldo played the conductor. At every catastrophe the rappers passed on the way, the bus stopped and they gave a commentary. Laconic and sardonic. Robbery and murder in broad daylight, drug dealers on every street corner, whores on the beach, bizarre religious sects: this was Rio. Unconcerned, cocky, Ronaldo looked into the camera. It was as if he was saying, 'If you come from Rio you take on the world.'

In his first season in Europe, Ronaldo scored 35 goals in all competitions and he ended up as the top scorer in Holland. The 18-year-old Ronaldo was not surprised at his own success.

'I have worked hard for my success. The game in Europe is very quick but is less rough than ours.'

Some of the big clubs were once more hovering in the wings. But Ronaldo insisted, 'It was a great season for me but I've no plans to move. I am aware there are a few clubs interested in me but I have a four-year contract with PSV and I hope to be a championship winner with them.'

Ronaldo reckoned he had come across the finest marker he has ever played against in the world — Dutchman Ulrich Van Goddel of Feyernoord. 'He was tough. I hope I never play against him again.'

In barely two years Ronaldo had risen from an unknown playing in the backwaters of the Rio second division to become the most expensive teenager in world footballing history.

His biggest chance to shine following the disappointment of not getting to play during the 1994 World Cup came when he turned out for Brazil in the Umbro Cup in England in the summer of 1995. By that time, Ronaldo had only played three times for his country, scoring once.

In England, he was even quite outspoken about not getting a game during the World Cup. 'I was a little unhappy, of course. Everybody wants to play. I never really understood the coach's reasons for not playing me.'

At Aston Villa's Bodymoor Heath training ground, a handful of onlookers watched the Brazilians training before the England game. Ronaldo back-heeled the ball through his marker's legs, spun around him and unleashed a ferocious shot that stung the goalkeeper's hands. They applauded.

On 11 June 1995, England lost 3–1 to Brazil and Ronaldo scored a goal on his début at Wembley Stadium. To the hundreds of watching journalists he was already a real force to be reckoned with. Pitta and Martins rubbed their hands in glee once more because their property had just virtually doubled in value.

The first half of Ronaldo's subsequent 1995–96 season at PSV was uneventful. His scoring rate slowed down quite considerably after a few injury problems. In Eindhoven, his current blonde conquest, Vivianne, and Sonia continued to be at his beck and call.

Towards the end of 1995, English Premiership side Arsenal were even rumoured to be in the hunt for Ronaldo after their then manager Bruce Rioch was spotted on a scouting mission in Holland.

His pursuit of Ronaldo was Arsenal's priority at the time as the club's executives were in desperate need of a player who could recapture the hearts and imagination of their frustrated supporters who were well aware that there was at least £15 million available for new signings.

Ronaldo, then aged 19, and his club PSV were supposed to give first refusal to Inter Milan if and when he decided to make a move. The Arsenal rumours were seen more as a bit of muscle flexing from Ronaldo's agents who wanted to keep PSV on their toes.

At Christmas, Ronaldo returned home to Rio for an extended break and seemed very relaxed to friends and family alike. His relatively low-key existence in Holland suited him perfectly. For the first time in two years, the pressure seemed to be subsiding and Ronaldo was really enjoying his football and learning his trade.

But it didn't last long.

CHAPTER 8

The Killing Fields

Ronaldo suffered a severe knee injury during a training session at PSV in March 1996. The injury itself was a fractured tibia just below the knee. It was a major blow, not only to Ronaldo's health but also to the financial plans of his agents. They genuinely feared that Ronaldo's value on the open market could be severely reduced although he was expected to be fit enough to play at the Atlanta Olympics in the summer.

The injury was given relatively little coverage by the press because both the club and Ronaldo wanted to make sure the seriousness of it was not going to damage his prospects of making a multi-million dollar transfer in the near future.

Following that injury, PSV agreed to Ronaldo's request to go to Rio to recuperate. They were greatly relieved when Ronaldo assured his coach he was intending to have treatment for his injury from Nelson Petroni.

Petroni, whose nickname is Filé (as in fillet steak), ran a

physiotherapy clinic in Rio's Barra de Tijuca, which had the atmosphere of a sweat-stained gentlemen's club. He had also spent a year at PSV as Romario's personal physio.

Filé, diminutive, fast talking and energetic, prowled the floor of his clinic offering words of advice, checking levels on ultrasound machines and chatting to many of his patients.

Today, Filé has no doubt that Ronaldo's injury problems at PSV were aggravated by growing pains. 'Basically, Ronaldo had the growing up disease. At that time he was still maturing physically.

'I treated him and got him back into good shape but I warned him and his agents that he would face more problems as long as he kept growing.'

In layman's terms, each time Ronaldo picked up certain bone-related injuries there was a danger that they might not heal correctly because he was still growing at a phenomenal rate.

In Rio, Filé was impressed by Ronaldo's sheer determination to recover from his injury. But he says today that he believes that Ronaldo probably did not adhere to the strict régime of exercises he'd recommended — and that might be why he picked up a number of serious injuries later on.

Initially — back in April 1996 — Ronaldo trained eight hours a day at Filé's clinic. His daily exercise schedule was rigorous and included 2,000 exercises on each leg, as well as 640 jumps on a trampoline.

Filé recalled, 'I've never come across a player with such immense strength in his legs.' And comparing him to Romario, his most famous regular patient, Filé perfectly summed up the differing skills of the two strikers. 'Romario is quick in confined spaces and resolves play instantly. Ronaldo, however, is superb at quick, sudden runs over longer distances. He explodes with sheer force. And because of that, Ronaldo's training depends on leg strengthening. He runs many metres on the sand. Ronaldo can do every exercise 25 times and two alternate ways.'

Filé gave Ronaldo a long list of exercises he would have

to stick to if his leg was to mend properly. He was also told that he would have to continue to work out in a swimming pool and continue with a régime of stretching and strengthening exercises once he had returned to Holland.

Ronaldo also received a few words of warning from one of the chief trainers at his favourite Rio club, Flamengo. 'Players like Ronaldo have to work harder than most, especially since they are now in Europe. Tomorrow they could be tackled by some German three times their size and that is when their physical fitness will save them from serious injury.'

The same trainer also voiced a warning to any players who were constantly travelling. 'That, and too many games, can have a very bad effect and often stop a player from properly recovering from an injury.'

Still in Rio, Pitta and Martins were so worried about protecting their property in case of any future injury problems that they altered an insurance policy at the start of his career that cost $20,000 a year and paid out $3 million if his career was ended by injury. They trebled the premiums so that a $9 million windfall would be received in the event of any further injury disasters.

Just before his return to PSV, Ronaldo's agents decided that they would listen to offers for their Brazilian superstar. At first, some cynics suggested that they might be trying to offload an injury-prone player, but Pitta and Martins insisted that any such suggestions were nonsense. There were tens of millions of pounds at stake.

What PSV did not realise was that Pitta and Martins had already started top-secret negotiations with Barcelona after Inter Milan had told them that they were not interested in buying a recently injured player. When Barca, as the Catalan club was known to its supporters, first officially approached PSV Eindhoven some weeks later, they encountered deep resentment and resistance from the Dutch club. They were angry at the way the negotiations had been progressing and insisted that Ronaldo was not for sale at any price. He still had two years of his four-year contract to serve.

Ronaldo and his agents knew that a lucrative move to Barca would increase his value and pay packet ten-fold. They also felt *they* could dictate the terms, not PSV. Strongly urged by Pitta and Martins, Ronaldo took the bull by the horns and brought the situation to a head in a cold, calculating manner.

He called a press conference and labelled PSV coach Dick Advocaat 'stupid'. Two days later, he was Barcelona-bound.

In Spain, newly-appointed Barcelona coach Bobby Robson had carried out some careful research on Ronaldo before deciding that he could be the perfect player for his club. Robson — a former coach at PSV — even spoke to his old friend at the club, defender Stan Valckx, who told Robson that Ronaldo had scored goals 'for fun' from all sorts of angles, distances and situations, and that he could dribble and also take players on'.

Negotiations between Barca and PSV started at $10 million but PSV turned that offer down flat. Then the offer began climbing until it reached $17 million. Barca president Josep Lluis Nuñez hesitated, but Robson insisted that Ronaldo was worth it. Finally, PSV relented when the offer reached the $20 million mark.

One of the key factors behind Ronaldo's decision to join Barca was that his agents had sold his image rights for an extra £5 million, allowing the club to profit from the sales of replica shirts bearing his name and such items as gold-plated commemorative medals, plus a host of other endorsed goods.

Like many of Europe's best players, the image rights deals were an import from the high-octane world of Italy's Serie A, where it was regarded as a huge tax reduction scheme.

Lucrative fees from television appearances and commercial endorsements were to be paid into offshore 'image rights' companies, set up by Pitta and Martins to keep them from the taxman's clutches. Part of Ronaldo's wages were even to be paid into the same offshore tax haven accounts, as well as his signing-on fees.

Barcelona then intended to collect the money from Ronaldo's boot and shirt deals and other marketing contracts to recoup their vast outlay. It was a huge gamble, as many similar deals in the past had ended with the clubs concerned getting only a fraction of what they'd paid out.

As Barca president Nuñez knew only too well, in the new world of football's super-rich, all the stars insisted on negotiating their contracts net of tax, leaving the player a guaranteed salary and the club with the headache of having to pay all the taxes due.

The fact that Ronaldo was still injured did not seem to worry Barcelona who had sought three medical opinions which all concurred that Ronaldo would be fit for the start of the 1996–97 season. In any case, he was already in training with the Brazilian national squad for the 1996 Atlanta Olympics that summer.

By this time, Pitta and Martins had registered offices in Miami, Florida, because it was a more convenient location for tax purposes, where corporation tax was amongst the lowest in the world. A base in the States also helped them to avoid any problems with the Brazilian tax man. While in Rio, they worked from a bank of mobile telephones in their $1 million holiday homes hundreds of miles north of the city.

Martins and his wife Alzira, in fact, spent much of the year at a luxurious rented house in Homestead, Florida.

Back in Rio, super scout Jairzinho was once again nursing his empty bank account in the knowledge that he was not due any share of the Barcelona bonanza after selling out his rights following his protégé's move to PSV Eindhoven.

At the Atlanta Olympics, Ronaldo came into his own and scored five goals in the tournament as Brazil took the bronze medal after being beaten in the semi-finals by eventual winners, Nigeria.

Before his first game for Barcelona, Ronaldo proved that he always preferred to spend as much time as possible in Rio by turning up late for his new paymasters claiming that he needed an extra long rest following the Olympics.

* * *

In Spain, they soon started calling Ronaldo *una palabra mayor*, a big word. And even his first game for Barca, a 5–2 victory against arch-rivals Athletico Madrid in the Super Cup (Barca won Spain's equivalent of the Charity Shield 6–5 on aggregate), prompted a surge of excitement in his new boss Bobby Robson. 'He's going to be sensational,' exclaimed Robson. 'He's fabulous working in small spaces in the box, he can take defenders clean out of the game with a feint or a turn, and then he knows instinctively the right ball to play, whether to shoot or pass. He can also drop back 40 yards, pick the ball up and go off on runs taking on whole defences on his own. I think he'll be the key player in the Spanish league this year. He must be one of the greatest players in the world. And he's only 19!'

Robson had at one stage appeared to prefer the idea of signing Alan Shearer from Blackburn. Now he was saying there was no one to compare with the teenager, already nicknamed 'Little Buddha' by the Barca faithful.

But not everyone in Spain rated Ronaldo as a worthwhile investment. Athletico Madrid coach Radomir Antic claimed that Ronaldo and another of Barca's close season signings, Pizzi, top scorer in the Spanish league with Tenerife the previous season, would not play well together in the same side.

However, none of this seemed to bother Ronaldo. He'd been so happy to sign for Barca he tied himself to the club for the rest of his career — but then he was on over $1.5 million a year for the following eight years. Naturally, questions were soon being asked about whether this might affect his motivation and appetite for the game. Bobby Robson responded just a few days after Ronaldo's arrival.

'That's something you'd have to ask Ronaldo. I think he can handle it from what I know of him. It's not like he's going to say to himself, "Christ, I'm a $20 million player so

I've got to play like one, it's going to worry me." I don't think he'll be concerned about the money, to be honest. Personally, I think it's a great investment because we've got a superstar for the next ten years.'

* * *

Awesome is the only adjective which sufficiently describes the five-tiered Camp Nou skyscraper-cum-stadium in Barcelona. The world's most impressive football stadium was built in 1957 and the fans immediately started calling it *el camp nou* (the new ground) so a legend was born out of the most obvious name. The stadium itself makes Manchester United's Old Trafford look like a non-league ground.

On Saturday, 7 September 1996, the Camp Nou was seething with flags; the red and yellow stripes of Catalonia's *senyera*, the green and yellow of Brazil and the cross of St George. 100,000 people flooded into the stadium for that day's game against Espanyol, and most of them were eager to see Ronaldo.

It was hardly a classic game. With just six minutes to go, Espanyol were still clinging to a shock 1–0 lead. Then Barca's other new Brazilian signing, Giovanni, equalised. Finally, in the 92nd minute, Ronaldo picked up the ball 30 yards from goal, forced his way around one defender and then through another and unleashed a wind-assisted rocket that the keeper miraculously managed to parry straight into the path of Pizzi, who stuck it home before leading a team dash towards the corner flag.

As Bobby Robson admitted after the game, 'Every player in the team has his part to play, but if you've got a $20 million footballer like Ronaldo, it's logical that he makes the difference. That's his obligation.'

On Sunday, 15 September, in the 31st minute of Barca's league game against Racing Santander, Ronaldo caught a long ball on his chest from team-mate Guardiola and swept past his marker in one fluid movement. Then he sent the keeper the wrong way before going round him. It was a wonderful goal but it also marked the last time he received the ball from any of his Barca team-mates during that game, which ended in a dour 1–1 draw.

The following day, the notoriously over-exuberant Spanish press accused the Barca team of suffering from 'Ronaldodependencia'. In other words, the entire side relied too heavily on their $20 million man to score goals. Ronaldo himself insisted, 'I've got plenty of team-mates who can score goals, it's just that I'm receiving all the good passes. Our success depends on the whole team, not just one player.'

And along with the surprising rumblings of discontent, Ronaldo had his first taste of criticism from within his own camp when Barca assistant coach Jose Mourinho moaned, 'We've told him it's no good scoring a wonder goal and spending the other 89 minutes sleeping. I'm sure he's got the message.'

The following morning, Ronaldo hit back. 'It would have been better if he'd told me face to face, rather than going to the press with it. That would have been more professional. I played badly at Racing, but so did everybody else. I'm in the team to carry out the coach's orders, but if I don't get the ball there's not much I can do.'

In the end, Bobby Robson had to step in to pour oil on troubled waters. 'I've spoken to Ronaldo and he knows he enjoys our total confidence and that everything we do is for his own good. You have to put yourself in his shoes; he's only 19 and every single day he's in the papers and people are looking for a story from him. Our job is to guide him, to help keep him on track. I remember what happened to George Best. On the pitch he was unstoppable, but by the time he was 25 he was practically finished because nobody put the brakes on off the pitch — discos, parties, booze ...'

CHAPTER 9

Ronaldomania

On Ronaldo's 20th birthday (his official one) — 22 September 1996 — after barely a minute of play against Real Sociedad, the world's most expensive player crashed the ball home with such force that it suggested he was heralding a new era, and finally dismissing his teenage years. Up in the stands, Sonia missed her son's birthday present to himself because she was in the toilet. In the 89th minute he scored again and this time Sonia saw it all in glorious technicolour and promptly burst into tears. Barca won 3–2.

A measure of the Ronaldomania that was sweeping the city of Barcelona at the time can be summed up by the comment of one bishop who attended a mass to celebrate the 39th birthday of the Camp Nou. 'Where there used to be paintings of the Last Supper, now there are posters of Ronaldo,' he grumbled.

Within the Barca team, a certain degree of resentment was already starting to circulate about the Ronaldo machine that included his agents Pitta and Martins, as well as at least half-a-dozen assorted bodyguards and personal assistants.

Then there was the matter of the three mobile phones that Ronaldo carried with him everywhere when he was not actually on the field of play. During Barca's 0–0 away game in the first round of the European Cup Winner's Cup at AEK Larnaca in Cyprus, Ronaldo sat out the game as a precaution following an injury.

Ronaldo spent most of the game gabbling into his mobile phones in the stand. As one player commented afterwards, 'It doesn't exactly give us the impression he was closely watching the team's performance, does it?'

But within three days, Ronaldo won back at least some of his colleagues' hearts by scoring twice in a show-stopping 5–3 victory over Zaragoza in the Spanish league. One goal involved yet another inspired run with the ball past several defenders, and burying the final shot in the back of the net having sent the advancing keeper the wrong way.

In the stands that day, Ronaldo's agents purred with pleasure. They knew that if he kept up this form, he'd have doubled in value by the end of the season.

Ronaldo was being hailed by the Spanish press as the saviour of Barca. There were even glowing comparisons with all the usual suspects; Pelé, Maradona, Superman, *et al.* Ronaldo played the field brilliantly by flashing a smile when asked if he minded playing twice a week. 'I wish I could play a football match every day,' he replied. 'The part I really like is when I look at the fans and they cheer. I am a hungry player. I want to score when I get the ball. Barcelona coach Bobby Robson has given me total freedom. Barcelona is the best club in the world.'

Down at Valencia, Ronaldo's erstwhile hero Romario had scored four goals in the Spanish league taking his tally to one less than the $20 million man. Already a hint of rivalry was creeping into conversations about Ronaldo.

Romario commented, 'If I was the Brazilian team coach

I'd pick Ronaldo at the moment, too. But once I'm in form, I'm sure I'll get back in the Brazil side.'

Meanwhile, defenders in Barca's Spanish league were becoming understandably nervous about facing Little Buddha as some sections of the local press continued to call Ronaldo.

Asked before one game how he would deal with marking Ronaldo, the Tenerife centre-half responded, 'Pray a lot.' After the game, the same player conceded, 'That was the most difficult marking job I've done in my life. I feel like I've just played five games.'

* * *

In the city of Barcelona, Ronaldo was, not surprisingly, in great demand.

On one occasion, he was surrounded by a sea of cameras, microphones and notebooks. While he answered everyone patiently, his eyes sought a gap to escape the throng. Suddenly he disappeared, as if he possessed a sixth sense for escape routes nobody else had noticed.

On 9 October 1996 Ronaldo appeared in a slushy TV show called *Sorpresa*, hosted by a Cilla Black lookalike. Appearing a little uncomfortable, Little Buddha made one 12-year-old's dream come true by taking part in a kickabout and then he feigned injury so that a curvaceous masseuse could come on and give him a body rub.

Ronaldo showed all his finest diplomatic skills through rounding off his performance by donating £7,500 to charity. One wag pointed out that the cost of flying Ronaldo, his two agents, mother and brother to Madrid for the evening would have cost about the same.

During yet another interview, one TV producer made the mistake of telling Ronaldo to sit down when he had tried to get up. The producer explained that he still needed to shoot some more close-ups of the interviewer. He gently pushed Ronaldo back into his chair.

A dark cloud crossed the face of the Brazilian. 'Why didn't you come with two cameras?' he rightly asked. He stopped smiling from that point on.

Not long after this, Ronaldo was invited to a restaurant opening in Barcelona which was also attended by Cindy Crawford. On the spot, he was offered many thousands of dollars to pose with Crawford for the cameras. Ronaldo refused. 'They should have asked Cindy Crawford to pose with *me*,' he said whimsically.

Many believe that Ronaldo's finest moment at Barca came when he ripped apart Compostela on Saturday, 12 October 1996. It was Little Buddha at his finest. After just 30 seconds he strolled through the right flank of the opposition's desperate defence only to find fellow Brazilian William so rattled on his début for the opposition that he scored an own goal.

Fifteen minutes later, Ronaldo galloped down the opposition flank to create a sitter for fellow Barca Brazilian, Giovanni. After 30 minutes, another surging run had the crowd on their feet. In the dugout, Bobby Robson placed his hands on his head in amazement and turned to the tiny 12,000 crowd, arms wide apart in admiration.

Then Ronaldo received the ball and freed himself from a ruck of players. One grabbed his shirt but he escaped and went on to beat five men, turning them one way, then another, and then leaving them for dead. His upper body swayed from left to right, he tempted and teased, threatened with feints, stepped this way and that. Opponents lunged desperately or grabbed him (one even tried to stop him with both arms) but they fell away like saplings in the path of a hurricane. The finish was of an improbable precision. Apparently off balance, with two players tackling him and the keeper to beat ahead of him, he netted the ball flawlessly.

After the game, Robson was ecstatic. 'You can go anywhere you want in the world, and you won't find a player who can score goals like that. Can anybody, anywhere, show me a better player?'

During the flight back to Barcelona, Ronaldo hijacked the captain's microphone to run through a litany of Robsonisms. It was a fascinating insight into another, lighter side of Ronaldo's character, something that few had encouraged him to show in the past. Ronaldo actually felt confident enough to reveal himself to others.

Down in Valencia, Romario's earlier words of warning for Ronaldo had a hollow ring to them when the older statesman turned up late for training and claimed that his alarm clock had not gone off. Romario's threat was seeming ever more hollow.

Meanwhile, the Ronaldo legend was growing by the day. Former Real Madrid boss Jorge Valdano responded to the $20 million man by exclaiming, 'I don't know about Brazilian, he's more like a Martian.'

On 16 October 1996, Ronaldo headed for Brazil to join the national team squad for a get together. Coach Mario Zagallo decided it was time to bring Ronaldo back down to earth. He told reporters, 'I had a long chat with him and told him not to get too carried away with all the praise. Personally, I don't like the hype; it's ridiculous that all the responsibility at a club like Barcelona falls on the shoulders of a 20-year-old.

'Ronaldo's not very good in the air and he still doesn't understand the meaning of teamwork. He's going to be an all-time great but Pelé was a more complete all-rounder at 20.'

Yet on 19 October 1996 — just two months after signing a supposed six-year contract with the Spanish giants — came the first rumblings of activity in connection with Ronaldo's long term future at Barcelona.

Reports from Brazil claimed that Inter Milan were willing to pay Ronaldo's 4,000 million pesetas buy-out clause (all players in Spain have one, and if they pay they can walk). Ronaldo fielded questions with great skill. 'I'd obviously look at any offer, but why would I leave Barcelona? I've only just arrived.'

The truth was that Pitta and Martins believed they had undersold Ronaldo for $20 million and Inter Milan had kept an eye on Ronaldo's progress and acknowledged that they should have come in for him before Barca. Inter were talking about making an offer in the region of $40 million.

Bobby Robson was so bemused by the rumours that he told a packed press conference, 'It snows in Milan in January and I know Ronaldo doesn't like the snow.'

Back on the field of play, Ronaldo was now such an attraction that during a pre-match warm-up for Barca's game against Logrones, centre forward Manel made a beeline for Ronaldo with his camera and a photo request. Little Buddha happily complied. A couple of hours later, Manel was sent off for angrily insulting the referee after Ronaldo had scored a hotly-disputed penalty.

On Saturday, 26 October 1996 Ronaldo scored a hat-trick during Barca's 3–2 victory over Valencia, who had just sold Romario back to Flamengo, thus depriving the Spanish of a classic encounter between the two Brazilian superstars.

Bobby Robson, who had coached Romario at PSV, had no doubts as to who he felt was the better player. 'Ronaldo will be better than Romario. They've got a similar technical level, they're both very quick over shorter distances and great dribblers. But Ronaldo is bigger, stronger and far more dangerous over longer distances.'

Undoubtedly, Romario would not have been able to live with Ronaldo on the form he showed that evening. As Robson said after the game, 'A player is obviously not at his peak at 20, so he should get better.'

Ronaldo's Barcelona had managed eight wins, two draws and 33 goals — their best ever start to the season. Even without Ronaldo's 12 goals Barca were still the league's highest scorers.

Off the pitch, Ronaldo was becoming just a trifle petulant. He dumped his Spanish classes and admitted, 'I

After winning the 2002 World Cup final, Ronaldo celebrates Brazil's victory and his own personal triumph over the setbacks of the last four years.

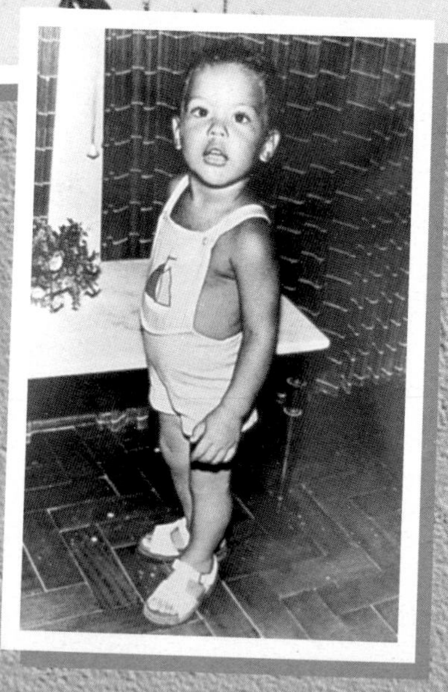

Top: **The tiny backyard of Ronaldo's childhood home in the Rio *favelas*.**

Bottom: **Aged nine *(third from right)* at a family wedding, in happier days before his parents split up.**

Inset: **Dreaming of an extraordinary future... Ronaldo aged two.**

Top left: **With his father, Nelio just after he'd sold his son to two agents for the princely sum of $7000.**

***Top right*:** **Ronaldo aged fifteen with his mother Sonia. It seemed even then, that this talented prodigy had the world at his feet.**

Bottom: **The team line up at São Cristovão. Ronaldo stands seventh from left.**

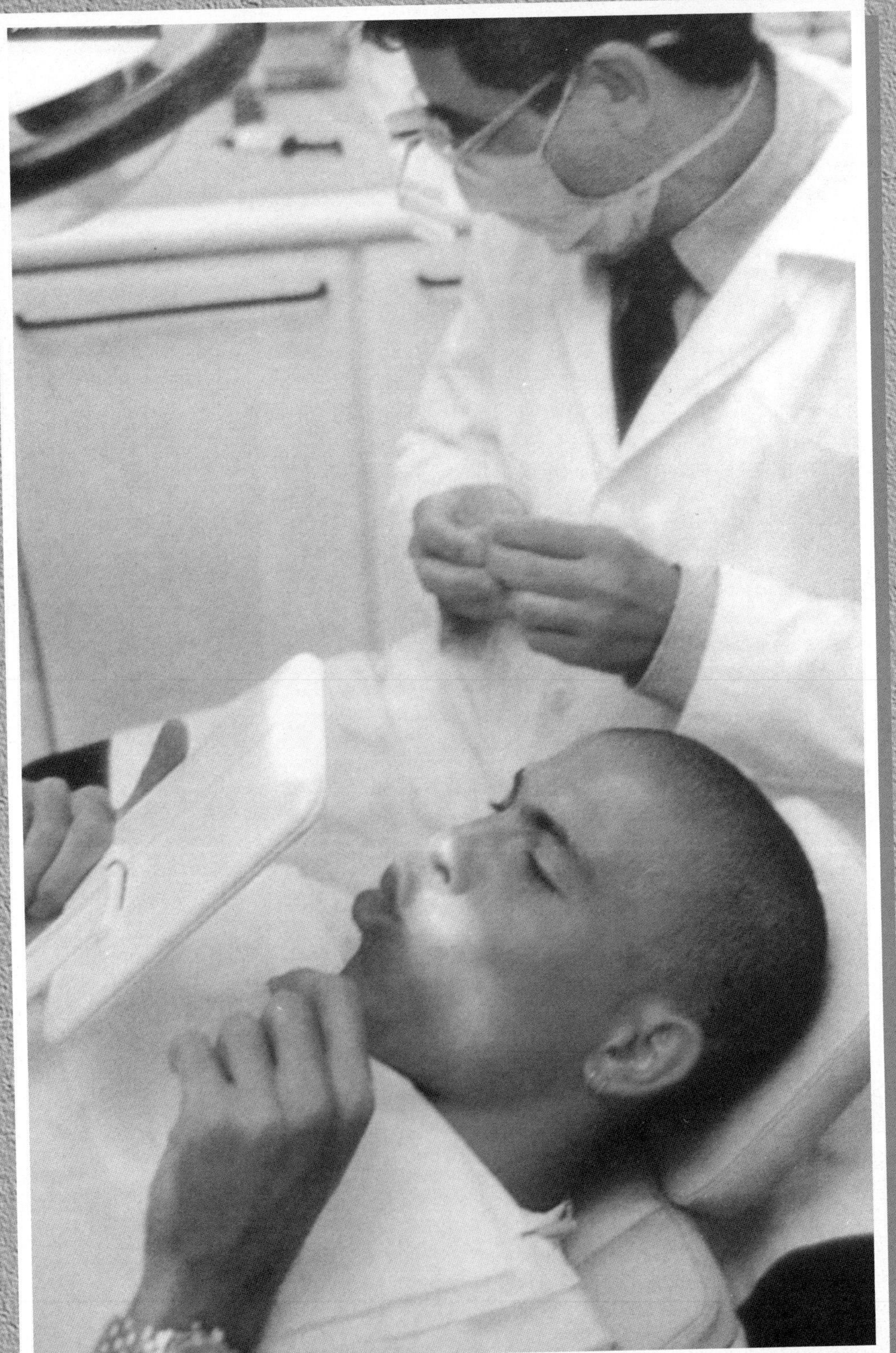

Ronaldo's teeth were rebuilt as part of his agent's plan to make him a world-wide sex symbol.

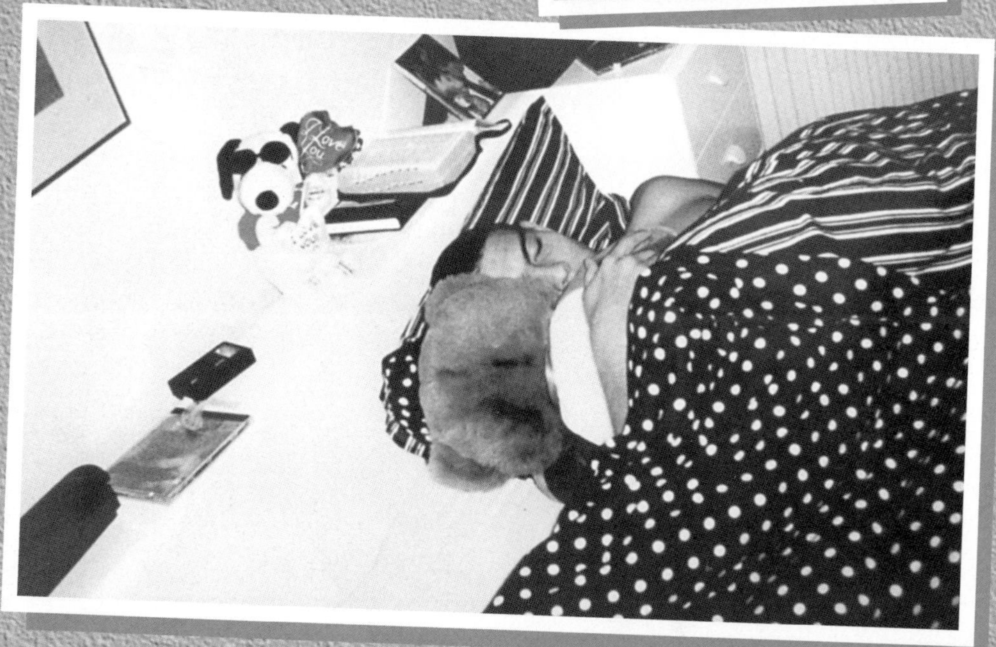

Top left: **Ronaldo and Mum cuddle after a successful match at São Cristovão. Their relationship has always been close.**

Top right: **With great friend and team mate Calango. The two teenagers dated girls, drank beer and came close to dying together in a freak accident.**

Bottom: **Fast asleep. Even at eighteen, Ronaldo liked to cuddle a teddy bear.**

Nadia and Viviane, two Ronaldinhas – Ronaldo girlfriends. After seducing him, they became celebrities. This picture is from the front cover of Brazillian *Playboy* magazine.

Top left: One of Ronaldo's finest moments for Inter Milan came with their UEFA cup victory over Spartak Moscow.

Top right: With ex-girlfriend Susanna Werner.

Bottom: Ronaldo's debut for Inter Milan v. Manchester United, July 1997.

Top: **Susanna discovered that even on Copacabana beach, her boyfriend could be very competitive.**

Bottom: **Romario, Ronaldo's Brazilian team mate was the inspiration for Ronaldo in many ways, but he was determined to avoid Romario's wild lifestyle.**

don't like studying or reading but I am reading a biography of Garrincha.' He paused for thought, then immediately spoilt the impression he'd just made. 'I expect to finish it within six months.' No one knew whether he was joking.

Most of Ronaldo's spare time was taken up at home with girlfriends, his mother, sister and brother, all of whom spent long periods of time with him in Spain. He had a bizarre penchant for playing with his baby nephew's toys. As sister Ione explained at the time, 'The only problem is that Ronaldo doesn't let my son touch the new ones until he's stopped playing with them.'

Ronaldomania even managed to cross the Atlantic on 27 October 1996 when *USA Today* actually gave him shared front-page billing with New York Yankees catcher Joe Girardi, as the Bronx Bombers celebrated their first World Series triumph in 18 years.

Back in Barcelona, there was concern that Ronaldo could start being illegally targeted by some of the games more physical defenders. Bobby Robson commented, 'The only way to protect him would be if the press didn't write so much about him. How about only four pages a day instead of ten?'

On Thursday, 31 October 1996, Barca played out a workmanlike draw at Red Star Belgrade to move into the next round of the Cup Winners Cup. But Ronaldo struggled throughout the game with a thigh strain.

Behind the scenes, that injury was significant because Ronaldo needed to concentrate more on certain aspects of his training, otherwise he could start to pick up more and more injuries just as his physio, Filé, had predicted back in Rio earlier that year.

Even more significant was Bobby Robson's response to criticism from the press that he had kept an injured Ronaldo on the field for far too long. With striking similarity to the events of the World Cup Final in 1998, he told a packed conference: 'If we'd lost 2–0 everybody would be asking why he didn't play. At half-time we asked him if he wanted to carry on and he said "Yes". People should praise his attitude. Anyway, it's not a bad thing that people should get used to us playing games without Ronaldo, there's no way he'll play all 60 games.'

It is natural for any male *Carioca* always to be on the lookout for a woman. Hooking up with a new partner specifically for romantic purposes was a personal challenge to any *Carioca*, and that included Ronaldo. When the opportunity presented itself he did not think twice.

So it was no surprise that by November 1996 Ronaldo seemed to be dating at least two girls at the same time. As his old friend Calango later explained, 'He was like a kid in a candy store. After years of being the odd one out when it came to girls, they were now lining up for him. He deserved it.'

In Rio, there was a pretty brunette called Raquel Fernandes Pinto, a reigning spring queen of the Rio suburb of Coelho Neto. She was just 16 years old with long, wavy dark hair and a childish smile.

Raquel had met Ronaldo in a Rio disco in August that year. Raquel's mother, Jurena, told one local newspaper reporter that her schoolgirl daughter was planning to visit Ronaldo in Spain in December.

But back in Spain there was another Brazilian, Adeli. The 17-year-old had met Ronaldo in a bar in the exclusive Rio suburb of Barra and had then flown out to Barcelona. Her sister insisted that Adeli was the girlfriend who really counted. 'He's only kissed this other girl. It isn't a proper romance,' she told one friend.

In fact, both girls were completely wrong, for Ronaldo had fallen in love with another girl who wouldn't even give him her phone number! Blonde *Carioca* actress and model Suzanna Werner had danced a very sexy, grinding pagode (a slow, intimate form of samba) with Ronaldo at a club in Rio during the late summer. The couple chatted all night and Ronaldo told Suzanna all about his life in Spain and how difficult it was living away from his home and family.

But when they said goodbye and Ronaldo asked her for her phone number, she coldly snubbed him. 'I'm not in the habit of giving my personal number to people I've just met,' she told Ronaldo. He was stunned ... and besotted.

In fact, the real reason behind Suzanna's rebuttal was that she had been dating the same man for four years and he was incredibly jealous. 'I couldn't bring myself to leave him,' she later explained.

By this time, Ronaldo had already reached superstar status in Barcelona. The local press were saying he was better even than Pelé. They were superimposing his smiling profile with a halo and running headlines like: words fail us.

Down at his beachside house near the city in Castelldefels, Ronaldo was still enjoying the company of the shapely Ipanema beauty Adeli, despite dreaming about Suzanna. Sonia was also in attendance most of the time. The locals were very impressed because Ronaldo only drank fizzy water and he rarely was seen out in any of Barcelona's wild nightspots.

FC Barcelona had even insured Ronaldo's legs for £20 million and, for the moment, everything in Spain seemed perfect. Ronaldo promised he'd glide above the deluge of press interest and get on with the business of scoring goals.

The fractured tibia injury earlier in the year actually sparked a whole series of injury problems for Ronaldo that were not helped by the constant pressure on him to play for his paymasters. He was not fit enough to play for Barca against Athletico Madrid on 9 November.

Ronaldo's absence was a blow to the club's balance sheet because Ronaldo made the decision to declare himself unfit publicly days before the game and it had a negative effect at the box office. He was told in future to keep his injuries to himself so as to keep the fans guessing until the last ticket was sold. Ronaldo did not appreciate being treated 'like a slab of meat', as he later told one friend.

At the Camp Nou stadium, a new restaurant called the Magic Barca opened serving food and football simultaneously. Specialities included the 'Ronaldoburger'.

But despite the hero worship of tens of thousands of Barca fans, Ronaldo was feeling increasingly isolated from the main core of the club. Many of his team-mates were jealous of his huge pay packet and undoubted influence. And he rarely socialised with any of them.

He kept away from many club functions, including a farewell dinner at Camp Nou for Jose Mari Bakero, the 32-year-old club captain. Ronaldo spent that evening at a concert given by the Brazilian singer Caetano Veloso. His absence was noted.

On 30 November 1996, yet more rumours of a move involving Ronaldo began to circulate. This time there was speculation that he might be transferred to Italy or England. Many at Barca believed Ronaldo and his agents were playing a dangerous game.

Ronaldo, however, seemed happy to comment on the speculation because it was obviously good for business. 'The offers are real and we're talking about incredible amounts of money. We've got to sort out this situation as soon as possible so I can settle down and concentrate on my game. Barcelona knows my intention is to stay but I'm a professional and I've got to consider offers from other clubs. Alexandre Martins and Reinaldo Pitta will be here next week and I'm sure the club will do everything in their power to find a happy solution.'

It wasn't hard to work out Ronaldo's strategy. He was working the room for more money. He'd already proved himself capable of great influence during the PSV negotiations. Signing an eight-year contract for Barca was looking more and more irrelevant.

By the beginning of December, reports were coming from England that Manchester United were prepared to pay £20 million for Ronaldo. Ronaldo even told one reporter,

'I've got no problem with English clubs.' Bobby Robson insisted that the stories were nothing more than rumours.

Manchester United's Scottish coach, Alex Ferguson, made discreet inquiries about Ronaldo after being told that the player had that extraordinary buy-out clause in his contract.

When news of Ferguson's interest leaked out he immediately refused to talk about the offer, but it was a very serious bid to take Ronaldo to Old Trafford.

United were convinced that they could put together a package which would prove irresistible to Ronaldo. What they didn't realise was that they were being used as pawns in a very long-term series of negotiations that had already started between Ronaldo's agents and Barca executives, including the club president Nuñez.

It was only a few days later that United conceded that they hadn't got anywhere near signing Ronaldo. The player himself artfully agreed to be interviewed over Manchester United's interest after pressure from his trusted agents.

'I know of the interest of Manchester United. I am proud to be wanted by such a famous club because it is so flattering, but I want to repay Bobby Robson for having the confidence to sign me.'

In fact, Manchester United had been unwittingly used as part of a warning shot being fired by Ronaldo's agents, who were planning to re-negotiate their client's contract with Barca or find him an even richer club to play for. Pitta and Martins were also happy to let all these rumours fly around the football world because that would hopefully increase the value of their star client.

Early December also saw the build up to one of Barcelona's biggest games of the season — an away game at Real Madrid. The rivalry extended back to 1902 and was fuelled by the animosity which developed during the years of the Spanish Civil War.

All 106,000 tickets were snapped up within hours of going on sale. And even the players like Ronaldo were selling the game as if their lives depended on it. 'It's the most important occasion of my life,' he told a packed press conference before the game. 'Even in Brazil, the build-up to a big game doesn't last two weeks.'

At Real Madrid, Brazilian Roberto Carlos joined in the rivalry by telling his terrified goalie, 'You don't have to kick Ronaldo to stop him. You've just got to make sure he doesn't get the ball. Then he gets really frustrated.'

Then Roberto Carlos let slip his real feelings about the young superstar, with whom he would later find himself embroiled in controversy.

'Everybody has put him on a pedestal, but nobody asks why he didn't get a single game at the 1994 World Cup. He's still a beginner, that's why. When he gets the ball he forgets there are other people playing. He's just obsessed with scoring great goals.' It was hardly a subtle dig.

But Roberto Carlos wasn't quite finished. 'I'm worried about Ronaldo; he's made such a good start that people demand too much. And wherever he goes, he gets stared at like a freak.'

Certainly, Ronaldo was feeling the pressure. He found the harassment in Spain much more relentless than in Brazil. 'Everywhere I go, I've got 30 people following me to the car wanting something from me and trying to touch me.'

The ultimate evidence of Ronaldo's superstardom in Spain came when the Barca team touched down in Madrid before their match against Real. It was a bank holiday, Friday, 6 December, and 2,000 screaming fans packed into the capital's airport to provide a reception that was reminiscent of that for the Beatles in 1966.

'I've never seen anything like it,' exclaimed Barca spokesman Nicolau Cassus. 'Two thousand people at Madrid cheering Barcelona. Amazing.'

The so-called match of the century came packed with staggering statistics: 106,000 fans, £1 million taken at the gate, touts charging £500 for £75 tickets, 500 accredited journalists, a thousand police ... Then there was Ronaldo. He had three chances and missed them all as Real beat Barca 2–0.

Within hours of the defeat, Ronaldo was boarding a flight to Rio for a few days' break and then to join the national team for their match against Bosnia. But before he departed, he tried to defend his performance in the Barca side. 'I'm not Superman and I can't win games on my own, I'm just a 20-year-old footballer who hates losing. I'm sorry but I do miss chances sometimes.'

As Ronaldo flew out of Spain, Pitta and Martins flew into Barcelona determined to thrash out a bigger money deal with the club. There was talk of a double-your-money £50 million get-out clause and a two-year contract extension that would keep him at Barca until 2006. In return he would get at least £2 million a year.

Then Martins threw a spanner into the mix by making cutting comments about the quality of the coaching at Barca. The banker-turned-agent appeared to have become an overnight tactical expert when he told one writer: 'Ronaldo spent too much time against Madrid dropping deep because he wasn't getting any decent service. If he has to drop into midfield to pick up the ball then his goalscoring ratio is going to fall. I suppose Robson has got his system, but maybe the players still haven't caught on.'

Martins' comments really grated with Bobby Robson and the Barca board. It was the first time an agent had commented on a client's team tactics and they found it very irritating. Caught in the middle was Ronaldo. His first loyalties were always going to be to the two businessmen who had 'bought' him for $7,000 in 1990. And much of what they said undoubtedly came from Ronaldo's own lips.

Bobby Robson had his own opinions of what the negotiations really meant. 'Some say we bought a parcel of trouble when we got Ronaldo but not me. He was a great player and a brilliant boy to work with. He likes a joke in the dressing room but he respects the senior players. He is a fine boy who trains well and, as far as I'm concerned, he wants to stay with Barcelona a lot longer.'

Then he paused. 'Will he have to move every time his agent says so? Certainly one was quoted as saying that the whole world deserved to see him play, suggesting that he would be packing his tent and moving like a gypsy from country to country.

'I was shocked when all these problems materialised because I thought we had signed him for eight years. There was no indication that he wanted to leave or that he was in any way unsettled.'

Robson also insisted that the main negotiating problems were caused by Ronaldo's agents and their new Italian partner, Branchini. He later claimed that Pitta, Martins and Branchini were demanding $15 million for the rights that Ronaldo had signed over to them when he was a schoolboy otherwise Barca would stand no chance of keeping their star player.

Robson claimed that the final bill to Barcelona would have been something in the region of $80 million.

Still determined to stop him leaving, Robson pulled Ronaldo into his office one morning and tried to talk him out of the move.

Robson recalled, 'Ronaldo had a magnificent house overlooking the Med in the richest area in Barcelona, he drove a fabulous BMW and he had no problem with the language.

'I told him I didn't want him to go and he replied that he didn't want to go either but his agents had told him he was here to play football and they were here to make money.

'I have to do what they say,' Ronaldo told Robson.

He would live to regret those words.

CHAPTER 10

Rat Woman

In the autumn of 1996, Ronaldo was speaking to a friend in Rio on the phone who told him that Suzanna Werner, the beautiful blonde model he had danced with in Rio a few months earlier, was no longer attached to the man she had talked to Ronaldo about. Ronaldo had been unable to get Suzanna Werner out of his mind. Now, by a strange twist of fate, the possessive boyfriend she had when they first met had died in a motorcycle accident.

Ronaldo begged his friend to get a number for Suzanna Werner and then called her and tried to offer his condolences about her boyfriend's death.

The call from Ronaldo had come like a bolt out of the blue for Suzanna Werner.

'I was so stunned that I didn't believe it was Ronaldo at all. Since our meeting in the club he had become a superstar. I thought it must be someone pretending to be him.

So four or five times she put the phone down on him.

'After a week of slamming down the phone I asked the caller to describe where we met. And he remembered every minute detail. I finally knew it was really Ronaldo.'

Suzanna says she then burst into tears while talking about her dead boyfriend.

'I felt a sort of guilt and pain for his death. In Brazil we say, "My man dies, I will let myself die," and a lot of women mean that,' she later recalled. 'I might have done the same if it had not been for the people around me — family, friends and others.'

For the following few weeks Ronaldo called Suzanna every day at her home in Barra de Tijuca and talked her through her feelings for her dead boyfriend. Finally, he plucked up the courage to blurt out what he had felt from the first moment in the club: 'You are the most beautiful girl I have ever met. I have been in love with you ever since I first saw you.'

* * *

The brash, new suburb of Barra de Tijuca is a far cry from the crumbling colonial buildings and skyscrapers of old Rio, ten miles further along the Atlantic coastline. Many *Cariocas* believe that Miami Beach was used as a blueprint when they created this sprawling mass of drive-in *hypermercados* and duplexes that mushroomed along a wide strip of land on the edge of an endless, white-sand beach, to the west of Ipanema. Barra was supposed to represent the affluent side of a mini financial boom in Brazil. It is here that many of Rio's most famous playboy footballers and soap stars come to play foot-volleyball. It is also here — and not Ipanema or Copacabana — where Rio's beautiful people parade themselves at weekends.

The player with the number 10 shirt certainly caught the eye on Barra beach that afternoon. This was the same strip of beach where Romario liked to show off his footballing skills as the girls lusted after him. And on most evenings and every weekend literally thousands of wannabe Romarios and Ronaldos took part in their own version of the beautiful game.

But this skilful forward was particularly eye-catching because she was wearing a skimpy bikini and possessed the ultimate in Rio accessories — golden blonde hair. Suzanna Werner had the perfect combination: good ball skills and a perfect body to match. During games of *pelada* she'd be lining up a perfect shot one moment and then diving into the sea to retrieve the ball the next. She also happened to have been the summer queen of Rio.

At 18 years of age, Suzanna was already part of the landscape in her home suburb of Barra. They called teenagers like her the 'condo generation' because they all lived in plush apartment blocks just a short distance from the Atlantic Ocean.

Suzanna was as ambitious as she was beautiful. And as part of a long-term strategy, her modelling agency even managed to place an article in one of the Rio dailies about this 'bold beauty with a touch of innocence'. In journalistic terms, they are called 'puff pieces' — articles written more like advertisements for their products; in this case Suzanna Werner.

But Suzanna revealed some interesting views when she was interviewed for the article. It was published at a time when the Brazilian government were having so many problems with the poor in the *favelas* that they'd sent the army in to deal with them.

'I am very optimistic about everything. I think it is very good what the army are doing,' said Suzanna sweetly. No doubt many of Ronaldo's relatives in the *favelas* might have felt rather differently.

Next came a quote from one of Suzanna's best friends which seemed to sum up the ambition of the condo girl from Barra.

'Suzanna? She's a real cat woman, a nymphette and a

true *Carioca* even though she's light-skinned. She has the brightness of the sun, the face of the summer.'

Suzanna was a girl who knew exactly where she was going. When she was not studying at school she was in the local gym sculpting her body to perfection. As the same article pointed out, 'Don't you think little Suzanna's body is muscley? She just loves to swim.'

Suzanna also loved beach football, cycling and often went surfing on Tuesdays and Thursdays. The residents of the Novo Leblon condominium complex where she lived knew Suzanna well. She'd starred in numerous TV commercials by the age of ten.

'She was a pushy, well-organised girl going places in a hurry,' says one.

Suzanna's only regret was that she had not been to many big football games thanks to a very nasty incident at the Maracana Stadium when she fell off a balcony while not looking where she was walking.

As far as her future was concerned, she had definite plans. 'I don't know how long I'll be a model. It's not a profession you can do for so long. One day I'm gonna go to Japan or São Paulo but I know I'll miss Rio so much. One week away from here and I start to cry.'

Suzanna's mother, Katia, was a little more down to earth. 'We never encouraged her to model. She just wanted to be one. We were proud but worried because we didn't want her to forget her values. That's much more important than her beauty.'

Suzanna's father, 47-year-old Avelino, was an economist at the local university. They had all moved from a rougher part of Rio to the Novo Leblon condo just three years after Suzanna's birth on 27 July 1977.

'I like living here and I feel safe,' Suzanna said in that same article. Then she added something which would also have no doubt upset Ronaldo and his family. 'The only thing I am afraid of is the poor people waiting to get us at the crossroads down the street.'

Suddenly, she changed tack entirely and spoke in serious, heart-rending terms about the death of her favourite character in a soap opera. 'It was so upsetting,' said Suzanna.

She even admitted that her favourite non-sporting activity was spending entire afternoons at the local shopping mall. 'I guess I am a bit of a shopping mall rat.'

But it's Suzanna Werner's comments about the importance of being faithful in a relationship that are most revealing. 'This is something that has been questioned by many young people. It is so difficult today. I don't believe much in faithfulness, especially from men.

'Women give themselves more. They are sentimental, they are the ones who insist on using a condom and that kind of stuff.'

Seconds later she returned to her little girl role by admitting, 'I love ice cream and marshmallow chocolate, but I tend to keep to fruit, pasta and beans.'

Then green-eyed Suzanna attempted to persuade readers of the article that she was 'not beautiful'. She explained, 'I don't think I am beautiful. I hate my ears and I think my teeth are too small. Women with dark hair and blue eyes are just wonderful.'

The article ended with a reference to Suzanna's measurements. She had the perfect body for a *Carioca* fantasy; small on top, shapely below the belt.

So this was the girl of Ronaldo's dreams ...

* * *

During December 1996 and January 1997, Ronaldo qualified for the endurance record of 'Around the World in Forty Days'. His travel schedule between Rio and Europe would have exhausted any airline pilot. Ronaldo's attempt to break the world record for airmiles had serious implications. It was very obvious to many in Rio and Barcelona that he was missing Brazil but at what cost? Back in Spain, coach Bobby Robson was becoming more and more anxious, wondering what side of the Atlantic his star buy was actually in.

Ronaldo's movements were positively exhausting:

8 Dec	—	Barcelona–Rio (12 hours)
16 Dec	—	Rio–Manaus (5 hours)
19 Dec	—	Manaus–Rio–Barcelona (17 hours)
22 Dec	—	Barcelona–Rio (12 hours)
27 Dec	—	Rio–Barcelona (12 hours)
30 Dec	—	Barcelona–Rio (12 hours)
1 Jan	—	Rio–Barcelona (12 hours)
10 Jan	—	Barcelona–Rio (12 hours)
15 Jan	—	Rio–Barcelona (12 hours)

Time in the air: 106 hours
Cost: $15,000 approximately

While Ronaldo lapped up life in Rio and found himself a new girlfriend, Barca manager Bobby Robson was having second thoughts about Ronaldo's off-the-field activities. On 10 December he even admitted to one reporter, 'There is a definite connection between his declining form and the recent pay talks. It's unethical that a player is re-negotiating a contract just four months after joining the club.

'The kid started the season playing very well, and his people are very clever so they start talking about Manchester United and Arsenal and Milan.'

In fact, Robson was privately so incensed by the well-fed rumours, that he told Barca, 'Don't panic about that, they're not coming in, they haven't got the money for him.'

Robson was convinced that Ronaldo and his agents were trying to bind him to Barcelona by raising the get-out clause which then meant they would have to re-negotiate the contract from scratch.

Robson later explained, 'I don't think it was right, but I suppose it was inevitable. It's very sad to talk openly about money because it alienates the fans. The less you let on about money and what people are earning the better.'

Robson was at a distinct disadvantage because back in England he would have been personally in charge of such negotiations, but at Barca, chairman Joseph Lluis Nuñez called all the financial shots.

At the Camp Nou, Ronaldo's two heavyweight agents were trying to force Nuñez into a corner where he would effectively have to more than double the existing Ronaldo deal in order to hold on to his star player.

And Ronaldo's team-mates at Barca were becoming increasingly disheartened by the non-stop supply of Ronaldo-in-pay-talks stories that filled virtually every sports page in the Spanish press. The decidedly sober sports editor of *La Vanguardia* newspaper even claimed that Ronaldo and his fellow Brazilian at Barca, Giovanni, had been virtually ostracised by the other players because of jealousy over their pay deals. The result was, according to the paper, a general reluctance even to lay on passes to the two South Americans during games.

Some even pointed out that the problems had existed for some months. The fact that Ronaldo's two best goals had come when he had had to drop deep and win the ball himself seemed to add weight to the rumours. Match statisticians pointed out that during the game against Real Madrid Ronaldo received half the passes compared with his Portuguese team-mate, Figo. Even Bobby Robson got wind of the problem but it was extremely difficult to solve.

The Spanish players at the centre of the rumours emphatically denied the deliberate isolation of their two star players. One team-mate, Sergi, claimed, 'The idea is ridiculous. There's no racism in the dressing room, no split and no boycott. It's stupid thinking that just because the foreigners are more famous and get paid more money that they are isolated from us.'

Back in Rio, Ronaldo's name was now so synonymous with

football that it was impossible to travel around the city without being reminded of him. On the drive along the Barra seafront, Ronaldo's striking features stared out from billboards advertising drinks and sports shoes.

Ronaldo had been calling Suzanna Werner every night until he arrived back in Rio from Spain in mid-December 1996. 'He would tell me that he would make me happy again, give me back my smile and look after me.'

It was a bonus for Ronaldo that the girl of his dreams was a skilful player in her own right for the Fluminense Club's women's football team.

Fluminense perfectly summed up the social background of this self-confessed 'shopping mall rat'. In contrast with working-class club Flamengo, it has always traditionally drawn its support from more aristocratic, white stock. Flu's nickname as 'the rice powder club' originated back to the day in 1916 when it secretly slipped a darker-skinned player into its whites-only side. A reporter discovered that player covering his face in rice powder in the dressing room before the kick-off. Flu fans responded to the taunts by christening the black-dominated Flamengo the 'coal dust' club. Even when both clubs eventually gave way to multi-racial selection policies, the difference between them remained black and white.

The first romantic meeting between Suzanna and Ronaldo was held in secret because of fears that the Rio press might ruin the situation. On a dark street corner in the upmarket suburb of Leblon, Suzanna pulled into the sidewalk. She was wearing dark glasses even though it was night-time. She got into the back of the car and lay on the floor.

Two minutes later, Ronaldo jumped into the car and drove off. The couple giggled uncontrollably. 'All he could see was my feet. When we stopped the car we kissed for the first time. It was wonderful.'

But those secretive love trysts eventually led to a frosty meeting with Suzanna's parents who were not convinced that Ronaldo was the right man for their daughter.

'My mother burst into tears when I told her I was dating Ronaldo and my father wouldn't speak to me,' she later admitted. 'They had dreamed of a different kind of man for me, not a footballer.

'They kept saying, "You will never have peace," and "You will always run the risk of being left for another woman." But they eventually agreed to meet him and over dinner they changed their tune.'

That meeting between Ronaldo and Suzanna's parents occurred during his Christmas break from Barcelona. Suzanna recalled, 'The atmosphere was electric. Ronaldo put on his best suit and wore it like a strait-jacket he was so nervous.

'Then my father took him into the smoking room after two hours for a private man-to-man talk. And when they came out it was obvious my father had changed his opinion and that Ronaldo had won him over.

'Now my mother and brother also love him. Ronaldo has kept all his promises. He sends me flowers and treats me like a princess. He wants me constantly by his side to show me off.'

On Wednesday, 18 December, Ronaldo scored Brazil's only goal in their 1–0 victory over Bosnia, played in the city of Manaus in the country's Amazon rainforest region. Then he rushed back to Barcelona for a Spanish league match.

On 22 December, Ronaldo made yet another trip back to Brazil for Christmas. But before he left Barcelona, he made a bizarre statement about the disgruntled fans at the Camp Nou.

'I've gone four games without scoring and have been unlucky in front of goal, but I'll be back to normal. I won't forget the fans that barracked me, though. They're just a group of frustrated individuals who go to football to let off steam and forget their problems at home.'

It was an immature response to a difficult problem and,

within hours, Barcelona's official supporters' club issued a hearty protest: 'Ronaldo should do us all a favour and stay in Brazil. He got off lightly for being such a bloody clown, running around with girlfriends instead of concentrating on his game. We pay him a fortune to score goals, so he should shut up and start hitting the net again.'

Privately, Ronaldo was furious about the controversy and he begged his two agents to get him out of his Barca contract as quickly as possible. They told him to calm down and leave the negotiating to them.

Ronaldo managed to celebrate Christmas with his family and new girlfriend. Suzanna gave him a black teddy bear for Christmas after he'd told her how heartbroken he'd been when his last teddy had been lost in the move to Spain. Ronaldo gave her a watch.

He arrived late at a family Christmas gathering much to the concern of his relatives, all waiting expectantly for expensive presents from their multi-millionaire soccer star. Ronaldo eventually turned up with nothing other than some stationery for his mother. He spent the following three hours trying to convince the rest of his family that gifts would eventually follow.

'I went to a shopping mall to get you each something but a crowd of kids wouldn't leave me alone so I had to leave after ten minutes,' he explained earnestly.

What he had failed to mention was that the week before Christmas he'd bought his mother a $500,000 house on an exclusive development a world away from the slums of Bento Ribeiro.

While in Brazil, Ronaldo also arranged the purchase of a penthouse apartment on the Avenida Sernambetiba, a 15-mile long boulevard by the beach at Barra de Tijuca, near Suzanna's family home. Looking up from the white sand you could see the giant Jacarazinho *favela* that almost reached the clouds. It housed almost half-a-million people. Jacarazinho had once been the home to some of the most famous footballers the country had ever produced. It stood there like a reminder of what might happen if it all went wrong.

During those visits to Rio, Ronaldo secretly met with physio Filé who'd helped him on the road to recovery following that career-threatening knee injury at PSV the previous March. He was especially worried about an ankle injury he'd picked up in a Barca game just before he headed for Rio.

To the outside world, Ronaldo seemed to be playing at peak fitness, but Filé was genuinely concerned that Ronaldo hadn't fully recovered the explosive force in his leg muscles, even though his thighs had regained their previous muscle bulk. Filé compared the scenario to topping up half a pint of milk with water: in the end you've got a pint, but it's not the same as before. That made him even more susceptible to other injuries as well.

And he told Ronaldo, 'Your play is all about sheer physical force all the time. If you lose the quality of your physical strength, just the quality of your muscular strength, your performance level will begin to drop.' Then he said ominously, 'You're playing because you're 20 years old. When you're 25, 26, if you haven't recovered, you'll begin to fall and fall dramatically.'

Ronaldo was extremely worried by Filé's words, particularly as the physio was probably the most respected person in his field in Brazil. Pitta and Martins were even more concerned and decided there and then to start moves to guarantee that Ronaldo (and, therefore, they) would be financially secure for the rest of his footballing life. They knew that it had become even more imperative that Ronaldo was the subject of a lucrative transfer.

Ronaldo was their property and they fully intended to get the maximum return on their investment.

CHAPTER 11

Escape from Gringoland

On 27 December 1996, Ronaldo and Giovanni arrived back to disturbing scenes at Barcelona airport. Ronaldo was so jet-lagged he couldn't remember where he'd parked his BMW. Then after a ten-minute jog around the airport car park, he jumped in the souped-up sports car hotly pursued by numerous paparazzi. Driving through red lights, he arrived at the Camp Nou in nine minutes instead of the usual twenty. But he was still two days late and had missed the first post-Christmas training session. Bobby Robson was so annoyed he booked Ronaldo and his two compatriots into a hastily arranged New Year's Day detention.

Ronaldo was furious about this as he considered Robson to be treating him like a naughty schoolboy rather than a multi-millionaire footballer. But his coach was unrepentant and he was particularly pleased that the detention would mean Ronaldo abandoning plans to fly back to Rio yet again for New Year.

The club claimed it couldn't stop Ronaldo spending his time off wherever he wanted but his continued absences raised a crucial question — if a player was receiving £1.5 million a year, surely it was fair to expect him to be free from semi-permanent jet-lag? Robson believed that the incident would enable him to prove once and for all that he was not giving Ronaldo any preferential treatment as some of the other players believed.

'When the other players have their day off, these three will come in to train,' explained Robson. 'I've told Ronaldo that it was a bad idea to fly to Rio again, anyway. You can't do that kind of return journey in two days and expect to be in a condition to play.'

Robson even went to the trouble of explaining to Ronaldo that even though England was only an hour-and-a-half away, he still would be spending New Year in Barcelona. Ronaldo reluctantly agreed to his coach's demands and even admitted, 'I am very sad about this. I would have preferred to spend the New Year with my family, but I have to accept the coach's decision.'

He still managed to return to Rio for two days by slipping out of Spain on 30 December and returning in the early hours of 1 January.

Ronaldo and Suzanna lapped up the sunshine of New Year's Eve 1997 on a beach on the Angra Goareif resort, four hours north of Rio. Before the end of that day, he had his bag packed and was facing a gruelling trip back to Spain.

Ronaldo even assured his agents that he would not miss any Barca training sessions. 'But no one can stop me travelling when I have time off. I can go where the hell I want,' he snapped.

The dreaded extra training session for the three bad boys who turned up late from Brazil went ahead on New Year's Day but it wasn't exactly a low-key affair. The players were outnumbered ten to one by journalists. When coach Robson, just short of his 64th birthday, decided to do sprint training with Ronaldo, it brought a smile to the faces of even the most cynical. Notably, it was Ronaldo who did not seem to see the lighter side of things.

In Rio, driving lanes mean nothing. Most people pass other vehicles whenever a space appears on either side. They say if you really want to drive like a true *Carioca*, never stay in one lane for more than eight seconds.

On 9 January 1997, Ronaldo — back in Rio once again — and Suzanna had a lucky escape when his brand-new black Vector car hit a traffic island on a dual carriage way in Barra. The couple had been on the Avenida de Ayrton Senna when Ronaldo was distracted by a car full of star-spotters alongside them.

Taking his eyes off the road momentarily, he hit the island in the centre of the highway and a tyre burst instantly. Suzanna said later she was terrified that they might be recognised and robbed or killed. Such crimes were an almost daily event in Rio. As it happened, they called her father on a mobile phone and he picked them up shortly after the accident.

Back in Barcelona, Bobby Robson and Barca president Nuñez rolled their eyes skyward thinking about how close the most expensive player in the world had just come to being wiped off the face of the planet. It also further compounded the problem of why he wasn't back in Spain with the rest of the Barca team.

In the second week of January, Ronaldo left Rio for Spain for just four days so he could play in a league game. Then he was planning to return to Rio for just two days so he could spend some more time with Suzanna. 'It's worth it to be here in Rio,' he told one reporter.

It was a crazy schedule but no one dared stop Ronaldo in case he decided to dispense with their services or stop buying them presents.

'I don't care about travelling backwards and forwards,' he insisted. Those who saw him playing beach football with

Suzanna in Rio said he looked tired, and he even became angry with his blonde lover when she dribbled past him for a goal. As the game progressed, it developed from a bad-tempered needle match into a lovey-dovey, kiss-and-make-up session, rounded off when Ronaldo and Suzanna started French kissing. After the game, he did have the good grace to admit, 'I think we get on better when we are not playing on sand. I'm not used to playing football on the beach. Suzanna is more used to it.'

Meanwhile, Suzanna flounced off the beach, insisting, 'Ronaldo is bullshitting. I haven't played for about five months. I was really bad. I was ashamed.'

Back in Barcelona, Ronaldo's team-mates were growing increasingly impatient because he still hadn't scored for five games and they felt — along with Bobby Robson — that he should end his now regular forays across the Atlantic.

Despite being so besotted by Suzanna Werner, Ronaldo honoured a promise he'd made to another girl around the time he and Suzanna first started going out together. Strangely, this new girl, Claudia, also happened to be a women's football star, and played for the same club as Suzanna — Fluminense. Ronaldo had apparently promised to take her out one day.

So Ronaldo, Claudia and her brother took a rowing boat out for a picnic near the $1 million condo owned by one of his agents, Pitta, in the exclusive beachside resort just north of Rio. This place was so snooty that Romario's bid to buy an apartment there was turned down because other residents considered that he might be too rowdy.

Unfortunately, the Rio papers had a field day and published photos of the happy threesome. Back in Rio, Suzanna accepted Ronaldo's explanation as to why he was out with another girl. But she told him in no uncertain terms that he would have to devote himself entirely to her from then on — otherwise their relationship would go nowhere.

In Rio, Ronaldo was feeling the full impact of his fame and the strain was beginning to show. He was fed up with being asked to play football on the beach and hated the way people expected him to perform like a circus animal. He decided to play down his absences from Barca and even refused to be drawn on commenting about the way the Spanish fans had booed him following a recent defeat.

Over on Copacabana, he played a brief game of basketball with his father Nelio in front of the apartment he'd just bought him. Ronaldo assured his family that they would never go short of money again. His move to Barcelona had guaranteed him an everlasting fortune.

A visit to a Rio orphanage was slipped into his busy social agenda almost as a way of sanctioning his trip back home.

Ronaldo also attended Filé's clinic where the trusted physio examined the knee which Ronaldo had injured back in March 1996. Suzanna turned up a few hours later and immediately whisked her lover off for a romantic lunch. On the same day, the Barcelona women's team faxed her an invitation to join the side. It seemed that the Barca board were prepared to do anything to get Ronaldo back to Spain.

The truth was that Ronaldo was extremely homesick during this period. He'd met Suzanna, whom he genuinely cared about, and he didn't want to leave her behind when he had to go back to Spain. Suzanna even told one journalist at this time that Ronaldo would have done anything to play back in Brazil.

But Pitta and Martins could never have allowed that to happen. Their plan for Ronaldomania to infiltrate every corner of the world had only just begun.

* * *

In Spain there was a growing belief that Ronaldo was lapping up sea, sand and blondes while most of his team-mates were attending training sessions. In the Barcelona paper *Sport*, a headline screamed RONALDO IN LOVE and was accompanied by a photo of him and his new blonde. Another paper, *El Mundo Deportivo*, had much the same story as well as an interview with Suzanna in which she revealed the 'inside secrets of their romance'.

Perhaps his sister Ione had the last word on this particular subject. She remarked, 'He's had so many girlfriends nothing surprises us now. The only real surprise would be if he stuck to one girl.'

Also in Rio, physio Filé talked about Ronaldo's injury problems and caused quite a storm.

'After his injury and before the Olympic Games, I sent PSV a video and a summary of what kind of exercises Ronaldo should be doing. I don't know if it was passed on to Barcelona, but looking at him, I'd say his training leaves a lot to be desired. A player who is valued at $50 million should have a personalised work programme to keep him in tip-top shape. At Barcelona he does plenty of work on his speed but not nearly enough on other aspects. And it's no good training just once a day. Ronaldo should be doing an hour-and-a-half of special exercises on his own as well.'

In Barcelona, Bobby Robson was furious when he heard about Filé's claims and hit back, 'I'm quite happy with the general level of fitness in the side. We've played 20 games; if the players are not fit now they never will be. It's the old Liverpool philosophy — you play twice a week and in between you rest and recover.'

But Robson was entirely missing the point. He saw Filé's criticisms as a direct attack on himself and the team in general. In fact, those comments were aimed at the fitness of only one person — Ronaldo.

And in the Barcelona dressing room, four clearly-defined camps were emerging which simply further endangered Bobby Robson's career prospects. Ronaldo and Giovanni had joined forces with at least three Spanish players to mount a round-the-clock deputation on certain player-power issues.

Giovanni even let it be known to the Spanish press that he and the others were behind Robson but only with certain reservations.

'We take risks as a team because we only play with two players in midfield. As a unit we need to improve our tactical preparation. I respect Robson but we need to bolster the midfield.'

Ronaldo — just crowned *World Soccer* magazine's Footballer of the Year — was in a much more defiant mood than his colleague Giovanni.

'Robson needs to change his tactics, not just for my benefit but for the whole team. His system might have worked at first, but as soon as we've faced stronger sides we've had difficulties. I prefer Zagallo's formation. The team is more compact and I receive the ball more often.'

Behind the scenes, the pressure was mounting on Ronaldo to act the tough guy to help his two agents strengthen their hand during the complex ongoing negotiations with Barcelona.

Bobby Robson was furious with Ronaldo's increasingly frequent habit of sending barbed messages through the media.

'I can't believe it sometimes,' Robson claimed. 'Everybody's at it: the board, the players. It's like the papers today with Ronaldo criticising my tactics again; he's 20 years old for Chrissakes ... it's diabolical. Ronaldo says the system doesn't work, but he doesn't work ... or hasn't worked for the last few games. He wasn't complaining when we were winning 8–0 and 6–0.'

On another level, Ronaldo was finding the all-consuming aspects of life at Barcelona quite difficult to handle. He just couldn't switch off, especially since one of his three mobile phones seemed to be going off at all times of the day and night. There was no escape from either the club, the Brazilian national team, his agents or his family ... especially his mother.

Sonia tended to call her son at least once a day to ask

him either for money, to complain that something didn't work at the house, or simply to remind him to be home in time for dinner.

Ronaldo reckoned his life now involved many more complexities he didn't even realise existed until after his departure from PSV. The pressure was constant and his sleeping was starting to suffer.

It wasn't helped during December 1996 and January 1997 by semi-permanent jet-lag, thanks to the numerous trips back and forth between Spain and Rio.

Now his increasingly frequent clashes with Bobby Robson were creating a feeling of dread about coming back to Barcelona from his Rio trips. One night, on the eve of a Barca home game against Celta, he and his team-mates found themselves forced to stay in a city hotel even though most of them lived no more than 20 minutes' drive away. During that uncomfortable evening, Ronaldo was censured by Robson and ticked off like a naughty boy. He did not take too kindly to that type of discipline from anyone.

Barcelona's 1–0 victory over lowly Celta in a muted Camp Nou did nothing to improve the relationship between certain players and their English coach. Ronaldo also received a distinctly unenthusiastic welcome from the 90,000 crowd.

Four weeks earlier, the notion that Ronaldo would be barracked at the Camp Nou would have seemed ridiculous. But four goalless games, ten days of holiday, a high-profile love affair and some multi-million dollar pay talks, had incensed many of the fans. Every time he stumbled with the ball or failed to connect with a pass, he was met with booing and hissing. As the team trooped off at the end, the fans once again raised their hankies and waved them in derision of the players. It was a sorry night for all concerned.

Bobby Robson was so concerned by the fans' attitude towards his $20 million man that he made a point of publicly defending Ronaldo despite the recent outbursts.

'I don't think the fans whistled Ronaldo out of disapproval, it was more a case of frustration. But you have to give him credit for trying the clever stuff on his bad days; the dribbles, the spectacular goals that made people go "Wow!" before. Despite the fact he's reached a dry patch and is not getting the run of the ball, he keeps going for it.'

But Robson knew much of the problem with Ronaldo was that he was physically and emotionally drained after returning from Rio. He was also aware that Ronaldo had never quite fully recovered from the knee injury in 1996. Robson believed that if he kept getting into good positions on the field, then his luck would eventually change. 'The key is to not put too much pressure on him,' he told one journalist. There seemed little chance of that.

At least there was some consolation for Ronaldo; Suzanna Werner was offered a job as head cheerleader for the Barcelona Dragons rugby team. On the same day, the publicity-hungry Suzanna turned up on the front cover of Madrid's *AS* magazine sporting a ball and little else, proclaiming, 'I'm a Real Madrid fan. Ronaldo made a big mistake signing for Barca, a mistake he's already regretting.'

Behind that statement was a message. Ronaldo was exhausted, fed up and deeply restless. He could also hear the dollar signs ticking ever upwards as his two agents continued their protracted negotiations with FC Barcelona.

After 458 minutes without a goal, Ronaldo began to realise he needed all the friends he could get. The background pressure from Ronaldo's agents' negotiations with Barca was immense and Ronaldo even later conceded that activities off the field were definitely affecting his form.

One Wednesday, in January 1997, Ronaldo had to be woken by a club official after he failed to turn up for training. He later claimed he'd been told by another player that it wasn't scheduled until the afternoon. For whatever reason, Robson surprised press and fans alike by not punishing his young superstar for this particular misdemeanour.

The power struggle behind the scenes continued. Barcelona issued a statement confirming that Ronaldo's contract would not be re-negotiated until the end of the season. It seemed like a classic ploy until another money-spinning contract appeared on the horizon and diverted Ronaldo's attention away from his pay talks at Barca.

In the middle of all this, sportswear giant Nike finally wrapped up negotiations with Pitta and Martins to make Ronaldo their biggest ever football signing in a deal that guaranteed the 20-year-old £1 million a year for the next decade. A Ronaldo leisurewear line would also follow. Ronaldo insisted, 'The contract with Nike isn't going to change my life. Money doesn't make you happy. I know because I was poor and happy before.' Not many people believed him.

The Nike deal was a brilliantly orchestrated contract painstakingly negotiated through Ronaldo's agents, but some inside the game were concerned that it would put even more pressure on the player who was already being hailed as the greatest footballer in the world.

On Monday, 20 January 1997, Ronaldo flew to Lisbon to receive an award as FIFA World Player of the Year. After a few recent knock-backs, he was in a modest mood.

'I still don't consider myself the world's best player; to be the world's best you should be a complete footballer and I've still got an awful lot to learn.'

Fellow nominee Alan Shearer saw little room for improvement. 'Ronaldo can do it all: he shoots with both feet, he's good in the air, and he knows how to play for the team. Only God knows what he can achieve in the next four or five years.'

Back in Barcelona, the club fans voted overwhelmingly in favour of Luis Enrique as Barca's best player. Ronaldo saw it as yet more evidence that Barca was not the team for him in the long term. He urged his agents to get back to the negotiating table and thrash out some kind of early release from his long contract.

Not even the ecstasy of a 3–2 victory at the Camp Nou over arch-rivals Real Madrid dampened Ronaldo's determination to escape from Spain, even though he was giving a completely different impression to the outside world.

A night of wonderful football was complemented by some exemplary behaviour, including Ronaldo and Roberto Carlos swapping jokes during breaks in the game. Ronaldo then broke the Barca cardinal rule and swapped shirts at the final whistle (something he has never done since). But despite all the smiles and back-slapping, Ronaldo had made up his mind.

Then Brazil's national team coach, Mario Zagallo, joined in the condemnation of Bobby Robson. 'Barcelona have a squad of extraordinary players, but the whole is disappointingly less than the sum of the parts. Robson's team lack tactical organisation and rely on individual inspiration. The midfield is uncompetitive and there's far too much space between the lines; any decent counter-attacking side would have a field day against Barca.'

Zagallo's carefully measured comments were, in fact, part of the psychological war that Ronaldo and his team of agents and advisers were waging in their battle to prove that Barcelona had broken the terms of the contract because Robson was a defective coach. It was plainly a no-win situation. The only victim at that time was Ronaldo himself because these off-field pressures were continuing to have a detrimental effect on his footballing ambitions.

And without his skills, he was a dead duck.

CHAPTER 12

Last Dance in Rio

In early February 1997, Ronaldo managed somehow to wangle enough time off from playing to make it back to Rio for the world-famous Carnival. The photos that found their way back to the Barcelona newspapers further infuriated the club supporters.

There was Ronaldo discreetly clad in a gold lamé jumpsuit, glittering green shoulder pads, a star-spangled headband and enough blue feathers to fill a duvet. Other shots showed him crashed out in the backseat of a limo with lovely Suzanna close at hand.

Sport newspaper's Miguel Rico echoed many sentiments when he wrote, 'The photos are an insult to everyone connected to FC Barcelona. The club is in the middle of a raging crisis and its biggest star is given special leave of absence to parade around at a carnival. It's beyond belief that Robson gave him permission to go to Brazil when he's got to go back there next week for an international. What happened to discipline and the club's image? What must the fans think about his all-night partying? Not to mention the other players. Ronaldo is Brazilian, he's 20, his girlfriend lives in Rio, he's got two days off and plenty of money in his pocket — he's not to blame. If he thinks he can get permission, of course he is going to take advantage of it.'

Then Ronaldo's team-mates joined in the chorus of disapproval.

'It's not about dancing in Rio,' said Guillermo Amor, 'it's about who gave him permission in the first place with all that's going on here.'

Even fellow Brazilian Giovanni was astounded. 'I love Carnival, too, but as a professional my duty is to be here. A return journey to Brazil for the sake of two days is really heavy going; even if I'd had the time off I would have stayed here.'

In fact, Robson had made the crucial decision to let Ronaldo go back to Brazil even before the Real Madrid game. Ronaldo had asked if he could miss the following Monday's training session. Robson had taken the attitude that from then on the team would be playing twice a week so there would be no further opportunities for him to disappear after this. He'd also secretly done a trade-off with Ronaldo when he made him come back from Rio on New Year's Day and he'd promised he could go back for Carnival.

Behind the scenes, Robson was under immense pressure to keep Ronaldo happy until the end of the season in the hope that his contract could be successfully re-negotiated.

Robson later admitted off the record, 'I can't control players 24 hours a day. When they have time off, I expect them to behave like professionals. But he's only 20. He's always got people saying, "Sign this contract, more money, do this, do that," yet when these guys go to Rio with him they don't say, "Hey, Ronaldo ... duck!" I'd spoken to him and said, "Look, go back to Brazil, see your family and friends, but keep a low profile." Then I come back from England and he's splashed all over the front pages like Joseph in his technicolour dreamcoat.'

On Ronaldo's return from Rio, he was greeted with an army of aggressive Spanish journalists at the airport and accused them of being 'a pain in the neck'. He even insisted he had done nothing wrong. He was clearly as fed up with the Barca fans as they were with him.

'I'm not surprised by the fuss,' he commented, 'nothing surprises me here any more. I've played lots of games lately so its perfectly normal that I get a chance to spend some time at home. When I was at PSV it didn't cause a row but the press here are different.' Then Ronaldo rounded on the reporters. 'I suppose you would have stayed at home if you'd had a chance to go to Carnival. Don't you guys ever get dressed up?'

Significantly, he then blamed his problems on Robson's decision to let him go in the first place.

'That's Robson's problem not mine. I'm just a worker like anybody else, it's his job to run the club.' It was another slap in the face from Ronaldo and one which Bobby Robson would never forget.

It can be safely be presumed that it wasn't until Ronaldo scored a hat-trick against Zaragoza on 23 February 1997 that he started to feel that he was once again enjoying his football.

His agents' negotiations were still continuing but Ronaldo himself took their advice and tried to pull back from direct involvement to concentrate more on his football. But then Martins and Pitta knew that Ronaldo's value would start to take a dive unless he recovered form very quickly.

At the end of February, Ronaldo got another boost when Brazil beat Poland on the début of the so-called 'Ro-Ro tandem' — essentially, it combined Ronaldo and Romario as a strike force to die for. Barca team-mate

Giovanni — keeping Juninho out of the team — even managed two goals of his own.

Once again, Ronaldo's presence back in Brazil prompted more dissent aimed directly at Barca. His agents stated publicly that they were hurt and confused by Barcelona's failure to confirm an upgrade of Ronaldo's new lucrative contract.

'We've given the board plenty of time to finance the new deal; we can't wait much longer,' announced Reinaldo Pitta.

His partner, Alexandre Martins, went one further. 'The train was at Barcelona's station and they let it pass by. From now on, we're not going to say anything about Ronaldo's offers, we'll just let him get on with playing while we study his future. We only have to pay his buy-out clause and he can walk.'

The money games were only just beginning ...

Two days later — on 28 February — Ronaldo publicly insisted, 'I am very happy at Barcelona.' As he came through Barcelona airport following Brazil's victory over Poland, Ronaldo added, 'The only thought in my head is to stay here and win things; there'll be plenty of time to sort out my contract at the end of the season. I know there are clubs prepared to pay my buy-out clause, but if Barca want me to stay, I'll do everything possible to make sure they get their wish.'

The truth behind this complex situation was that Ronaldo and his agents had signed a draft agreement but Barcelona had not stuck to the document's 20 January deadline. Then they asked for another week to sort out a new offer but, by the end of February, Ronaldo and his team had run out of patience. Ronaldo explained, 'I don't understand it, I actually had a ten-year contract in my hand to sign. We only left it because of a few minor details.'

It was a hard-faced attempt to force Barca's hand but the club's laid-back response seemed extremely shortsighted. Many within the club wondered if they realised what a bargain Ronaldo had been in the first place.

Back in Rio, Ronaldo's father Nelio was being seen regularly out on the town in the company of pretty blondes. He'd persuaded his son to invest in a pizzeria in Copacabana which Nelio was going to run. But Ronaldo's father spent more and more time hanging out at bars and in his penthouse flat (also bought by Ronaldo). Far from houseproud, Nelio seemed to use the flat as a virtual ashtray, with a constant fog of cigarette smoke obscuring the cluttered surfaces. Cigarette butts were left everywhere.

'Nice flat, isn't it? Did you see the porter with the gun? If I want to, I can call room service just like that,' Nelio proudly told one visitor.

Nelio also had planned to start up an estate agency in Copacabana, but the firm he had an eye on went bankrupt before he could put a bid in. And he still delighted in telling visiting journalists about the day that his son was named after the 'doctor who closed off Sonia's tubes after his birth. Ha, ha. Doctor Ronaldo, his name was.'

On 1 March 1997, Nelio, aged 47, left his penthouse apartment near Copacabana Beach at 5.00pm to buy some beers from a nearby store. Two policemen came up to him as he got out of a taxi in Avenida Nossa Senhora de Copacabana. They claimed they'd found a bag of 1.5 grams of cocaine on him and demanded $100,000 to cover up the offence.

There had been heavy traffic at that time of day yet no one ever came forward to say they had witnessed what happened next. It says a lot about the relationship between the residents and the police in Copacabana.

What neither of the policemen said at the time was that they knew he was Ronaldo's father because Sonia was living with an ex-policemen who had worked out of the same precinct.

For six hours, Nelio was driven around in a police van

while he 'thought about' the proposition which had been put to him by those two officers. When he refused to hand over the money, he was finally taken to the police station — the 12th precinct station in Copacabana — and charged with possessing cocaine.

Nelio immediately called his lawyer who arrived at the station and announced that his client would not plead guilty to lesser charges of drug possession because he wanted to clear his name completely.

At 11.20pm that evening, he was bailed after paying $110. He left with his lawyer, Neosanero Irica, and a blonde woman who was apparently lying in the back of the Chevette taxi when the police swooped.

When Nelio finally got home in the early hours of the morning, he immediately called Ronaldo only to discover he'd just left for Spain. When father and son eventually spoke, they each sobbed down the phone line as Nelio explained what had happened.

When news of Nelio's arrest leaked out a few weeks later, one Rio newspaper pointed out that Ronaldo's team-mate, Romario, had had similar problems with his father, who had been arrested in May 1994 for drug possession.

* * *

Back at Barcelona, the continual saga of Ronaldo and team-mate Giovanni's constant transatlantic commuting continued to haunt Bobby Robson. Both Brazilians arrived exhausted in the Canary Islands for Barca's match against Tenerife with only 12 hours to spare. Despite jet-lag, they both made the starting line-up.

It was a disaster. Ronaldo wandered around the pitch for the first 45 minutes in a trance. As Tenerife midfielder Alexis commented after the game, 'Ronaldo looked knackered. Maybe he has to play to justify his salary. I can't see any other reason.'

In fact, just minutes before the kick-off, Ronaldo had

been told about his father's arrest back in Rio.

Back in the Barca boardroom, club president Nuñez was still insisting that there would be no re-negotiation of Ronaldo's contract until the end of the season.

Unfortunately, the contract negotiations just would not go away because Ronaldo and his agents wanted the situation resolved before the end of the season. The player himself once again joined in the battle. 'If the president said they didn't agree terms with us, then there's really nothing more to be said.'

Ronaldo's agents were even more forthright. 'The only way that Ronaldo will stay at FC Barcelona after 30 June is if we don't receive a single offer from another club,' barked Alexandre Martins.

Then Nuñez hit back. 'These Brazilians change their tune every five minutes. One day they're saying they'll take Ronaldo somewhere else, the next they say he'll stay here for eight years. Which story are we supposed to believe?'

The last word at the time went to Bobby Robson. He justifiably pointed out, 'The more that's said in public about Ronaldo's contract, the more difficult it'll be to handle the situation properly. I've told the lad to forget about it for now and I suggest everybody else does the same.'

Unfortunately, that seemed extremely unlikely ...

On Wednesday, 12 March 1997, Ronaldo took part in one of the most bizarre games in Barcelona's history. Barely a week after Robson had asked his players for less drama and more skill, a 3–0 deficit at half-time left Barca looking dead and buried. Five goals later, it became one of the all-time great comebacks and it included a hat-trick by Ronaldo.

A few days later, the first of numerous ominous stories that questioned the influence of Nike, Ronaldo's main sponsor, appeared in the Spanish press. *AS* magazine cited a Nike spokesman claiming the company could not justify their investment in Ronaldo if he stayed at Barcelona.

'We can't possibly wait three years until Barcelona's deal with Kappa (the team's existing kit sponsors) ends. That's three years of Ronaldo photos in another kit.'

An inside source suggested that Real Madrid were in a position to link up with Nike and place themselves at the head of the queue for Ronaldo's services. The importance of this story was that it exposed the influence of Nike when it came to their number-one property, Ronaldo.

Meanwhile in Italy, sources claimed that Juventus were prepared to pay for Ronaldo's well-publicised buy-out clause and offer him $25 million for eight seasons.

The following day, Nike insisted they had no involvement in decisions about Ronaldo's future. 'Our job is to manufacture sportswear for the world's best athletes. We are not involved in deciding which clubs our stars play for. Speculation about Nike's involvement in Ronaldo's negotiations with Barcelona or any other club is simply absurd.'

Madrid president Lorenzo Sanz backed the sportswear giant. 'We've had absolutely no contact with Nike or Ronaldo.' By a strange coincidence, at almost precisely the same time, Juventus chief Luciano Moggi called a press conference to insist that his club 'cannot afford to sign Ronaldo'.

Someone had to be wrong. In fact, it was Ronaldo's hard-working agents who were the most likely source of the original story. In Rio, a press conference at which it was expected that they would announce Ronaldo's move to another club was cancelled at short notice. The mystery deepened.

In Barcelona, Bobby Robson tactfully steered clear of the 'Ronaldo for Madrid' stories and simply concentrated on his star striker's immediate future.

'I spoke to him about his fitness on Monday. I want him to eat properly, to sleep well and get plenty of rest. He plays an awful lot of games, in most cases for 90 minutes, and then there's all these trips to Brazil.

'When he gets back, he hardly has time to recover; that's hard for a 20-year-old kid.'

Then why not give him a rest?

'He's our player, we paid a lot of money for him and we want to use him. If Brazil haven't considered giving him a rest, why should we?'

Then, as fate would have it, Brazilian national team coach Mario Zagallo decided to rest Ronaldo for a friendly against Chile. Then he changed his mind. There were rumours that Nike expected Ronaldo to play in all 21 of Brazil's 1997 fixtures, although this was not true.

The following day, 25 March 1997, Italian side Lazio stepped right into the middle of Ronaldo's buy-out clause saga by announcing they were prepared to offer him $4.1 million a year for eight seasons as well as splashing out on the buy-out clause.

Club president Sergio Cragnotti even announced, 'We're working on the loose ends with financial backers, but Ronaldo has agreed to join us.'

Five days later, with all this transfer talk still ringing in everyone's ears but no firm news, Ronaldo once again flew off to Brazil. Before he got on the plane he made one short, curt statement that seemed to sum up the situation. 'My future doesn't depend on whether we win the league; it's purely an economic question.' At least he was being honest.

Back in Barcelona, it was clear that many of the club's hierarchy were growing angry about the continuing Ronaldo 'Will he? Won't he?' saga. Club vice-president of communications Jaume Sobreques told one TV reporter that Ronaldo was 'a troublemaker' and described his agents as 'birds of prey'.

In Brazil, Ronaldo lost his cool. 'I'm furious. Pitta and Martins are like parents to me and Barca should show them more respect. They've been looking after me since I was 14, and my life has changed for the better thanks to them.'

Reinaldo Pitta was even more blunt. 'The more fuss Barcelona kick up the worse for them. They're the vultures;

they promised to improve Ronaldo's contract and haven't kept their word.'

The tide seemed to be turning when Bobby Robson told a press conference at Barca, 'I'm the coach, it's not my decision to take sides in this argument. But if the club's decision is to sell Ronaldo, I can understand it. I've got my own opinions, but Nuñez still hasn't asked me. I was the one who said "Buy, buy, buy" in the summer, even when they warned me the price was going up. But however much I've insisted, it's the board who pay, they have to make the final decision about what's right for the club.

'Ronaldo is probably the best footballer in the world but a club can't depend on one player. I suppose Nuñez doesn't want the other players feeling aggrieved. It's a problem that's difficult to solve and if Ronaldo does go, you're transferring the problems to another club.

'It's also a race with no end in sight. In the summer, we thought he was worth the money we paid for him, now it's 25 million, but where does it all end?'

Then Robson rounded on the traditional whipping boys — Ronaldo's agents. 'The situation is caused by his agents. Ronaldo is their principal source of income so they're constantly testing the market and the possibilities of making a fresh profit. But if I was Ronaldo, I'd look closely at what I'm getting into; he might earn more money elsewhere, but he'll pay more tax and more commission to his agents.

'And where's he going to find a better club and city than Barcelona? It makes me laugh when his guys say one of the reasons Ronaldo wants to go is because he doesn't like playing in my system. Can anybody tell me what club Martins played for? Who has he coached? Did I miss the World Cup he took part in? The day I take any notice of what an impresario says about football is the day I'll be ready to retire. Meanwhile, I'll treat their declaration with the contempt they deserve.'

Barca president Nuñez reckoned that the total cost of

bringing Ronaldo to the club was in the region of £80 million. On the day Robson was lashing out, Ronaldo was further increasing his value by sharing four goals with Romario in Brazil's 4–0 win over Chile.

But the saga was far from over. On 6 April, Ronaldo scored a goal in Barca's 4–0 victory over Sporting Gijon. Then he implied that any move from the club was still definitely on ice. After a meeting with Nuñez, he told waiting journalists, 'There's more possibility of me staying now. Nuñez has told me he wants me to stay, and he knows that I love it here.'

The following day a press conference called by Lazio apparently to announce their acquisition turned into a farce when president Sergio Cragnotti admitted he had not signed and sealed and the ball was firmly back in Barca's court once more.

'I've told Ronaldo's managers that we accept their economic conditions, now it's just a question of waiting. I'd love to bring him to Rome, but as he's already in Barcelona it's easier for them to reach an agreement. We don't want this thing to turn into a soap opera, so our offer only stands until the end of the month.'

It seemed that Nuñez was changing his tune following his meeting with Ronaldo the previous day. He even adopted a paternal-like role when he explained the current scenario to waiting press.

'I'd advise Ronaldo to stay. Italian football is extremely complicated, that's why so many great players struggle there. Look at Laudrup; he was a great player but things didn't work out for him in Italy, yet he was happy here at Barcelona.

'Maradona was the best player in the world and things still didn't work out for him at Naples; Romario hit his peak and won a World Cup while at Barcelona, too. Ronaldo has just come back from Brazil so it was important to talk to him and clear up the confusion about what's been said. I've told him that not only will we improve his salary, but we'll extend his contract.'

Ronaldo's situation was not improved by a lacklustre display the following week during Barca's 1–1 draw at the Camp Nou with Fiorentina in the Cup Winners' Cup semi-final first leg. Even Robson felt sorry for him and commented, 'It was a difficult night for him, he always had two men tight on him.'

Club president Nuñez saw things slightly differently. 'Fiorentina have given Ronaldo first-hand experience of what I told him about Italian football; he'll have far more problems in a league where the accent is on defence.'

And Nuñez's words did not go unnoticed in Italy. *La Gazzetta dello Sport* pronounced, 'Ronaldo's performance was very unimpressive: he demonstrated a woeful lack of initiative and the mobility of a 1950s centre-forward.'

Ronaldo tried to shrug off the criticisms but deep inside he was burning with a desire to prove them all wrong. 'The comparisons don't bother me,' he shrugged. 'Let's see who comes out top before passing sentence.'

On Sunday, 13 April he scored a hat-trick as Barca demolished Athletico Madrid 5–2 in a topsy-turvy game that was a joy to watch and a tactical nightmare for both coaches.

Ronaldo's first two goals were accompanied by a single finger to the lips which sent an unmistakable message to his detractors. But he dedicated his third goal to Athletico's fans with a strident 'Up Yours' gesture which Ronaldo later described as a 'banana'.

'It was just a spontaneous reaction,' he said coolly afterwards. 'They spent the whole game insulting me and my girlfriend.'

To say the pressure was getting to Ronaldo would have been a gross understatement.

CHAPTER 13

Mucho Dinheiro

Barca's $20 million man may have been causing them headaches off the field, but his promised goal-a-game pledge had brought his tally to 40 in 41 games.

On Monday, 14 April, Reinaldo Pitta announced that his star client was staying at Barca after all. 'Barcelona have accepted our conditions, and the contract that'll keep Ronaldo at the club until 2006 is waiting to be signed.' Pitta paused, then added, 'As soon as we receive a bank guarantee confirming the money is available, we'll come straight to Barcelona to sign contracts. We don't want to come over in vain again.'

The umpteenth addendum to the contract saga seemed to be drawing to a close on Sunday, 20 April when Barca's Nuñez announced that Ronaldo's tens of millions had been safely deposited in a bank and his new contract was being drawn up.

Even Ronaldo sounded convinced. 'I know the board

have made a big effort and I'm extremely grateful. I spoke to Nuñez last week and my mind's now at rest. Although I've received serious offers from Italy and England, I've always told my representatives that I wanted to play for Barcelona. I'm very happy to be staying.'

Four days later, Barca surprised everyone in football by beating Fiorentina 2–0 away and securing a place in the Cup Winners' Cup Final. The fact that Ronaldo failed to score did not go unnoticed by the hyper-critical Italian press.

Within hours, he was flying out to São Paulo to make a beer commercial, despite pledges not to advertise alcohol or cigarettes. In fact, it was part of an earlier sponsorship deal signed before Ronaldo left for Europe.

On Saturday, 26 April, just when everyone at Barca thought that the Ronaldo contract saga had finally been resolved, his agents decided to move the goal posts once again. Not only did they demand $5 million a year for their client but they also wanted Barca to pay all his tax as well.

In São Paulo, Ronaldo sent out very confusing signals. 'I still haven't agreed anything with Barcelona. I've not even received a concrete proposal from the club,' he said. 'The board are saying they've reached an agreement with several sportswear manufacturers, but that's impossible. In the first place, I'm not going to get involved with more than one company, and in the second place, I've got a contract with Nike.'

Three days later, Pitta admitted from his base in Miami that 'four or five clubs are willing to pay Ronaldo's clause and Inter Milan are top of the list. He wasn't born in Barcelona, he was born in Brazil. It was a business decision to leave PSV and join Barcelona; he went there to make money. If he receives a better offer elsewhere, he'll go. Business is business.'

On Friday, 2 May, Ronaldo arrived back in Spain from yet another trip to Brazil to play in the national side. This time, he made training but Bobby Robson told him to go home and get some rest. Over the entire season, Ronaldo had gone round the world the equivalent of four times. He'd clocked up 160,000 kilometres and ten countries since September.

Then one of Ronaldo's closest associates told a Rio journalist, 'I know which team Ronaldo is going to sign for and how the deal will be done.' The biggest clue came when Ronaldo's newly-appointed European agent Branchini confirmed, 'Ronaldo has a new club and it's Italian.'

But five days later, Barca's Nuñez was still trying to dissuade Ronaldo from leaving. At a club lunch on the eve of yet another Barca v. Real Madrid match, he pulled Ronaldo aside to lecture him personally on why he should remain part of the Barca set-up. Ronaldo looked far from impressed by Nuñez's words although the following day he did go out and score the only goal of Barca's 1–0 victory in front of 110,000 people.

* * *

Sportswear giant Nike imbues its products with a kind of spiritual superiority, implying that entry to this virtuous and meritorious world can be achieved simply by investing in a pair of trainers or a tracksuit.

But there are only so many pairs of feet in the world and therefore only so many people prepared to succumb to the latest marketing wizardry of pan-global companies like Nike. In 1996, Nike, whose name was taken from the Greek goddess of victory, was brand leader, boasting a 30 per cent share of the world's training-shoe market and sales of almost $10 billion.

Back in 1978, the company had first found its feet, so to speak, when it was claimed that Nike was paying college basketball coaches in the US to use its shoes, or certainly supplying them with free shoes which were passed on to their players. While Nike had not actually broken any rules, the publicity they attracted was enough to scare its competitors — namely Adidas, Converse, Pro-Keds and

Puma — into down-playing any endorsements they had. Nike ignored the negative publicity and made a concerted effort to snap up everyone in sight, forging relationships with global sports stars like Michael Jordan, Michael Schumacher, Pete Sampras and Tiger Woods.

By the early 1990s, the company was still on the lookout for new opportunities despite a predicted slump in the market. It was then that Nike decided to push fast and hard into football.

The company believed that the beautiful game could be its saviour. So immediately after the World Cup in the USA in 1994, they actively began sponsorship deals with entire teams at club and international level, as well as approaching many of the finest players in the world on an individual basis.

In 1995, the Brazilian national team became Nike's highest-profile acquisition, having been snatched from under the noses of arch-rival Umbro for a 10-year deal worth $40 million. In addition, Nike had to pay out more than $5 million in compensation to Umbro. Part of the deal required Brazil to play five exhibition matches a year for Nike, which the company would promote as well as control the TV rights.

Those five games could be played anywhere in the world. Some inside football worried about the fact that that would heavily increase the workload on players already committed to 60, sometimes even 70 games a season at club level. But those fears were ignored by Ricardo Teixeira, the Brazilian Football Federation president. Teixeira, son-in-law of the head of the world football governing body FIFA, Joao Havelange. Watching all these proceedings with bemusement was the legendary Pelé, newly installed as Brazil's Minister of Sport.

As one of Nike's most senior Brazilian executives explained in an exclusive interview in Rio in August 1998, 'Teixeira is like the owner of Brazil. He calls all the shots. He is the money man and no one argues with him. It's as simple as that. But Pelé did not like what he was seeing.'

Within months of the Nike deal there were clashes between Havelange–Teixeira and Pelé over issues involving the national team. Pelé's problems began when he dared to suggest that the structure of Brazilian football was open to the abuse of power and match-fixing.

Perhaps significantly, back in 1960, Pelé's own lucrative player's contract with Santos included a clause that stipulated he had to play for 65 of every 90 minutes, something that it had been rumoured Ronaldo had also agreed to for Nike.

Pelé's war, especially with Havelange, had developed into a personal dogfight, and culminated in Havelange personally banning Pelé from the draw for the 1994 World Cup.

In the two years following the '94 World Cup, Nike contracted its tick trademark to the jerseys of teams from Italy, Holland, the US (Nike has given US soccer $120 million as a 'gift' to help promotion of the game in North America) and Olympic champions Nigeria and South Korea. They also personally sponsored at least 40 individual players, including Ronaldo, Roberto Carlos, Leonardo and Italy's Vieri.

In Brazil, sales of Nike goods went up 20-fold between 1995 and 1997, which was seen as definitive evidence that the company's aggressive marketing activities were well worth pursuing.

The Nike empire in Brazil had been developed from virtually nothing in the early 1990s to become a formidable commercial force by 1996. In Brazil, it was openly acknowledged that the company's top executives in Rio were in regular contact with Pitta and Martins. They helped broker the deal that won PSV Nike sponsorship and they were committed to help any club with which Ronaldo was connected.

In 1997, Nike built a new headquarters in Rio. The

conference rooms were called '1958', '1962', '1970' and '1994', after the years in which Brazil won the Cup. One conference room had no name. The plan was to call it '1998'.

And Ronaldo couldn't wait. 'If Brazil wins the World Cup and I score more than 13 goals, then they can name the room after me.'

In the spring of 1997, Martins made a comment that probably says more about Ronaldo's future than anything else. He told Italy's *Gazzetta dello Sport* that Ronaldo would probably eventually be purchased outright by Nike.

It was a remark that sent shockwaves through European football because if players started to become the property of corporations then the traditional influence exerted by managers, coaches and chairman could be seriously affected.

Martins knew what he was talking about. He and his partner had already calculated that Ronaldo needed at least two more big money moves within Europe before that ominous prediction became a reality. Both agents had narrowed the field down to two clubs: Paris St Germain and Inter Milan. Inter had already started selling off some of their talent and it seemed clear to Ronaldo's men that they were preparing to make a huge offer once they had their finances in place. And, of course, they had already formed a close relationship with Ronaldo and his agents.

In fact, in the spirit of safeguarding the interests of *nosso garoto* (our boy) as they called him, Ronaldo's agents were rumoured to have already secured Ronaldo's deal with Inter Milan as early as December 1996. There was even talk that they'd first spoken about a deal with Inter the previous summer before their client signed for Barcelona.

Meanwhile, back in Barcelona, Ronaldo was still in such demand that a restaurant owner paid him £100,000 just to walk on to his premises. He did not even have to eat there, just to be visible for a few minutes. Despite the transfer uncertainty, the Spanish papers still wanted as much of

Ronaldo as they could get — what he ate, wore, where he went, what he said, and they'd print shot after shot of his latest wonder goal, how he scored it and where his inspiration came from.

Ronaldo had stated that he had always dreamed of this kind of life, so he could hardly complain now it was actually happening. He'd been winning since the age of 14 and learned to overcome many obstacles. Fame was just another irritation.

But further evidence of Ronaldo's on-field unhappiness came during Barca's hard-won 1–0 victory over Real Madrid at the Camp Nou. It was a scrappy game won by an even scrappier goal; after the goalkeeper had parried Ronaldo's under-hit penalty, the Little Buddha had little choice but to nudge home Figo's point-blank assist from the rebound.

More than 200 million TV viewers around the world watched the so-called clash of the titans and all agreed that Ronaldo, allegedly the hottest property of all, was infuriatingly apathetic.

On Monday, 12 May, FC Barcelona's flight to Rotterdam for the Cup Winners' Cup Final was delayed for four hours following claims that a bomb had been planted on board the team's chartered aircraft.

Ronaldo disembarked with his Brazilian entourage that included his mother, Sonia, a bodyguard and his secretary. They retired to a secluded corner and awaited the flight. When the time came, Ronaldo found himself remonstrating with his mother who was not keen to reboard the aircraft.

To many of Ronaldo's team-mates, that incident highlighted the problems facing Ronaldo on a day-to-day basis. Besides having to turn on the magic for 90 minutes of every game, he also had to contend with contract wrangles, a staff of half-a-dozen at any given time and a mother who could often be extremely demanding.

It eventually took Ronaldo all of 20 minutes to calm Sonia down and finally persuade her to board the plane. In the middle of all this, his mobile phones were constantly ringing.

When the team finally arrived in Holland, they found that the Dutch were taking a keen interest in the final at the De Kuip stadium. But then Cruyff, Neeskens, Koeman, Romario, Ronaldo and newly-announced Barca coach Van Gaal had long made the team big news in Holland.

On Wednesday, 14 May, Ronaldo managed at least to put some of those many diversions behind him by scoring a penalty to seal a 1–0 win against Paris St-Germain in front of a 45,000 crowd. It wasn't a classic Ronaldo performance but at least he was threatening every time he found himself within range of the goal.

The following day, the city of Barcelona played host to a euphoric round of celebrations but there was one player among the happy faces of the team who seemed distant, almost detached from the occasion. Ronaldo had to be dragged to the microphone to say *gracias*. To many of his team-mates and the watching crowd it was clear he was about to leave the club. Ronaldo was also made blatantly aware that he was not the Barca fans' favourite hero.

Ronaldo looked on with a blank expression as the crowd shouted for their homegrown heroes, De la Pena and Luis Enrique.

Back in the Spanish league the following Monday, Barca managed a 3–1 victory at Celta Vigo with Ronaldo scoring in the 64th minute, the ninth consecutive league game in which he had scored, overtaking a 53-year-old Barca record. Barca's next game against Deportivo would probably be his last for the club, although no-one had actually said he was definitely leaving yet. When asked by a reporter if he was going, Ronaldo would only say, 'We'll see.'

The following day, 20 May, the Italian press boldy announced that Ronaldo had already signed an eight-year contract for $4.5 million a year with Inter Milan. There was even a promise of more cash and perks depending on results.

In Rio, Ronaldo's agents insisted, 'Everything's ready to take Ronaldo to Italy.'

Ronaldo himself tried to avoid commenting any further on the latest reports and instead chose to tell journalists how disappointed that he was that would be missing Barca's last three matches because of international commitments. 'I know I'm leaving at a bad moment. I'd love to play the last three games and the [domestic] Cup Final, but I can't split myself in two.'

Then Ronaldo was once again asked to comment on whether he was actually leaving the club for good.

'I don't know. All I can say is that it'll hurt me to go. I've got a great lifestyle here. This morning I was sunbathing by the pool in my garden and I said to a friend, "Gee, if we were in Holland now, we'd be locked inside watching telly." But I've got to think about my future well-being and my family, too. If I go, it'll be purely for money. Barcelona is the best football club in the world, but life doesn't begin with Barca, Manchester United or Milan. If I have to leave, *no pasa nada*. Life goes on.'

Two days later, Ronaldo scored his last goal of the season in the last minute of what many presumed would be his last game in Barca colours. Even the 95,000 fans seemed vaguely forgiving of the 20-year-old who had scored 45 goals in 48 games in the pressure-cooker environment of FC Barcelona.

As soccer writer Jeff King explained at the time, 'Ronaldo looked disinterested and when the ball was forced upon him he seemed intent on playing on his own. His future in the balance, you'd have thought a heaving Camp Nou would have been at pains to make their boy wonder feel wanted. On the contrary, there was not a "Please Don't Go" banner in sight or a token chorus of "We love you, Ronaldo, we do ..." In fact, the 20-year-old superstar was whistled as early as the 11th minute, and then successively, for his flagrant individualism. The lack of communion was summed up perfectly, if inadvertently, by the kit man's oversight; Ronaldo spent the first half in a shirt minus the Barca badge.

'He was back to proper gear after the break, but despite the significance of his late winner, Ronaldo's behaviour at the final whistle was indicative of where his heart really lies. While his team-mates headed for the centre circle to say goodbye for the season to the fans, Ronaldo preferred to exchange pleasantries with Deportivo's Brazilian clan on the touchline.'

Once again, Bobby Robson showed what a true gentleman he was by refusing to criticise his $20 million superstar, even though many Barca fans considered Robson's demise to be directly related to the Ronaldo 'problems'.

Later, off the record, Robson admitted to journalist Jeff King that Ronaldo had a terrible game against Deportivo. 'But he gets off the ground and wins the game with a remarkable goal so everybody writes about him. But his performance in the game didn't merit more marks than some of the other players; Sergi, for example. He was up and down the left flank non-stop for 90 minutes.

'Ronaldo was very static, and he lost the ball a lot. Maybe it was a case of getting by on natural talent, but he'll improve and participate more. When he learns exactly when to be selfish, he'll be even more effective.'

Behind the scenes, president Nuñez and his assistants secretly contacted Sonia and tried to get her to persuade her son to stay at the club. It was an unprecedented step but they felt that she could exert the most powerful influence on her son.

Her involvement did lead to a meeting being held but the moment Ronaldo realised the club had tried to influence him through his mother, he stormed out of the gathering and yet another twist had been added to the epic struggle for control of the world's most marketable footballer.

CHAPTER 14

Taking Care of Business

On Monday, 26 May, a group of executives in sombre suits, who looked like the characters from the film *Reservoir Dogs*, turned up at the offices of Barca president Nuñez. As word spread that the Ronaldo affair was finally entering its showdown stage, such a large crowd gathered that police had to put up barricades outside the building. The visitors, all wearing shades and carrying briefcases, had assembled to call an end to the situation once and for all. They were all going to decide on the future of a 20-year-old footballing commodity called Ronaldo.

The opposing factions — president Nuñez, his son Joe and fellow Barca board member Joan Gaspart on one side, and agents Martins and Pitta, and their Italian associate Giovanni Branchini on the other — were each accompanied by an army of bodyguards, secretaries and 'assistants'.

In the early hours of the morning, Nuñez left the

meeting, and proclaimed, 'We've agreed on 90 per cent.' Everyone was confused.

Ronaldo himself had flown to Oslo that morning to join the Brazilian squad for a game against Norway. As he rushed through the airport he told journalists, 'I'll be in touch by mobile and, despite what's been said, my managers work for me, not the other way around. They'll follow my instructions, and I want to stay.'

The following morning, it seemed as if Ronaldo's words had been heeded. At a 4.00pm press conference, president Nuñez announced that Ronaldo was staying. 'He's ours for life,' said Nuñez, who insisted that Ronaldo's contract would be extended until June 2006 with a rising wage scale that would net him an average £2.3 million a year. It was a package that, including Ronaldo's tax obligations, would cost Barcelona a cool £55 million.

It finally seemed as if the entire matter had been settled. Ronaldo told reporters in Norway, 'I've spoken to Nuñez to thank him for the club's efforts.' Ronaldo was so delighted he even immediately ordered a bottle of Catalan champagne and sprayed it Formula One-style over the Spanish press contingent in Oslo.

'If I'm World Player of the Year it's thanks to Barca; when I was at PSV I scored just as many goals but nobody noticed. My managers had told me not to build up my hopes, and I'd convinced myself that moving to Milan was not the end of the world; it's Italy's fashion capital and Inter are a big club, too.

'But I was so desperate to stay I couldn't take in what they were saying. So I insisted and insisted and now they've finally settled it. As I'm getting more money I'll have to score even more goals! This year I've scored 35, but next year I want to do even better. My aim is to smash the Spanish record.'

He had actually scored 34 but, unlike the rest of Spain, Ronaldo claimed that a disputed own goal had been scored by him. Others were astonished that he should claim a goal that was clearly not his. But as one former Premiership striker explained, 'I don't know a top-class forward who *doesn't* try to claim own goals on his personal tally.'

In Oslo, Ronaldo continued gushing to the assembled sports hacks, 'I'll do anything for Barca now. I'll even take dual nationality if it helps them. And if I've got a Spanish passport I won't have to queue so much at Barcelona airports [laughs]. With a Brazilian passport, they always tell you to wait or get in the queue.'

At 8.00pm the following day, Barca's team of lawyers sat down with Ronaldo's representatives once again in president Nuñez's office to iron out the minor details. At 1.00am, the Brazilians stormed out of the building and agent Reinaldo Pitta told waiting reporters, 'As soon as we began to draw up the definitive contract, the problems started all over again.'

At 3.00am, Ronaldo's agents called Nuñez to announce the deal with Barca was off. The following day, rumours swept round the club like wildfire. Then at 7.00pm that evening, Nuñez emerged from his accountants' offices in the city to admit, 'It's all over. Ronaldo is going.'

Two hours later, Ronaldo's agents released a statement confirming that the negotiations had completely broken down. Ronaldo's supposed love affair with Barca was over.

Over in Oslo, Ronaldo's mind was on anything but Brazil's game against the Norwegians. He launched a bitter attack on the Barca board from his hotel.

'It's all over. They've spent seven months deceiving me. I'm leaving and that's that. We'll never sit down to negotiate with Barcelona again; the only thing that matters now is our dignity, it's not an economic problem.

'Nuñez can say whatever he likes but my managers were working for me and I know exactly what happened. He's a liar and he'll carry on lying. We've tried everything to reach a deal but we can't trust the board any more, they're not men of their word. They blame my representatives, but I trust them far more than Nuñez.'

Ronaldo trusted his agents more than he trusted Nuñez. Not surprisingly, bitter, acrimonious comments began circulating in Barcelona. Some said Ronaldo's negotiators had already accepted $5 million commission from Inter through their Italian representative, Giovanni Branchini, himself a Milan resident and close friend of the club president. Others claimed that his agents only sat down with Nuñez to keep Ronaldo happy as they had already signed him away to the Italians. And there were stories that Ronaldo's advisers were so greedy they had asked for his salary for the ninth and tenth seasons to be paid across years one to eight.

Nuñez added fuel to the fire by commenting, 'I'm sure they'd already made a deal with Inter. It was obvious they wanted talks to break down. I accepted things I never should have: they asked for £5 million by ten this morning and we said "Yes"; they asked for ten million more in seven days and we said "Yes"; they refused to pay five per cent of Ronaldo's taxes as previously agreed and we said, "OK, we'll pay them."

'We even agreed to pay everything in dollars. Then they refused to accept that Televisio de Catalunya could pay 15 per cent of Ronaldo's contract or my word as a guarantee. It's clear they only came here because Ronaldo forced them to. I feel sorry for him; when I spoke to him yesterday he was so happy.'

Alexandre Martins hit back almost instantaneously.

'We're not interested in a war of words. We're just sorry that once again it's been impossible to get down in writing what was agreed verbally. Barcelona knew Ronaldo's heartfelt desire was to stay and they thought they could take advantage of that.'

Reinaldo Pitta was even more blunt.

'We're disappointed. They told us Televisio de Catalunya would pay 15 per cent of Ronaldo's contract but when we asked for guarantees they couldn't give us anything, that's why we broke off negotiations.'

But president Nuñez wasn't finished yet. The following

day he hit back once again. 'If Ronaldo was as happy as he says he was and really wanted to stay, I don't understand how he can say no to nearly £50,000 a week. It could be he was playing a three-way game all the time to push up offers from elsewhere.'

Ronaldo was furious at what he saw as slurs on his character and that of his agents.

'They had seven months to sort things out with my managers and all they did was mess around. I'll never let my people sit down with Barca again, there's not that much money in the world.

'All I'm interested in now is having a great season in Italy and preparing for the World Cup in France. I know Nuñez is trying to justify himself by blaming us, that's natural. I just hope the fans understand me. While I was there I did everything to make Barca champions — my conscience is clear.'

The pressure was clearly affecting him. Ronaldo had tired, sunken eyes following a night of tears, his unique smile was absent and he even excused himself from breakfast with his team-mates because he wanted to be alone in his room.

And that pressure would build steadily until it reached bursting point just 14 months later. Ronaldo had genuinely wanted to stay at Barcelona but forces more powerful than him had ruled otherwise. He was no longer his own man.

And as if to compound this scenario, in the middle of all this Ronaldo and some of his team-mates were disciplined by Mario Zagallo for staying up late in Oslo watching pornographic videos at the team hotel. The truth was that Ronaldo was so stressed by the ongoing uncertainty that he couldn't sleep, or so he later claimed.

'Zagallo had to talk to us because he said the bill for porn films was getting too high. We were renting too many of the films. He asked who had been watching the films but nobody raised their hands,' Ronaldo told one amused friend many months later.

More importantly, Brazil suffered a shock 4–2 defeat at the hands of humble Norway. Ronaldo's problems off the field were definitely affecting his form.

By Saturday, 31 May, many were wondering if Ronaldo might still turn out for Barca in their domestic Cup Final. After all, he was still under contract until Inter actually handed over the cash for his buy-out clause.

But Ronaldo made it clear he was not in favour of such a move. 'I know I'm still a Barca player, but I've got no desire to wear the Barca shirt again — I don't want to go within a mile of Nuñez or anybody else from the board.'

The only person involved in this saga who seemed to appreciate the human side of it all was Bobby Robson. He said, 'It's very sad what has happened this week; the best player in the world was ours and now it seems we've lost him. I'd say one thing to Ronaldo: maybe clubs like Inter have got the money to take him away from Barca but that doesn't make them better clubs.'

Robson insisted that Ronaldo should be allowed to have the final word in this now farcical situation.

'It's logical that his managers fight to defend his economic interests but Ronaldo's the one who has to make the final decision. He has the key, he has to decide whether he wants to play in Spain or Italy. There are other great players around, but there's only one Ronaldo. This whole thing is such a mess.'

Amazingly, Barca president Nuñez still hadn't completely given up hope of keeping Ronaldo. He decided to test the strength of the sponsors Nike and their role in the saga. He claimed the sportswear giant was still desperate to see Ronaldo stay at the club.

The role of Nike at this late stage was significant because it was alleged to be the first time a sponsor had openly been able to influence the transfer of a player. It resulted in compounding an already extremely confused situation, with contradictory stories being offered from all sides.

On 1 June 1997, Martins and Pitta arrived at the Brazilian training camp in Lyons, France, where the team were preparing for the Tournoi de France. Ronaldo announced to the assembled press pack, 'Nothing has changed. I didn't open any doors. My decision is made and I'm not interested in talking to Barcelona again, no way.'

Barca vice-president Joan Gaspart even admitted: 'We have to forget about Ronaldo. His representatives have got too much power over him.'

In Lyons, Ronaldo's ever-present battery of mobile phones were in constant use. Some of his team-mates from Barca, including Couto, Figo and Baia urged him to think again. But there was an overwhelming feeling that this time his mind was made up.

On Wednesday, 4 June, Pitta and Martins shared a tense breakfast with their most famous client at the Brazilian training camp at Château du Pizay. Ronaldo was upset with them because of all the transfer confusion, but they convinced him that the best decision would be to go to Inter. Martins even told his client, 'Keep your sentiments for Brazil. You play in Europe to earn money.'

As Martins later explained, 'He understands that now, he's calmed down and accepts we've all got our roles — his job is to play football, ours is to take care of business.'

The two agents then jumped into a cab for Orly Airport. Their destination was Milan and they travelled there on Inter Milan president Massimo Moratti's private jet.

Back at the château, Ronaldo looked shattered. The realisation was finally dawning on him that he had lost control of the situation. He was in the hands of his agents whatever he might say in public. Theirs was a vice-like hold from which it was impossible to break free. At Milan airport, Branchini whisked Pitta and Martins off to a meeting with Moratti.

Back in France, Ronaldo tried to put a brave face on it by insisting, 'My decision is final — I've just signed the documents confirming my departure from Barcelona. Inter are offering the same money but there are more guarantees in the form of payment.'

Barca then stepped in and insisted that both domestic legislation and FIFA rules dictated that only Spanish clubs could sign players using the buy-out clauses. President Nuñez was not going to let his man go *that* easily.

'There's obviously some confusion,' he said. 'This is Spain, not Italy. Ronaldo is not on the transfer list and Inter are breaking FIFA rules by negotiating with him behind our backs.

'He can only join an Italian club if they reach an agreement with FC Barcelona. He can go ahead and rescind his contract via the buy-out clause, but the right to grant his international transfer remains in the power of the Spanish authorities. If Ronaldo doesn't want to play for us, he can't play for anybody.'

And so it went on. Ronaldo was permanently being dragged back into the battle when he should have been thinking, breathing, eating and sleeping football. Nothing else.

Back in France, he snapped, 'They should try reading my contract more carefully. It clearly states I can go to any club I choose on paying my buy-out clause. It was one of the details we took longest to negotiate when we drew up the contract last summer in Miami.

'We specifically asked that the clause be valid for Spanish or foreign clubs to avoid this kind of problem. At least this will show Barca fans why I'm leaving; the board don't even want to respect what's written in contracts.'

Pitta and Martins then provided a chorus line. 'One of the biggest mistakes Barcelona have made is to act behind our back with their dirty tricks. Their second big mistake is that they tried to buy us off. They wanted to give us $2 million more when negotiations broke down; we felt like telling them to stick the money up their asses.'

Then Real Madrid entered the battle obviously enjoying the predicament that their rivals Barca found themselves in. If Ronaldo could only sign for a Spanish club they'd happily act as a stepping stone. Club president Lorenzo Sanz even admitted, 'As president of Real Madrid it's my obligation to try and weaken Barcelona, and doing so seduces me. It's not our war, but if we can take advantage of it ...'

Back at the Camp Nou, Bobby Robson continued to sound like the only voice of reason in the whole sorry saga.

'I still can't believe he's going. The problem was the board's inability to get along with his managers; they've never managed to sit down with them and clarify all the problems.

'It's a crime the boy's leaving here. And it's crazy that the boy's been in Barcelona eight or nine months and the decisive negotiations are going on while he's away on duty for Brazil. My impression is that Ronaldo really wanted to stay, but his guys have influenced him, I don't think there's any doubt about that at all. A Barcelona with Ronaldo at 20 and improving all the time are far better off than a Barcelona without him. I'm very sad.'

In early June 1997, in France for Le Tournoi, Brazil enjoyed mixed fortunes; they drew 1–1 with France thanks to the now legendary thunderbolt free-kick from Roberto Carlos; then they had a nerve-racking 3–3 draw which featured a goal from Ronaldo; finally, they beat England 1–0 thanks to a Romario goal set up by a perfect pass from Ronaldo.

The movement of Romario, Ronaldo and Leonardo always threatened to upset the English composure and discipline. As England coach Glenn Hoddle pointed out, 'That Ronaldo, you think he's lazy and then suddenly he runs at you and he's opened you up.'

The British and Brazilian press tried to project the England game as a battle of the two strikers — Ronaldo and Shearer. But most admitted that the Brazilian was in a different class to Shearer.

As Brazilian skipper Dunga told one reporter, 'Shearer

has only played in England, and only really scored goals in England. Until he has played and scored in another league he cannot be compared to Ronaldo who has scored in Holland and Spain.'

A few hours after watching the Brazil–England game, Martins gave a clue, for the first time, that his opinions were not just going to be limited to money. 'It was a terrible game.' He said that the only memorable moment came when Shearer and Ronaldo kicked each other. 'Before the match, I told Ronaldo, "You should shake Shearer's hand." A nice picture: Ronaldo and Shearer, the most expensive players in the world. Instead of being grateful, Shearer kicks Ronaldo in the balls. Did you see how upset Ronaldo looked? But he gave him one back.'

When Ronaldo was in Paris during Le Tournoi, he found yet again that the sheer number of matches and non-stop travel were taking an awful toll on his nerves.

The risk of an early burn-out seemed a real possibility for the first time although Ronaldo insisted in France, 'I am only 20 years old. I can take more than a player of 30. Also, I am used to playing a lot. As a child I played football all day.'

He also voiced a very different opinion of where he was going to end up playing his club football. 'I don't care where I play next year. Inter or Barcelona — the Brazilian team remains the most important thing for me.'

But what was it about playing for Brazil that meant so much to Ronaldo?

'Everything. The atmosphere, the happiness. It is the only team where I am not criticised for my so-called egotism. Nobody ever complains that he is being passed over. You'll never see one Brazilian chastise another the way Frank and Ronald De Boer do it, with those horrible gestures.' It sounded a shade naïve and those words would come back to haunt Ronaldo one day.

On Friday, 6 June, Ronaldo's agents insisted that talk of legal problems over the Barcelona buy-out clause was simply a smoke screen. 'If Barcelona are trying to get us to negotiate again they can forget it,' said Martins. 'Ronaldo's clause is very, very clear. He can choose to go to the club he wants.'

Over in Milan, Inter president Moratti was positively ebullient. 'Ronaldo is mine. I've given myself a present.' Once again, Ronaldo sounded more like a product than a human being.

And Ronaldo himself contributed to the debate. 'I'm not going to Real Madrid because it's unnecessary. Once I pay my clause I can go wherever I want. Barca are powerless to stop me.'

One little known fact was that during his negotiations with Inter, Ronaldo tried to insist he be given the Number 9 shirt. He even told one Inter executive, 'I'll play the same football no matter what shirt I wear, but I really want number nine.' In the end, a compromise was reached and he was promised he could have it after he'd played one season at Inter.

The club were happy to agree to the condition. But what they didn't realised was that Ronaldo and his agents were more concerned with the commercial marketing potential of 'R-9' as a trademark than for any sentimental reasons.

As usual, business came first.

In the middle of all this, Barcelona president Nuñez bizarrely announced that he had tied up a very handy £90 million, ten-year kit deal with Nike, despite the fact that the club's existing contract with Kappa didn't finish until June 1999. Nike had even agreed a £9 million down-payment.

Some observers suggested that while Nuñez had accepted he'd lost Ronaldo he had gained an even more profitable acquisition.

Meanwhile, the supposed deal with Inter was still not signed and sealed. Branchini was still flirting with Roma in an unsubtle attempt to close the deal in Milan.

Behind the scenes, many in Barcelona were saying that Nuñez was delighted to say good-bye to Ronaldo. 'He never wanted to sign him in the first place,' said one local reporter with close contacts to Nuñez. 'On the day Ronaldo arrived, he spat at journalists, "You've signed Ronaldo, not me." He's never been happy about a player whose fee represents such a high percentage of the club's budget, especially when Ronaldo was uncontrollable because of the whole Brazil/Nike thing.

'When Barcelona failed to meet the January deadline for revising Ronaldo's contract, Nuñez didn't even bother to get in touch with his agents. In those kind of cases, it's standard practice to make a down-payment that's equivalent to their commission. If you keep the agents happy, you've generally got the player.

'Here in Catalonia, Ronaldo's entourage have been depicted as the villains of the peace; now I'm sure they're getting a nice commission from Inter, but basically their version is true.'

Two weeks later, on 20 June 1997, Ronaldo's lawyers deposited a 4,000 million peseta cheque ($27 million) at the Spanish league HQ in Madrid, leaving him free to join the club of his choice.

Half-way across the world at Copa America in Bolivia, Ronaldo signed a five-year contract with Inter Milan worth $7 million a season plus a $10 million signing-on bonus. Or, at least, that's what everyone was saying.

The issue remained unresolved even as Ronaldo and the rest of the Brazilian team played against host nation Bolivia in the final of the Copa America in La Paz, on 29 June 1997. The game turned out to be evenly balanced but two goals in the last 15 minutes gave Brazil a 3–1 victory.

It was an exhausting experience thanks to the high altitude conditions in La Paz. 'There was no air. I couldn't breathe. It was terrible. I ran and barely moved,' gasped Ronaldo to a packed press conference following the victory.

At least he'd managed one goal from a finely judged Denilson pass.

Barcelona, meanwhile, lodged a formal complaint with the Spanish league insisting that Inter were in breach of FIFA regulations. The league then announced that it would withhold Ronaldo's international transfer until the matter was resolved.

Incredibly, a few days later, Nuñez was still insisting that Ronaldo was an FC Barcelona player.

Inter president Moratti seemed remarkably unconcerned by all the complications. 'Ronaldo is going to be at Inter for ten years, so we can afford to lose a few months. I'm not going to lose any sleep.' Moratti had already confirmed that the Italian FA were completely behind him.

In Bolivia, Ronaldo insisted, 'I'm now an Inter player. When FIFA read the contract they'll realise that once I'd paid Barca the buy-out clause I was free to join Inter.'

In reality, Nuñez had accepted defeat and was already actively pursuing players, such as the Argentinian Gabriel Batistuta, as a replacement for his departing wonderboy.

Less than a year later, Bobby Robson reflected on Ronaldo and offered his opinion of what the future held for him. He made one ominous point: 'I believe only injury will stop him developing into one of the all-time greats, possibly the greatest of them all, and also if he loses his drive, becomes fed up with the game and looks for another side of life. In terms of potential, he is a cut above anything else I have seen.

'Ronaldo was portrayed as a greedy young man but I never had a problem with him or his attitude; in fact, the biggest problem I had with the lad was getting him off the training pitch because he would always say, "Please Meester, just a leetle longer, just a few more shots."'

CHAPTER 15

Nosso Garoto (Our Boy)

In late July 1997, Ronaldo took Suzanna Werner out for a 20th birthday treat when he got back to Rio. He also told her he wanted to tell the world about their love for each other.

Suzanna later explained, 'He asked me if I would come out for a quiet romantic meal with him. First, he took me to a boutique and bought me a beautiful dress.

'But we drove to a villa, not a restaurant, and once inside I came face to face with everyone I knew. Family, friends ... about 300 people. There was a splendid banquet with live music.

'Then Ronaldo took the microphone and announced, "This is to make our love official in front of everyone."

'He took a beautiful ring and slipped it on my finger. The next day I gave up my two parts in soap operas and flew to Europe with him. I'm profoundly in love. Off the pitch he's such a gentle, quiet man. He doesn't talk about football. We just play games like kids — cards and video games.'

Ronaldo even purchased a larger apartment in Barra de Tijuca where he intended to have a room built filled with computers for all his games.

'That is the house where we will live when we are married,' said Suzanna. 'It has an amazing view and is our little love nest.'

At that same engagement party, Ronaldo and Suzanna pledged they would marry by December of that year 'at the latest'.

Suzanna proclaimed proudly, 'The wedding will be in Rio in the St Agostino Church in the area where I was brought up. I took Communion there and when I was little went to that church every Sunday.'

Suzanna insisted to anyone who would listen that she didn't care about Ronaldo's tens of millions.

'I don't want villas, cars or jewels. He knows what I want ... a baby.'

Would those dreams really come to fruition?

In Rio in the summer of 1997, Ronaldo also agreed to appear on a TV chat show hosted by another ex-Bento Ribeiro resident, a shapely blonde called Xuxa.

She was already the most famous woman in Brazil thanks to an affair with Pelé after which she sold the story of their wild sex life together. Then she'd switched her attentions to Pelé's successor as Brazil's ultimate sporting genius, Ayrton Senna.

When she became pregnant, the Formula One champion rubbed salt into the wounds by saying that, 'If it is a girl, I will send it to France; a boy, I will send it to Switzerland; if it is black, I will send it to Pelé.'

Despite her background, Ronaldo seemed intrigued, almost bewitched by Xuxa and gave her what was probably his frankest ever interview and opened up about a number of subjects that many thought he should have kept to himself.

He admitted drinking beer regularly to overcome shyness, especially when he was dancing with a girl; he also told Xuxa he found it difficult to accept when Suzanna had to kiss another actor as part of her role in the Rio soap opera she had starred in.

'I am very jealous. The day I saw this scene on the teenage soap opera when Suzanna kissed another guy. I called her and told her she shouldn't have done that.' It was the second time he brought it up with Xuxa so many viewers not surprisingly concluded that he was obsessed by it.

He even talked about how he had wetted his bed after being confronted about the infamous pitch-wetting incident before the kick off of a Brazilian league match. He told Xuxa, 'I do it sometimes.'

Then he told her all about his sex games with Suzanna. 'Sometimes we do a lot of that. We like sex games. Sometimes we dream we're in a bathroom and it's happening. Anything between four walls goes as far as we are concerned.'

He also revealed Suzanna's pet name for him — 'Baby'.

Suzanna wasn't quite so happy when he told a television audience of 50 million that he was 15 when he first made love to a girl.

As far as sex itself was concerned, he said, 'I love to kiss from head to toe. I really miss Suzanna. She's about to spend three months in Italy so we are going to get to know each other much better.'

Then he told Xuxa what really annoyed him in women: 'I can't stand lies and fraud in a woman.'

As far as Suzanna's jealousy towards him was concerned, Ronaldo then told the vast audience a strange little tale: 'Suzanna got very jealous of me in a nightclub because a woman asked me to take a straw out of her mouth.' He did not elaborate.

When it came to romance, Ronaldo insisted, 'I am faithful. Well I try to be. When I enjoy myself I'm faithful. When I'm unhappy that's different.'

As soon as news of Ronaldo's confessions to Xuxa

reached Italy, he earned himself a new nickname: 'Pee-in-the-bed'.

One reason why Ronaldo left Barcelona was because his £46,153-a-week, tax-free wage packet was provided by 'ghost companies' set up by Barca president Nuñez. It was all perfectly legal but Ronaldo and his agents were fed up of never knowing where the cash was coming from.

They insisted that all his money should come from one bank at the end of each month — and that was what finally opened the door for Inter Milan.

A Spanish government crackdown on tax avoidance had forced Nuñez into a corner because, as was common practice in Spanish football, Ronaldo had signed two contracts — a playing deal and a second agreement for tax purposes, making him self-employed and a director of a limited company.

In Ronaldo's case, 56 per cent of his earnings went into that 'company' but that was then reduced to 15 per cent, giving him a huge loss in earnings and putting pressure on Nuñez to find a new way of easing his tax bill.

To continue to pay Ronaldo his full salary, Barcelona would have to come up with 60 per cent more to satisfy the Spanish tax man.

Ronaldo was already on £1 million a year from Nike, and Nuñez was angry that Ronaldo was called up so often to play for Brazil — also sponsored by Nike. Nuñez and his backroom staff had already worked out that if Ronaldo was selected for every Brazil fixture for the coming 1997–98 season then he would be away from Barcelona for *two-and-a-half months*.

The situation was perfectly summed up when one newspaper in Britain ran a photo of Ronaldo, looking exhausted on a plane holding his mother's hand as she sat beside him. The headline screamed: IF THIS MAN IS WORTH $45M, WHY DOES HE STILL GO TO SLEEP HOLDING HIS MUMMY'S HAND?

Yet another agent entered the ring while Ronaldo's tug-of-war between Barcelona and Inter Milan rumbled on through the early summer of 1997.

Venezio Fiorenelli, known in certain European football circles as 'the man without a face' because he was so keen to avoid publicity, insisted that Ronaldo's £50 million-plus transfer was 'cheap at the price'. He had actually represented Lazio during their eventually doomed transfer bid for Ronaldo.

He explained, 'He's the only player in the world who is worth so much because of the commercial spin-offs. Any club who invests in him can definitely get their money back. Everybody calls him the most expensive footballer in the world but he is one of the cheapest at that price.

'Ronaldo is re-financible, part of a concept. He is the only player in the world who can be part of a company's marketing strategy. He has a bigger following than any other sportsman anywhere and more publicity value than the next five top players put together.'

Fiorenelli even admitted that many clubs were frightened off by the massive sums of money that Ronaldo's three agents had been demanding. He said, 'The transfer rights to Ronaldo are not affordable to any club in the world. The total cost works out at £80 million over seven years. Even if he scores 50 goals each season and helps his team win their league and cup competitions, he's still not affordable in traditional terms.

'But this is where the marketing structure of the club and future policy is absolutely vital.'

Scottish champions Rangers were well aware of those financial possibilities and that was why they appeared on Ronaldo's final short-list of six clubs. But as Ronaldo pointed out at the time, 'What do I want at Rangers? There's no future for me there. There's no real competition.'

Just to make sure Suzanna Werner kept up with her high profile boyfriend, stories began appearing in various newspapers claiming that she was about to sign for the Bologna women's team in Italy. She even told Italian newspaper *La Gazzetta dello Sport*, 'I want to carry on playing football. I love it so much. I'll speak to Bologna as soon as I arrive in Italy.'

As an afterthought, she also said, 'But then I have my career to think of — modelling and television. And I might want to start a family ...'

In Rio, Ronaldo's father Nelio and brother Nelinho both shaved their heads bald. Nelinho looked so much like his kid brother that he started being chased in the street by autograph hunters. When Ronaldo heard that, he put Nelio on the payroll as a decoy so he could leave places without being swamped by the paparazzi.

Another inducement for Ronaldo to join Inter Milan was yet more corporate sponsorship. Inter's main backers, Pirelli, were keen to break into the South American market and they had pledged to underwrite any offer by club president Massimo Moratti. They had a 14 per cent stake in the club and wanted to see off rivals Goodyear. Pirelli even envisaged Ronaldo as an ideal pin-up for their famous calendar.

Back in Rio in December 1997, Ronaldo's ex-girlfriends Nadia and Vivianne posed together for a set of racy nude and lesbian pictures for the Brazilian edition of *Playboy*. It was the ultimate piece of exploitation but Ronaldo refused to take any legal action against them despite being urged to do so by Pitta and Martins.

A few months earlier, the two girls — now known throughout Brazil as the 'Ronaldinhas' — had even hosted the pilot of a TV sports series on nationwide TV in Brazil.

'They were trying to turn their experience into a virtual industry. It was a classic piece of exploitation,' said Rio journalist Ruth de Aquino.

And the soft porn spread of photos provoked an interesting response from Ronaldo's latest lover, Suzanna Werner. 'I'm not worried. They knew what they were doing.'

But then she had the satisfaction of knowing she had what both Nadia and Vivianne wanted; the long-term love of the richest, most famous footballer on the planet.

Nadia gratefully conceded, 'I have to thank Ronaldo for everything because I know this fame has only happened because of him.' Strangely, Nadia had just landed a small part in the same soap opera which had starred ... Suzanna.

Nadia insisted that Suzanna was angry. 'I think Suzanna is really angry because the magazine called up Ronaldo for a comment but we are not to blame for that.'

The other Ronaldinha, Vivianne, remained convinced that their pornographic poses were just what the Brazilian male population needed. 'People like to see girls together. They like to see the ex-girlfriends of idols like Ronaldo.'

Eventually, both girls joined a dance troupe that specialised in showing off their buttocks to men in bars and clubs. They had no doubt that their new-found celebrity was down to the fact they were Ronaldinhas.

A manager called Mauro Cardon took over all the business affairs of Vivianne and Nadia in much the same way Pitta and Martins had taken over Ronaldo when he was 14.

But the big difference was that the two girls specialized in a routine called the bottle dance where they would wiggle their rears down into a crouching position to the point where they would come very close to being able to pick up a bottle.

* * *

In the summer of 1997, Suzanna Werner let slip her ambitions when she told one journalist she was hoping to move to London to further her modelling and acting career. There was no mention of whether Ronaldo would be joining her.

New English ladies' champions Arsenal immediately made a bid to sign her up for their team. Manager Vic Akers said, 'With her looks and skill I'm sure she'd prove a massive crowd-puller.'

Suzanna made it clear she was open to all offers and said, 'I play football because I like it, but it's not my first priority. To tell the truth, I love working in fashion.

'I've modelled for all the top designers in Rio, but if I had the chance to work in London I'd do it with great pleasure. Europe is the centre of the fashion world and London would be the perfect base.'

Then Suzanna revealed another small motivating factor. 'When I really want something I get it. I hope that now I'm in the news as Ronaldo's girlfriend people won't forget what I've done for myself.'

Meanwhile, Ronaldo tried to explain to the world the reasoning behind his move to Inter.

'All the great players of the past have been linked with one team. Think of Pelé and Santos, for example, with one team shirt. I want to stay at Inter for a long while and play a big part in the club's history. Leaving Spain wasn't easy but the set-up at Inter is very impressive and I know that this team will be one of the biggest in Europe for years to come.'

But before Italy, there was yet more travelling to be done ...

* * *

Spanning the spectrum from deep pink to lizard green, the Art Deco structures on Ocean Drive, Miami Beach, were built to uplift the spirits of Americans and offer a distraction from the Great Depression.

Over 60 years later, they had helped turn the beach area into a lurid collection of icing sugar façades, earning Ocean its nickname of 'Deco Drive'.

The day after Ronaldo and Suzanna arrived in the so-called American Riviera for the Miami Beach Carnival, they found themselves caught up in the biggest news story in the world.

On 15 July 1997, world-renowned fashion designer Gianni Versace was shot twice in the back of the head and left to die in front of his $5 million South Beach mansion. Welcome to the USA.

Versace had been murdered by Andrew Cunanan, a cunning cold-blooded killer who had eluded police for three months on a cross-country murder rampage that only ended when he shot himself on a Miami houseboat eight days after Versace's death.

Ronaldo and Suzanna were like a couple of kids in a sweet shop when they hit Miami in the middle of all this drama. Instead of putting Ronaldo off America, it made him even more intrigued and he told Suzanna that he'd love to live there some time in the future.

When he and his fiancée took part in a local Brazilian carnival, they were hardly noticed. It was the kind of anonymity that really appealed to Ronaldo. He'd finally grown weary of stardom and looked forward to the day when he lived in a place where no one knew who he was.

On 27 July 1997, Ronaldo made his first appearance for Inter Milan in a friendly against Manchester United at the San Siro stadium in front of almost 50,000 people. However, the crowd was left disappointed when he left the field after just 17 minutes of play.

In Italy, the occasion was seen as second only to the night in 1985 when 80,000 Neapolitan fans crowded the São Paulo stadium for the arrival of Diego Maradona.

Typically, commentators seemed more concerned with the fact that the £550,000 gate takings represented a first instalment on Inter's massive investment in Ronaldo. Ronaldo's initial appearance on the pitch 45 minutes before the kick-off earned a rapturous standing ovation, complete with flares and firecrackers.

Even when Ronaldo was replaced by Chilean striker Ivan Zamorano, there were no complaints from the crowd who had been gripped by Ronaldo fever all weekend. The eventual result of 1–1 was of little significance as it was only a friendly, but the response to Ronaldo provided an insight into the air of expectancy his arrival in Milan provoked in many of the club's fans.

Ronaldo's move to Inter was a colossal gamble by both the player and the club. He was putting his reputation on the line and Inter had put up an estimated £30 million fee, including £8.8 million in payments to Ronaldo's three agents and himself, plus a nine-year contract worth an annual £3.7 million.

There was a lot riding on Ronaldo's move; Inter had been in the shadow of their neighbours AC for longer than most cared to remember. Meanwhile, other respected leaders in Italian football were far from convinced by the move.

Gianni Agnelli, former Fiat president and the man behind Juventus, said, 'I'm not entirely convinced that Ronaldo will turn out to be such a good buy ... he's a very good player, I think the best around at the moment, certainly the best striker, but having said that there's no certainty that Inter will win everything ...'

Agnelli's observation came hot on the heels of a claim by one Italian sports economist that Ronaldomania in the country would be so positive that over the following nine years, Inter would more than double their total £80 million investment in Ronaldo through increased revenue from season tickets, sponsorships, television rights, friendly match fees and merchandising.

No one bothered to consider whether Ronaldo could survive that long.

CHAPTER 16

Il Fenomeno

In Italy, Ronaldo immediately suffered from bouts of loneliness because Suzanna regularly travelled back and forth between Europe and Brazil on various work commitments. Inevitably, he turned to his mother when he was feeling at his most isolated. Sonia didn't hesitate to rush to her son's side.

Ronaldo was happy to put up with the constant barrage of phone calls on his mobile asking what he wanted for dinner, what clothes he needed washed and ironed and when he was coming home, because his mother had long since been the rock upon which he relied so much.

At Inter, his team-mates got fed up with the constant calls but Ronaldo ignored all their protestations. 'We advised him to switch off his mobile but he just didn't want to know,' one colleague said.

A few weeks after moving into a vast suite of hotel rooms in Milan, half-a-dozen of Ronaldo's old childhood friends turned up in the city. Naturally, they wanted

Ronaldo to go out partying with them.

But Sonia stepped in and wouldn't let Ronaldo go with them. At first, Ronaldo was furious and sulked in his bedroom like a child. Then Sonia explained to him why it wouldn't be wise only a few weeks after joining Inter.

Later even Sonia admitted, 'They wanted to take him out for a good time. I didn't let them do that and I fought with Ronaldo but in the end everything turned out OK.'

Undoubtedly, Sonia only had her son's best interests at heart. As she told one friend, 'Ronaldo doesn't complain about many things but he worries a lot about football. We have an understanding that we will not bother each other but I am his mother. I have a right to an opinion.'

One of the few problems between Ronaldo and his mother centred around her new husband, the same ex-policeman whose former colleagues had arrested his father (the case was still pending).

'I think he was a bit jealous of him at first,' said Sonia. 'I love my son and it's only natural that he should be slightly jealous of my new husband.'

Ronaldo's rather cold treatment of her new husband was directly related to his hope for many years that his mother and father would reconcile. Then Ronaldo went through a stage of hating his father for breaking up the family in the way that he did.

Only a few weeks earlier — just before Ronaldo arrived in Milan to start pre-season training in August 1997 — he spent two days in Venice with Nelio. It was ironic that all of Ronaldo's accumulated millions were now helping father and son to bond in a way they had never done when the family was still together.

Sonia insisted it was a good thing. 'It was very important that Ronaldo made peace with his father,' she said. But then she made a point of adding, 'We are giving Nelio all the support that we can now that he is free from drugs. There are people in the family who think I am crazy to let Nelio stick around with us but I think that my son's suffering is over and that's all that matters.'

Sonia continued to tell relatives, friends and even some journalists, that she would never interfere in her son's life. But then she'd admit, 'When I see him doing something bad I tick him off very hard. Like that time I stopped him going out with those guys. Ronaldo knows that I only nag him for his own good.'

Ronaldo still has to this day that old-fashioned Latin respect for his mother. He needs and wants her approval for just about everything he does — even down to his choice of girlfriends.

Sonia explained, 'When he meets somebody he always introduces me to them and asks for my opinion and whether I like or dislike the girl. He has put me on a pedestal I suppose. He respects me a great deal.'

Suzanna Werner had clearly passed Sonia's suitability test, but Ronaldo's mother was very guarded in her response when it was pointed out that Suzanna had already started telling friends back in Rio that she often felt very lonely when Ronaldo was away playing football.

Sonia said, 'Suzanna likes him a lot. She's different from the other girls and that is the most important thing for the family.'

But Sonia had been quite surprised when Ronaldo and Suzanna announced their engagement in the summer of 1997. She said at the time, 'I think it's a bit early but it's what he wants.'

In many ways, Sonia still saw her son as a boy in his early teens. She felt he had not grown up much since the day her ex-husband signed away ten years of his son's life at the age of 14. Talking about the marriage plans, she even commented, 'Ronaldo's still playing with his friends. One hour he wants to marry, then later he says something else, then a week later something else.'

Naturally, Sonia did not want the marriage to go ahead too soon because that would mean losing her son. 'I hope he doesn't marry too quickly.'

It was also extremely difficult for Sonia to accept that her son was a fully grown man, considered by millions across the globe as a sex symbol.

When one journalist pointed this out, she snapped back, 'No, he's not. The people who say this are just using him from a financial point of view. Nothing else. Many of the same people have written that he's ugly, he's got big teeth and so on. Ronaldo's not pretty, not ugly. He's just a normal guy.'

Sonia fully appreciated that without football her son would be just another kid from the *favela*. That meant she often took the beautiful game as seriously as him.

When asked what made her really angry, she replied with complete seriousness, 'To see my son miss a penalty. Then my day is finished. It looks so easy to take a penalty.' Then she added: 'Of course, I also get very angry when they push him around on the pitch and try to hurt him.'

Within weeks of arriving in Italy, the often hysterical Milan press had nicknamed Ronaldo 'Il Fenomeno' — the phenomenon. In his first eight games for Inter, Ronaldo scored six goals.

But perhaps not so surprisingly, Ronaldo soon discovered that he'd get few favours in Serie A, even from his old Brazilian compatriots. Playing against the skilful Aldair during a clash in Rome, Ronaldo received a distinctly unfriendly punch in the ribs early on. Ronaldo said nothing, climbed to his feet and minutes later set up an Inter goal after a brilliant turn of foot that left Aldair stranded.

Ronaldo had some very blunt words on the subject of Italian football.

'Italy is still the land of the *catanaccio*, even if they don't use the word any more,' he said. 'Now they talk about *ben messo* (well arranged) but it comes down to the same thing. Every team plays from defence. They let the opponent come, and then they surround you, cement you in and crush you to death. Every match I have three, four defenders with me. Thanks to my speed I can sometimes break away. But usually the first man brings me down.'

He sounded positively under-whelmed by life in Italy but still insisted he would not be looking for yet another move.

'I feel in my place with Inter, and I think I can play there for years. We have a team with strong internal ties. And I'm not afraid of a little resistance. A top-class player can only get better in Italy. Because the bit parts are also well performed, you automatically play a speed higher, with more concentration. In Holland, you have to show a trick ten times to get people clapping. In Italy, they're satisfied with just one move.'

Ronaldo's words sounded peculiarly reminiscent of those he had uttered less than a year earlier in Spain. The tight Italian defences were exhausting Ronaldo much more than most people realised.

Meanwhile, Ronaldo's new Inter team-mate Aron Winter summed up the massive influence he had at the club since arriving during the summer.

'As soon as he gets on the field, you can sense an atmosphere of fear among the opposing players. He gets the ball and immediately there is danger. You can feed him whether he has space or not because he will make it anyway. The part of his game people underestimate is the work he does for others.'

Back in Rio, Pitta and Martins were watching their earnings shoot into the millions. Thanks to their representation of the world's most famous footballer, a total of 66 other major stars — mainly Brazilian — had signed up with them since 1990.

But naturally they would drop everything whenever Il Fenomeno clicked his fingers. Pitta told one US journalist, 'He's kind, he's responsible, and he has an exceptional character. Ever since he was a boy, he knew what he wanted from life and he knew he could achieve it.' It all sounded like a well rehearsed advertising slogan.

* * *

Down in the depths of the San Siro stadium, in the VIP room, a huddle of people ignored the canapés, fruit juices and waiters in white ties to gather round a calendar that was mounted on a lectern.

On it was an image of Ronaldo standing with his back to the camera, perched on a plinth of a mountain gazing out over Rio, his arms outstretched, his index fingers pointing in opposite directions, imitating the statue of Christ the Redeemer. On the sole of his foot was the tread of a tyre.

The advertisement was commissioned by Pirelli, the sponsor of Inter Milan. The slogan above the image read: 'Power is Nothing Without Control'.

Whether Ronaldo really had control of his life by the time he found himself battling mid-season with Inter is questionable. But the way he dominated the club like no other before him was indisputable. He had become to Inter what Michael Jordan had been to the Chicago Bulls and the National Basketball Association.

The club was selling 2,000 Ronaldo shirts every week and in the beautiful Galeria in the city centre, scarves with his name adorned almost every store. Brazil shirts were also selling like hot cakes, and Brazilian flags hung over the San Siro constantly.

On Ronaldo's name, the club had sold 48,000 season tickets, more than any other team in Serie A and more than they had ever sold before. On the field of play, Inter were snapping at the heels of Juventus in Serie A — and that would hopefully mean a place in the European Champions League.

But back in Rio, Ronaldo's father had some pressing

'business' to deal with: his trial for possession of cocaine.

Nelio turned up for court in a navy-blue suit and white shirt with a thick gold medallion dangling on his chest. His new wife — Ronaldo's stepmother — 36-year-old Marilene Dexerra, accompanied him.

The hearing began at 2.15pm, on 3 October 1997. Nelio insisted to the court that the two policemen were trying to frame him. At one stage, Nelio even quoted a Greek philosopher by saying, 'When you declare war, my fate will come out.'

Nelio was eventually acquitted of possession after the court heard that the two arresting officers gave contradictory statements about what had really happened. Nelio reiterated that the drugs were not his.

The judge even pointed out that it was wrong for the two policemen to keep Nelio in custody in the police van for six hours before taking him to the police station. He even described it as a kidnapping in his summing up.

The judge also branded the police as liars after pointing out many of the contradictions in the case.

After the trial, Nelio called his son to tell him of his acquittal. 'It's the best news I've heard for months,' replied Ronaldo, who had been very worried about the case and what it was doing to his reputation.

Nelio insisted after the case, 'I just wanted to prove my innocence. I did nothing against the police but everyone says you have to be very careful with them.'

In fact, Nelio was so scared by that encounter he sold up his pizzeria in Copacabana — bought by Ronaldo — moved to the relative safety of the rich suburb of Barra, and put all his business plans on the back burner.

* * *

Milan was soon playing host to numerous members of Ronaldo's family. Sonia and her husband set up camp in the Savoya Hotel where she pledged to look after her beloved son, who had Suzanna with him in a room down the corridor, whenever she was in town.

Nelio eventually crossed the Atlantic and moved into a vast suite all to himself at the five-star Hotel Palace just up the street. Nelio even told one journalist that he'd learned how to speak Italian during one transatlantic flight accompanied by an Italian dictionary and cassette tapes.

At the Savoya Hotel, Ronaldo had a choice of two cars, both provided by Inter Milan. He preferred the Ferrari to the BMW. But whenever he tried to slip out for a drive, he tended to attract quite a bit of attention at traffic lights.

Just like his aversion to training, Ronaldo had great difficulty with the language and dropped his Italian lessons after only a few weeks.

Soon after arriving at Inter, Ronaldo did everything in his power to try to persuade the club to buy his Brazilian striking partner Romario. He even implied during the first round of negotiations that he'd only join Inter if they signed the veteran striker, but Inter had heard negative rumours about Romario being a troublesome player and decided to steer well clear of him. He'd just returned to his beloved Flamengo.

In November 1997, Ronaldo visited the central Italian town of Foligno after reading of the devastation caused in the region by persistent earthquake tremors over the previous month. It was an unscheduled, spur-of-the-moment trip, and back in Milan his agents and family panicked because they thought he'd disappeared.

In fact, he'd had a pang of conscience and decided to take the trip entirely alone. 'It was a learning experience for me to come here,' insisted Ronaldo. 'You see people suffer on television but only when you visit them yourself do you realise how bad things are.'

After inspecting the damage to numerous houses, Ronaldo surprised the regulars in a hall in the little town by turning up unannounced to watch Italy scrape through to the World Cup Finals against Russia.

Back in Milan, Suzanna persuaded Ronaldo to buy an apartment they could truly call home. It was located in the sophisticated neighbourhood of San Siro just a stone's throw from the Inter Milan stadium. Ronaldo flew over his favourite Rio interior decorator to apply some finishing touches. But Ronaldo's colour schemes were more akin to a 12-year-old schoolboy than a sophisticated man of the world.

'I just love blue as a colour and if all the walls were blue that would be great,' he told one friend. He also loved black. Building work inside the apartment began in mid-October 1997 and a few weeks later his possessions from Barcelona were shipped over.

The apartment had four bedrooms so Sonia could stay there whenever she wanted. His neighbours in the block — called Dia Dinarlo — included Chilean striker Zamorano and Argentinian Simeone.

All this rather conveniently coincided with Suzanna's career as a model in Milan taking off. Ronaldo and his blonde lover were looking every inch the perfect couple.

But beneath the surface there were some heated moments between them. When one Brazilian TV crew flew in from London to do an 'at home' feature on the glamorous pair, they were told by an embarrassed assistant that they weren't talking to each other, that Suzanna had booked her plane ticket back to Rio and would be leaving in a matter of hours.

Eventually, she agreed to stay at the apartment while the cameras turned over, but only on condition that she didn't have to be photographed sitting near Ronaldo. The producer managed to make it look as if everything was perfectly romantic in the finished programme. And the couple eventually kissed and made up. But it was clear that they were both extremely strong-willed, emotional people.

As the millions of dollars continued to flood in, Ronaldo found that more and more relatives required financing and he simply assumed he had to be generous to all of them. The kid who had collected coins off the street to buy a football just ten years earlier had given houses to his mother, father, brother, sister and an aunt. And then there were the cars; his brother received a souped-up Corsa, his sister a Golf, and his mother had a Vector. The family pizzeria had just been sold at a disastrous loss. Ronaldo even joked to one team-mate, 'I've got to keep working to service my family.'

As Ronaldo's Serie A season progressed, more and more media interest centred around the imminent World Cup in France. And all eyes seemed to be on Brazil, who were favourites to retain the trophy.

Ronaldo tried to dismiss the expectation that surrounded him and Brazil by telling one reporter, 'Everyone says that Brazil are favourites, but we who play here know that we may not win.'

Ronaldo was also under pressure to explain his apparent obsession with money following the highly publicised transfer problems at Barcelona. Was money his main motivation rather than a love of the beautiful game? He was also constantly being accused of trying to curtail his tax obligations. Ronaldo knew all about his agents' various 'safe' tax schemes and offshore accounts but he refused to accept the obvious conclusions. 'I am not a criminal. I do not try to avoid taxes,' he angrily told one interviewer.

The smiling façade was gradually fading, and behind it was a very stressed young man.

CHAPTER 17

Blondes Have More Fun

Towards the end of 1997, Ronaldo and Suzanna's love affair had become even more of a tempestuous on-off-on-off saga. It was summed up by the fact that every time they had an argument, he would spend thousands of dollars on gifts to placate her.

When one Brazilian journalist went to interview the couple as Ronaldo visited Brazil just before Christmas 1997, the football star turned up with a painting and a vast teddy bear, kissed Suzanna passionately and then handed her a jewellery box containing a pair of diamond earrings.

Both of them insisted they'd 'forgotten all the fights and we are just thinking about marriage now'. They said the marriage would happen immediately after the World Cup in France the following summer.

Suzanna said, 'The important thing is that we love each other and we are really happy when we are together.'

Ronaldo added, 'We should marry as soon as possible. It

should be just after the World Cup.'

Over on Suzanna's home turf of Barra de Tijuca, Ronaldo's new penthouse apartment was christened by a lively pre-Christmas party. The same Rio interior designer responsible for all of Ronaldo's other properties had decorated the flat for them.

Suzanna also gave Ronaldo yet another teddy bear for Christmas that year as well as a beach chair and a gold chain.

But when Ronaldo put his arm around Suzanna while they posed for a photographer, he made the mistake of patting her stomach affectionately. 'Take your hand off me, Ronaldo. It makes me look like I'm pregnant,' snapped Suzanna.

During those numerous flying visits to Rio, Ronaldo rarely got in touch with any of his old childhood friends. He told his family that Suzanna was his best friend and he didn't feel the need to socialise with anyone else. But some of his relatives believed that Suzanna had felt that he should always go out with her.

Some of Ronaldo's old friends from the two Rio clubs he'd played for before his departure for Europe were still waiting for a call from their old chum asking them if they wanted to join him and other millionaires at one of those luxurious foreign clubs.

In fact, the only one who ever got the call had been Calango who had briefly joined Ronaldo at PSV Eindhoven on a trial. His air fare and accommodation were paid by Ronaldo. Unfortunately, the Dutch club decided they did not need his services.

In late December, Ronaldo added yet another title to his collection when he won the European Footballer of the Year award organised by *France Football* magazine. He finished ahead of Real Madrid's Yugoslav striker Predrag Mijatovic, Juventus's Zinedine Zidane, Arsenal's Dennis Bergkamp and Ronaldo's fellow Brazilian Roberto Carlos.

Also in December 1997, Ronaldo and several of his Brazilian team-mates were flown by Nike to Brazil to appear in a $3 million TV commercial featuring their products. The intention was to screen the advert worldwide during the World Cup Finals. Nike hoped to cash in on the likely prospects of Brazil winning their record fifth World Cup.

Top Hollywood action director John Woo, the director of *Face Off*, was contracted to direct the commercial and it was to be shot at Rio's Galeao International Airport. The team members would be shown about to take off for the World Cup and having a kick-around inside the terminal. Other players included Romario, Juninho, Denilson, Leonardo and Roberto Carlos, as well as coach Mario Zagallo.

The Nike commercial which eventually aired was hailed as such a masterpiece by many that it actually helped Nike come away with some real dignity from the tournament, unlike many other major advertisers.

The story behind the filming of the commercial reveals a lot more about Ronaldo and his relationship with his Brazilian team-mates. One of the production staff described what happened behind the scenes in an exclusive interview in Rio in August 1998.

'It was one hell of a chaotic shoot. John Woo the director was not an expert on football and he treated the players as if they were actors,' explained the informant.

But far more surprising was the fact that all the stars appeared in the commercial for no money because they were all signed to Nike. 'That meant none of them were particularly keen to hang around,' added the source.

Ronaldo and Roberto Carlos grew bored waiting between shots that they invented a gambling game in which each bet the other they could keep the ball up in the air for as long as possible by balancing it on their feet. At one stage, there was a $2,000 bet on the table which Roberto Carlos won much to the annoyance of Ronaldo.

The entire set was surrounded by thick-necked security

men hired by Nike and the commercial's production manager.

But it can be revealed for the first time that the most famous sequence of the entire commercial — showing Ronaldo dribbling and then having a shot in the check-in area — had to be filmed in Italy after he announced he had to go back to Milan for a game.

'It was very annoying because Ronaldo had not been present for the complete shoot because he was filming a commercial for milk in São Paulo and travelling between the two cities constantly.'

Of all the players, it was Ronaldo and Romario who insisted on leaving the earliest and, as a result, director John Woo was often left with half his cast missing for the last few shots of the day.

But there was one good reason why Ronaldo was happy to appear in the commercial. It meant that he had to be released by Inter to go back to Rio for Christmas despite the fact he only had a few days' break between games. Nike's influence was extremely far reaching.

By the end of 1997, Ronaldo had played umpteen matches for Inter and the Brazilian national side. The rest of his time seemed to have been spent in airports and hotels, in press rooms and TV studios. It was a claustrophobic life. Outside a small circle of family, agents, team-mates, coaches and club directors he saw virtually nobody. But Ronaldo refused to complain, so nobody realised just how exhausted he was.

Shortly before joining the Brazilian national side in Saudi Arabia for the Confederation Cup, Ronaldo returned to PSV Eindhoven for a couple of days. He treated his former team-mates to the farewell which they had had to forego when he left in 1996.

First, they all went go-carting, and then clubbing in Belgium. The following day, he visited PSV's training ground to see coach Dick Advocaat.

'Now that you're here, you might as well train with us,' the PSV coach told Ronaldo. He borrowed some boots and had the best day of his life. Previous difficulties between the pair had been entirely forgotten.

Advocaat later said he was impressed by Ronaldo. There didn't seem to be any signs of a burn-out or an unwillingness to muck in with the other players. 'He seemed the same as always. Cheerful, happy. Some people say he's childish, but I think he's very mature and intelligent. Ronaldo knows exactly what he has to do and what he doesn't.'

But while in Saudi for the Confederation Cup, reports began circulating in the Italian press that seemed to point to some problems typical of an over-worked person in any profession. *La Gazetta dello Sport* said Ronaldo had fallen into depression during the Middle East tournament.

When the papers reached Ronaldo in Saudi Arabia, he read an article in one newspaper which forecast a Maradona-style descent unless he quickly cut his workload. Ronaldo read the article over and over again trying to absorb what was being said. He wondered if perhaps they had a point. He did feel exhausted and he had not enjoyed much of his life over the previous year.

The magazine article bluntly stated that Ronaldo was such a worldwide phenomenon that he would soon burn out and fall rapidly from the straight and narrow into a world not unlike that which consumed Maradona for at least the second half of his career.

As he continued to read the article, tears began streaming down Ronaldo's face. His Brazilian room-mate Cesar Sampaio tried to console him, but Ronaldo was by this time sobbing uncontrollably. He was convinced that what he was reading was a plausible prediction that he had been fearing ever since his move to Inter from Barcelona had first been suggested by his agents.

Ronaldo even insisted to Sampaio, 'We can all learn from what has happened to Maradona. There are many bad people in football who only want to use you. But I have a strong character. I know who to associate with ...'

But those tears had another significance. They showed he still had a childlike vulnerability and that he was feeling greatly under pressure in the build-up to the World Cup.

As he explained a few days later, 'It seems incomprehensible to Europeans but failure in moments of great importance are dramatic for people in my country. Zico, for example, was the best player in the world in the mid-Eighties but he is still remembered as being part of two sides who failed to win the World Cup.

'The World Cup is the real objective of any Brazilian footballer. If you win it, you go down in your country's history. If you don't, you could win everything else, but in Brazil you will be remembered for failure.

'We can only be truly happy when we win, playing good football and having individuals who stand out. That's what people in Brazil are expecting from us at the World Cup in France.'

It seemed as if Ronaldo was once again putting himself in the firing line.

Brazilian coach Mario Zagallo openly voiced concern about Ronaldo's form. His comments came after his dismal performances in the Confederation Cup in Saudi Arabia.

'He is absent on the pitch, with his thoughts elsewhere,' the veteran coach observed ruefully. 'A Ronaldo like this is no good to Brazil or, above all, himself.'

Zagallo was so concerned that he left Ronaldo out of a couple of the following matches but he felt that Ronaldo's collapse into tears of despair had been caused by other reasons. He told one player that he believed Ronaldo was suffering from the burden of having to lead Brazil to its hoped-for fifth World Cup victory.

'Leave Ronaldo alone,' Zagallo begged the Brazilian press. 'The boy has it hard enough. No other footballer has ever gone the way he is going.'

Profound words from a veteran coach who had literally

seen it all before.

On 12 January 1998, Ronaldo became the first player to be crowned World Player of the Year in consecutive years and confidently predicted he would add the World Cup and its scoring record by July.

National team coaches from 121 countries cast their votes and 86 of them put Ronaldo in first place, polling a total of 480 votes.

With an eye on the imminent World Cup in France, FIFA staged the vote for that year's award at Eurodisney, Paris. It was also to be the site of the International Football Hall of Champions. Beckenbauer, Charlton, Stanley Matthews, Pelé, Johan Cruyff, Alfredo di Stefano, Lev Yashin, Ferenc Puskas, Michel Platini, Eusebio and Rinus Michels were among the chosen few.

Only one of these legends disagreed with Ronaldo's award. Rinus Michels said, 'If you only look at spectacle and goals, then Ronaldo is the best. But if you judge it as a coach and professional, then the team deserves the most attention. In that case I chose Zidane.'

And Ronaldo's outburst at the podium during the awards ceremony seemed extremely big-headed to many in attendance.

'I would just like to say how sorry I am to England, Italy, Germany and France because Brazil are the winners of the World Cup and everybody else is just fighting for second, third and fourth place.'

Ronaldo then went on to claim that Juste Fontaine's record of 13 goals in a World Cup Final was there for the taking.

'In a team like Brazil, we make six or seven chances in every game so I think Fontaine's record is possible for me.'

But Ronaldo did admit that Brazil had one worry.

'Our main problem is time. The way the world treats football now, with so many demands in the league and friendly matches, there is no time to train together.

'This is a massive problem for our national team

because most of the players are based in Europe and there is never enough free time to do the training we would want because we can get better as a team.'

On 25 January 1998, Ronaldo appeared naked on US television in an advertisement during the Super Bowl. The advert for Nike featured Ronaldo, NBA basketball star David Robinson, women's basket heroine Lisa Leslie, double world and Olympic athletics champion Michael Johnson and fellow sprinter Suzy Hamilton.

In late January, Ronaldo's relationship with Inter president Massimo Moratti took a turn for the worse when the club chief openly criticised Ronaldo following Inter's dull 1–1 draw with Empoli.

Ronaldo had failed to score for the sixth successive match and Moratti said, 'He is not himself — he is playing badly. I don't know what his problem is but he's certainly got one.'

Asked if he thought his star player was in some kind of personal crisis, Moratti replied, 'It seems that way to me ...'

In early February 1998, Brazil failed to beat either Jamaica or even Guatemala in a tournament in Miami, Florida. Certain sections of the Brazilian backroom staff were angry that Ronaldo was missing because he was making a TV commercial in Tenerife with girlfriend Suzanna, although coach Zagallo had already said he intended to rest his star striker.

And then there were problems with other players such as Edmundo, sent off seven times in 1997, even though he managed a Brazilian record of 29 championship goals. Romario had already angered coach Zagallo by being hauled out of a nightclub, while three more players prompted even more negative publicity by forcibly shaving the heads of reluctant colleagues during the Copa America.

Back in Italy, Ronaldo was growing increasingly dispirited about the noisy Italian press. He'd had a bad run of not scoring and the newspapers were clearly getting on his nerves.

'It was the Italian press that invented that I was a phenomenon,' Ronaldo told Brazilian weekly magazine *Isto E*. 'I demand a little bit more professional respect ... find another description for me.'

The Italians even suggested that Ronaldo's goal famine was caused by his busy nightlife. Taking time off to shoot numerous TV commercials and pining for fiancée Suzanna didn't help either.

Ronaldo hit back angrily, 'I'm first to admit that I have played badly, but let's analyse the reasons seriously and not with lies. I haven't been in a discotheque in three months. I know perfectly well how I should behave.

'I miss Suzanna, but I don't mix my private life and soccer. Our relationship never cooled off, as they insinuated, but neither has it heated up to the point of setting a wedding date.'

Many were a little confused by Ronaldo's last statement as he'd told the world he'd become engaged to Suzanna six months earlier and they presumed that meant a wedding date had been set.

On the day that same magazine interview hit the news-stands, Ronaldo ended his goal drought by scoring Inter's winner against Bescia in Serie A.

In February 1998, reports from Spain suggested that Barcelona were plotting a £70 million bid to lure Ronaldo back from Italy.

Having only just ended a two-month goal drought for Inter, it was said that Ronaldo was not terribly happy. His Brazilian team-mate Roberto Carlos added fuel to the fire by saying, 'Ronaldo will be back in Spain next season. I can't say any more but I know it for a fact.'

Ronaldo himself tried to laugh off the rumours. 'Roberto Carlos is a practical joker. I don't know where he would have got that from. I haven't seen him or spoken to him for ages.'

In fact, they'd been virtually glued to each other at the FIFA World Player of the Year Awards two weeks earlier so

Ronaldo's denial was not taken *that* seriously.

Also in February 1998, Ronaldo shocked a few old fashioned soccer fans by declaring, 'Scoring a goal is as good as sex. Both are very important to me.'

Around this time Ronaldo was voted one of the top three most handsome players in Serie A despite his very unconventional looks.

In March 1998, Nike unveiled a super-lightweight soccer boot called the Mercurial which Ronaldo had agreed to wear exclusively. The company claimed it had been tailored to Ronaldo's own speed-driven style of play and it was going to be Nike's top-of-the-line boot, just like the Air Jordan had been to basketball in the US.

Many other European stars looked on with bemusement. One said, 'What would have happened if the boot had been no good? Would Ronaldo have turned round and refused to wear it? I think not.'

Nike were naturally proud of their new product and even announced, 'We know for a fact that Ronaldo is the most global of all athletes.'

In April 1998, Ronaldo was banned for two games after criticising the referee in charge of Inter's defeat at Juventus. The biggest controversy in the top-of-the-table clash concerned a 60-second spell in which the referee first denied Ronaldo a penalty, and then awarded a spot-kick at the other end.

It was the second time Ronaldo had got into trouble with Italian referees since his arrival in Milan and many believed it was connected to his apparent unhappiness in Serie A. As one soccer pundit pointed out, 'Ronaldo's disciplinary record had been exemplary until he arrived at Inter. Anyone could see he had a lot of problems on his mind.'

Ronaldo did much to improve his standing in Italy during the UEFA Cup semi-final first leg against Spartak Moscow. Ronaldo's brilliance in the first half was hailed as exhilarating by sportswriters. Those who witnessed his performance were privileged to have been there.

The Inter midfield dynamos Djorkaeff, Winter, Ze Elias and Zanetti fed him superb balls with frightening regularity. Fear gripped the Spartak defence. One run in the tenth minute was mesmeric. In a flash of sidesteps, feints, deceptive turns and changes of pace, Ronaldo danced his way through the massed ranks of defenders. Somehow, the last man managed to touch the ball and deflect it far enough away from Ronaldo for a team-mate to hack it away in panic.

Despite Ronaldo's superb display, it took the arrival of Uruguayan Recoba to swing the match Inter's way. They got their winner in injury time when Ze Elias hooked a shot from close range after a goalmouth scramble.

Having, at last, been able to confirm his standing in Italy as a genius on the pitch, it would remain to be seen just how far Ronaldo could cope off it.

CHAPTER 18

Muchas Problemas

Ronaldo's world transfer record was never going to last for ever. The successor to Ronaldo's crown was fellow countryman Denilson, who surprised many by turning his back on some of Europe's biggest clubs to sign for unfashionable Spanish side Real Betis.

Denilson explained his decision. 'I felt the club wanted to sign me more than anyone else. They are a genuine club on the rise.'

Denilson believed it was grossly unfair to compare him to Ronaldo because they played in different positions. Denilson told one reporter, 'People will look at the transfer fee, and that's where the comparisons will be made. Ronaldo is a tremendous player. He has lived up to his fee and more. But Ronaldo is a striker, I'm a winger. There is a difference.'

Ronaldo was actually delighted to lose the transfer record to Denilson because he hoped that the youngster would take some of the immense pressure off his shoulders. He raved about Denilson to anyone who would listen.

'Denilson has the potential to become one of the big stars of the World Cup this year, if he keeps his feet firmly on the ground. He is a very quick player, he's very alert and he unsettles defenders by running at them.'

* * *

They say the Maracana stadium smells even on the days Brazil wins. At the end of April 1998, Ronaldo and his team of hot favourites were brought rudely down to earth, sounding the alarm bells in Rio even though the rest of the world remained convinced of their superiority as a footballing race.

It was the national side's only game at the biggest football stadium in the world since 1993. Maracana had become something of a crumbling wreck in the Nineties and had twice been closed down due to poor safety standards. The Brazilians must have wished it had remained closed when the Argentinians came to Rio.

They disposed of Brazil with a last-ditch goal but the national side seemed rattled and uncomfortable up against their fellow South Americans. In Rio, the air of confidence that had pervaded for the previous few months was fading fast.

The old offices of the CBF, the Brazilian Football Federation, were located in a run-down building on a narrow side-street in the heart of Rio's old business district. It was here in early May 1988, that coach Mario Zagallo announced not only the squad of 22 players he intended to take to France '98 but also the 11 he wanted to field against Scotland in the tournament's opening match.

Many interpreted the early release of the actual team as an attempt to intimidate the opposition, but there was a definite trace of self-flattery in that assumption. Coach Zagallo was actually more interested in reducing the furore of journalistic speculation that constantly assailed him in Brazil, and especially in countering the recurring allegation that indecision had been the defining characteristic of his second tour as national team coach.

Opting to start with Denilson on the bench sparked enormous controversy because many Brazilians considered the 20-year-old, left-sided midfielder as a classically talented player capable of turning any match. Zagallo defended his decision by pointing out, 'Though Denilson is not in the first team, I value him highly and know how to employ him. We cannot win the World Cup with just 11 players.'

Zagallo insisted that the recent defeat against Argentina was not relevant to their World Cup chances. 'Forget that game. It meant nothing. Argentina came to get zero–zero. They won because my players did not even reach the field. Maybe their heads were in Paris. Nobody wants to be injured so near to the finals.'

Even in early May 1998, the pressure was mounting on Ronaldo. Zagallo did not hide his feelings about certain aspects of his star striker's play.

'It is vital for the national team that Ronaldo moves around more than he has done in some recent matches.

'He must not copy Romario but complement him. He has the young legs and he must cover more ground in seeking the ball and looking for openings. It is no good if both strikers are fairly static, lurking, waiting for the ball. If Ronaldo operates like that, it will be easy for the defenders to cut off the supply to him.'

Zagallo's inclusion of Romario despite a thigh injury sustained while playing for Flamengo was also controversial because the coach seemed to be saying that, without Romario, Brazil might not win the World Cup. The two men had clashed on numerous occasions in the past but Zagallo believed that Romario would relish the world stage more than any of his other players, including Ronaldo.

There was also a feeling that Romario's inclusion took

the pressure off Ronaldo because the focus of world attention would be aimed at two players instead of just one. Zagallo was well aware of how stressed Ronaldo had seemed during the Confederation Cup the previous Christmas.

Also in Rio, Ronaldo's fiancée Suzanna Werner had secured her own place at France '98 by getting a job as a World Cup commentator for Brazil's TV Globo. She'd already been assured of the full backing of Ronaldo's sponsor Nike who wanted her to wave their products around whenever she was on camera.

This scenario was a dream come true for Nike because TV Globo camera staff would constantly be cutting back to glamorous Suzanna at every Brazil game.

Meanwhile, Sonia was so worried about the pressure on her son that she insisted he should rent her and Suzanna a house in Paris for the entire World Cup so she could be on hand if he needed her support. She'd seen enough bouts of loneliness during the previous three years in Europe to know that her son needed all the support he could get.

Sonia was particularly concerned because she had noticed in the few months before France '98 that her son had become much more distant and distracted — and she sensed that he was extremely stressed from the expectations of the entire Brazilian nation.

Part of that pressure had been a constant stream of newspaper articles comparing Ronaldo to other so-called soccer superstars. Every aspect of his play was analysed and re-examined. It was an endless process. One of those he was compared to was England's Alan Shearer, who had clashed with Ronaldo during that game in Paris the previous year.

Shearer's first impression was hardly surprising. 'He seemed a nice, level-headed sort of guy,' said Shearer. But he did make some valid points about the immense pressures on Ronaldo.

Shearer explained, 'I can relate to the kind of pressures he's facing because it's not easy to be up there, leading the line, with everybody looking for you all the time. The goalscorer's life can be a great one but it's not adulation all the time.

'He seems to be coping with the pressures really well and that's a tribute to someone who's so young. He's a very strong player, with a great first touch, who can beat three or four players from the half-way line and stick the ball in the back of the net.'

Rarely had a team — or one player — set out for a World Cup campaign such firm favourites. Everyone cited Ronaldo as the key player and talked about the supreme confidence of coach Zagallo.

But back home in Brazil, they were not so sure ...

ACT III

Copa do Mundo

'In my time, it was the army generals running Brazil who tried to pick the team. Today, it's the sponsors, the businessmen, the media moguls. The World Cup Final is the world's biggest TV show.'

Carlos Alberto Perreira,
coach to Brazil's 1994 World Cup-winning team

CHAPTER 19

Nada Especial (Nothing Special)

On 24 May 1998, Ronaldo was due to arrive in France to join the rest of the Brazilian squad at their team headquarters at Château de La Romaine, in Lesigny, less than 20 miles from Paris's Charles de Gaulle aiport. But he managed to vanish for at least three hours after flying in. No one really knows where he was during that period but when the Brazilian management tried to locate him there were very real fears that he might have panicked and flown home to Rio; they were *that* concerned about Ronaldo's psychological state at the time.

When Ronaldo did finally turn up at the hotel in the early hours, he claimed there had been no one to meet him when he arrived from Rome late on the evening of the 24th. He said he had finally hailed a taxi but the driver had got lost.

But what concerned the Brazilian backroom staff the most was that Ronaldo was virtually hysterical by the time the taxi dropped him. He was so agitated that team doctor Lidio Toledo gave him a 'bluey' tranquillizer to calm him down.

It brought back memories of the Confederation Cup when Ronaldo had been edgy, highly emotional and considered in serious need of a break.

* * *

At Brazil's training camp before their world-shattering victory at the 1970 World Cup in Mexico, most of the players had shown a typically laid-back attitude towards training. Captain Carlos Alberto explained many years later, 'We would go out after training and say to ourselves, "I'm going out today, I'm going to make love with my wife, she's waiting for me at the hotel." We went and came back without any problems,' he smiled. 'Of course, no one would stay out the whole night drinking, we just liked to make love. It energised us.'

How Ronaldo and all his team-mates at their training camp for France '98 must have sometimes wished they could have enjoyed the same level of freedom. But in the sponsored, money-driven 1990s, no sane coach could even allow his players to nip down the street for a morning paper.

Ronaldo found this tough because Suzanna and his mother were staying at a house just 30 minutes' drive away and he'd actually presumed he might be allowed out whenever he wanted to see them. He was starting to feel like a caged bird within only a few days of arriving in France.

At Brazil's training camp, coach Zagallo had other things on his mind; he wanted to impress upon Ronaldo that he was going to be in for a rough ride from many defenders during the World Cup tournament.

Zagallo's words rang warning bells in Ronaldo's mind and greatly worried the young player. Instead of firing him up as Zagallo had hoped, Ronaldo began to fear taking the field in case his very lucrative career was ended by the boot of a clumsy, bullish defender. Ronaldo had already been warned by Pitta and Martins to try to avoid any heavy injury. They wanted to make sure their property was going to be ready to start the season in Italy fresh and healthy at the end of August. Ronaldo's bosses at Inter had already been in touch to impress upon them that they expected a fully fit Ronaldo to arrive in Italy for the new season.

Ronaldo himself gave away a hint of his unhappiness when he admitted to one reporter during the pre-World Cup build-up, 'People tell me how Pelé was kicked out of the World Cup in 1966 and I have only seen films of 1970 when he was at his best. Players have such short careers, it is tragic when they are cut down when they have so much to offer.

'I am really worried about these criminal tackles from behind. They've already wrecked the career of Holland's Marco Van Basten and others. It's something people talk about a lot, but nothing is done. I just hope the referees will be strict in France.

'Referees can only do so much but with the right kind of guidance and by applying the rules evenly, these terrible tackles can be stamped out. Clamping down in the World Cup is the ideal way to send out the message that these tackles are unacceptable.'

* * *

One of the most outspoken characters in the Brazilian squad was Edmundo — the so-called 'Animal'. His label did not come without reason.

He was rude, abrasive and brutally honest. As one Brazilian FA official said, 'He is like Eric Cantona. He has been involved in fights with opponents, team-mates and managers. He also pushed a referee to the ground once.'

Edmundo had actually been banned for four months

for that offence. He had also lashed out at opponents in a game at São Paolo and caused a 15-minute hold-up as rival players brawled. Six were sent off.

Unfortunately for Edmundo, his reputation in the lead-up to the World Cup had not exactly been enhanced when he was involved in a car accident which killed three people. He was eventually ordered to pay £377,000 compensation to the family of one of the victims.

Edmundo — full name Edmundo Amves de Souza — had ploughed his four-wheel-drive Cherokee jeep into a Fiat Uno while driving at 100mph along a busy road that runs around Rio's central lagoon. However, judicial hearings against him were delayed until after he returned from the World Cup.

Edmundo rarely stopped berating his team-mates and opponents and, during one of Brazil's games against Sweden, he was told to shut up by team skipper Dunga. He'd also been sent off five times playing for Palmeiras.

As he stormed off the field following one dismissal, his progress was blocked by a cameraman. The red mist descended and Edmundo attacked. The camera fell to the ground, perfectly framing the deranged face of The Animal as he repeatedly kicked his prostrate victim.

Inside the Brazilian World Cup training camp, Edmundo was proving a very strong presence — and he believed he was capable of playing as Ronaldo's striking partner throughout France '98. Any suggestion that The Animal had been tamed seemed rather premature to his fellow squad members.

But Edmundo's disruptive influence was having a detrimental effect on some of his team-mates, especially Ronaldo who rapidly was growing to live in fear of him.

He found his compatriot's ferocious attitude towards training very worrying, especially since The Animal tended to crash into people so harshly that many — including Ronaldo — feared injury. He also had a habit of berating team-mates even in training. Edmundo was

Top: **Brazil's first World Cup '98 started inauspiciously. There are many theories as to why...**

Bottom: **Ronaldo has finally found lasting happiness with beautiful wife Milene and son Ronald.**

Top: **Snatching a few minutes sleep on yet another transatlantic trek. In one four week period Ronaldo travelled between Europe and Brazil ten times, and still managed to play in six games.**

Bottom: **Ronaldo and ex-girlfriend Luciana.**

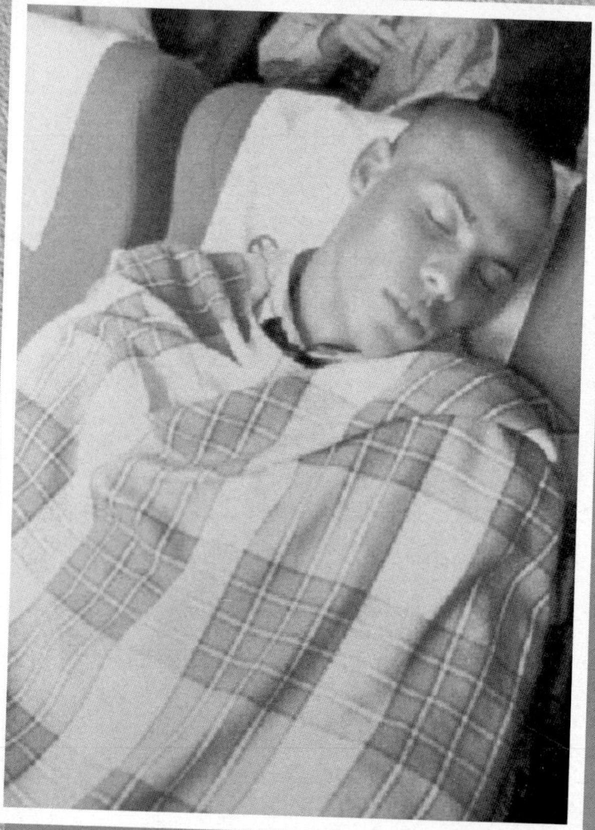

Top: Ronaldo wearing the number 10 shirt before his multi-million dollar move to Inter Milan from Barcelona, which projected him instantly into the realm of mega-money soccer stars.

Bottom: A brief moment of joy in the ill fated World Cup '98, after scoring against Chile in the second round.

Tennis star Anna Kournikova and Ronaldo, pictured at the Roland Garros tennis tournament in Paris in 1998. When Susanna saw this picture, she was *not* happy.

Ronaldo broke down in tears at the end of the '98 World Cup final match between Brazil and France. His dream was shattered.

Top: **At the World Player Awards, with soccer champion Pele, and fellow nominee Roberto Carlos.**

Bottom: **At the gate of his mother's house in Rio, shortly after the disastrous World Cup final.**

Top: **Ronaldo's relationship with room mate Roberto Carlos was complicated by their interest in bizarre black magic rituals.**

Bottom: **On the flight home from World Cup '98, Ronaldo still found time to pose with a young fan.**

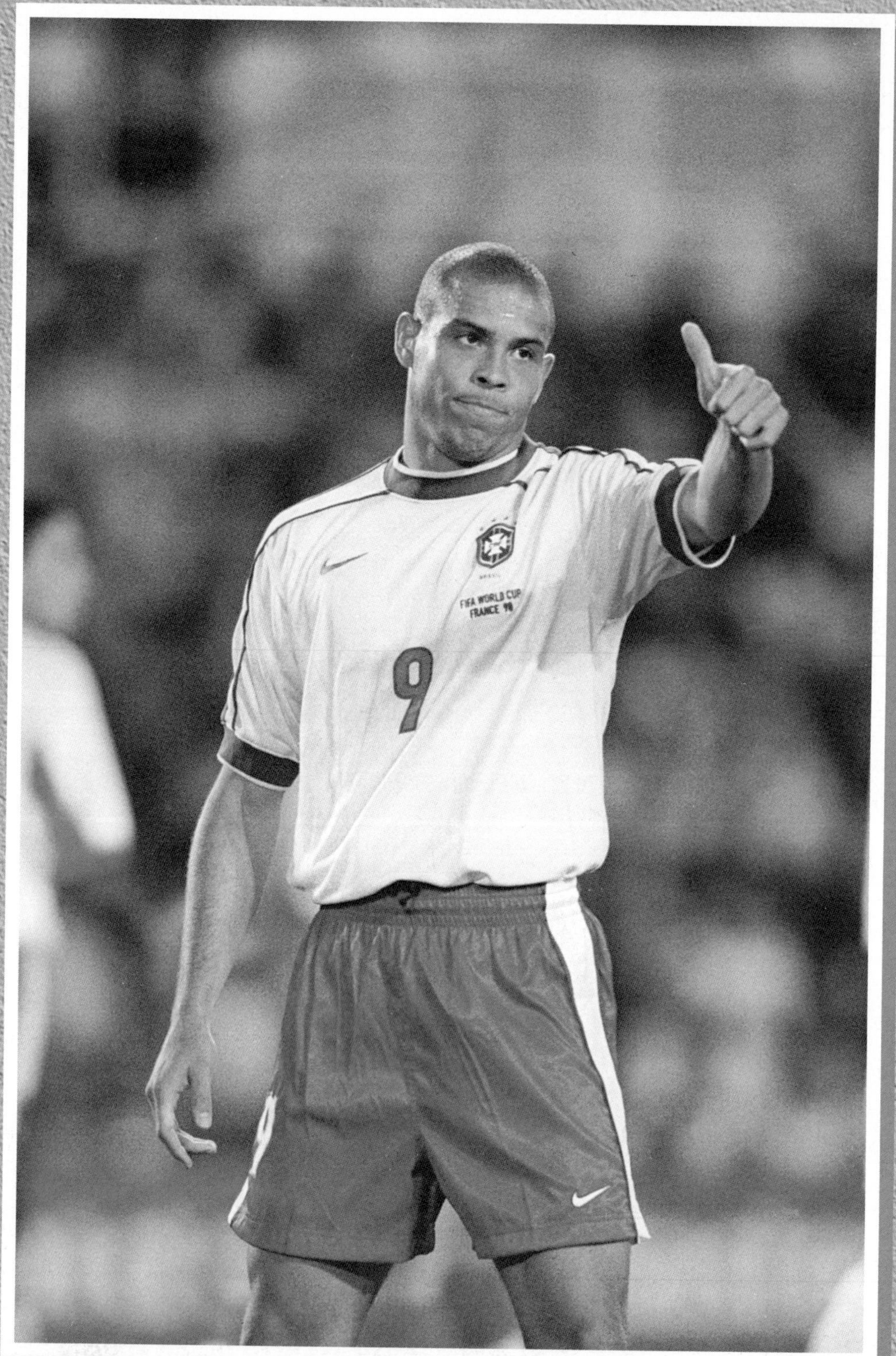

Ronaldo – what does the future hold?

particularly ferocious towards veteran striker, Bebeto.

* * *

However the press liked to portray it, it was Brazilian coach Mario Zagallo who really held the key to Brazil's potential. He was a notoriously superstitious man despite his reputation as a straight guy who took few risks. Since marrying his wife on 13 June, he had let the number 13 dictate virtually all the major decisions of his life.

He lived on the 13th floor of a Rio apartment block, had the number 13 on his car licence plate, and always wore the number 13 shirt in training. Many in Brazil presumed that it could not have escaped his notice that the World Cup final of 1998 was scheduled to be played on 12 July.

But one simple, if astonishing, fact about Zagallo remained: Brazil had never won the World Cup without his involvement, whether as a player, assistant coach or coach. It was hardly surprising, therefore, that the 66-year-old told every journalist who would listen, 'Copa do Mundo — it is in my blood.'

The tournament was also in the blood of Brazil's 160 million other residents. And during the weeks before the World Cup kicked off, three of Brazil's foremost footballing citizens started publicly questioning Zagallo's methods and his mental state.

The views of Carlos Alberto, Gerson and Toastao were not dismissed lightly because they were three of the pillars of the greatest national side of the century, the 1970 Brazilian team. Carlos Alberto even went as far as to accuse Zagallo of 'betraying everything Brazil are famous for'. He was talking about the victorious 1994 side but the 1970 captain bluntly told anyone who would listen, 'What you will see in France is not real Brazilian football. We have some wonderful players but Zagallo will not let them improvise. He has no right to manage the national team.'

Carlos Alberto even publicly insisted that Zagallo should get no credit for managing the 1970 side because he was only installed in the job three months before the World Cup began. Brazil was a military dictatorship then and Zagallo's appointment was seen by many as a political move.

Zagallo's track record for club and country seemed second to none but still the critics were lining up to take swipes at him. Throughout his career, critics had charged him with having a preference for pragmatism over glory.

Zagallo himself tried to defend his attitude in the countdown to France '98.

'Football has changed,' he said. 'Today, there are not only more people behind the ball, *most* people are behind the ball.

'Football is not always changing for the better. There is much less space in which footballers can express their ability. At the '94 World Cup, Colombia and Argentina tried to turn the clock back and play a happier, free-flowing game, but without much success.

'They reminded me of 1982 when Brazil were voted the best 'pure football' team of the tournament. But Brazil forgot to play to win and were knocked out in the second round, unlike in 1994 when they did not put on a show but did play to win.'

Mario Jorge Lobo Zagallo was brought up in Tijuca, a suburb of Rio, by parents who aspired to a career other than football for their son. The boy acquiesced, to the extent of completing his studies, but at 18 he joined America, a local club.

'I played everywhere as a child,' Zagallo recalled. 'In the street, on the beach, in the square, in the house. As far back as I can remember, I had a ball at my feet.'

At 19, he joined Flamengo, where he was nicknamed The Ant in recognition of his industrious, self-effacing style which included working back and forward as probably the first wing-back in international football history. Three consecutive Rio championships prefaced his selection for the 1958 World Cup Finals, in which he played in all six matches, scoring in the final 5–2 victory over Sweden, the hosts. A year later a serious spinal cord injury was diagnosed but he made a miraculous recovery by 1961 when he moved to Botafogo, where he and the legendary Garrincha led the side to the titles of 1961 and 1962.

The second World Cup medal, in Chile in 1962, was his ultimate reward for refusing to accept the doctors' pessimistic forecasts. Three years later, he retired from playing and became an apprentice coach, in charge of Botafogo's youth team.

In 1967, he took over the senior squad, and performed so impressively that early in 1970, when the Brazilian FA sacked one-time journalist Joao Saldanha only three months before the finals in Mexico, Zagallo was their choice as an emergency replacement.

'I was very young,' he later recalled, 'and I was lucky to take over such a fabulous team — the greatest, I think, in the history of football.'

But the circumstances surrounding his appointment have always led to hints, probably unfairly, that the team was Saldanha's, not Zagallo's.

Afterwards, there was an interlude as a club coach, with Rio rivals Flamengo and Fluminense, before Zagallo resumed the national job in time for the World Cup campaign of 1974 — the tournament to which other Brazilians always refer when things are going badly.

Seven years in Middle Eastern exile was Zagallo's 'punishment' for that appalling campaign. During this period, he amassed a small fortune and was even able to buy a vast mansion by the sea in Tijuca for his wife, Alcina, and their four children.

But in 1994, Zagallo was recalled to the national team as an adviser to Carlos Alberto Perreira, who had been Zagallo's physiotherapist in 1970. Together they planned and executed Brazil's first World Cup win in 24 years.

Shortly after returning from America with the trophy, Zagallo took over once more at the helm. Thanks to the £40 million coming in from Nike, Brazil were even able to pay their head coach £600,000 a year. He soon surrounded himself with his own backroom team — Americe Faria, the general manager; Nelson Borges, the press chief; Lidio Toledo, the physio; and, eventually, Ronaldo's all-time footballing hero, Zico.

Ironically, it had been Zagallo's own defensive inclinations which saw him dropping Zico from the 1974 World Cup squad, a competition which resulted in fresh abuse for the manager owing to Brazil's alarmingly destructive tactics. Three months before France '98, Zico was appointed to work alongside Zagallo by the CBF, apparently worried by Zagallo's negativity and his use of 117 players since that World Cup victory in Los Angeles in 1994.

Mind you, Zagallo did enrol his own grandson in Zico's football academy which many saw as a sign of solidarity between the two men. They also both shared a lack of faith in Romario, which many predicted would be bad news for Ronaldo because it would heap even more pressure on his shoulders.

The three of them had had very public differences of opinion in the previous couple of years. Romario had even once referred to Zico as a 'loser'. To the outside world, those differences seemed to have been put behind them but, in reality, they were just beneath a very fragile surface.

But the one player Ronaldo truly admired in terms of his skill as a striker was Romario. The Romario–Ronaldo partnership had been a surprising discovery for Zagallo. They had only started playing together in February 1997 but the goals had flowed in from both players with Romario (33) and Ronaldo (10) accounting for a total of 43 goals.

*   *   *

Zagallo became increasingly suspicious of the habits of some of his stars in the weeks following the Brazilian squad's arrival in France. He was particularly concerned by the way that many wives and girlfriends had moved into rented accommodation near the training camp, despite his warning to the players.

Zagallo even re-issued his orders that wives and girlfriends should stay away from the team as Brazil launched its defence of the trophy.

No one could ever recall a Brazilian coach laying down such strict guidelines. But much of it stemmed from the 1994 World Cup in the United States when there had been a number of incidents involving players being caught in their rooms with girls and going out nightclubbing.

But the re-issued ban was especially bad news for Ronaldo. He was sharing a room with Roberto Carlos and while the two men had got on well in the past, they had never shared accommodation before. Roberto Carlos spent most of his time either listening to his Walkman or chanting with the various *macumbo* artefacts he'd brought with him from Brazil. Ronaldo had asked to share a room because he did not want to feel lonely but Roberto Carlos wasn't quite what he'd had in mind.

They never seemed to have a proper conversation even though Ronaldo did try his hardest. Roberto Carlos had his own agenda and Ronaldo didn't necessarily want to be part of it.

On the footballing side of things, Ronaldo fully appreciated how important an easy victory over their first opponents Scotland would be. He felt it would help wipe away the nervous tension that had been building up to virtual boiling point in the Brazilian training camp in the weeks before the tournament kicked off.

In public, Ronaldo insisted that he could live with the pressures. But privately, he wasn't entirely confident about the abilities of one or two of his team-mates. He voiced his concern in one-to-one meetings with his mentor and hero Zico, who was working as assistant coach for the side.

On the surface, Zico was expected to show complete support to Zagallo, but Zico was privately concerned about certain aspects of the Brazilian team tactics. Zagallo was well aware of this and it added to the tensions within the training camp.

Some inside the Brazilian camp believed that Ronaldo was showing clear signs of exhaustion. He even admitted to one journalist, 'If I do start to tire as the tournament progresses, I'll just keep on playing until I drop. Life is full of sacrifices and this is just one of those occasions.'

On 1 June 1998 — less than two weeks before Brazil's World Cup opener against Scotland — the first serious crack appeared in Ronaldo's relationship with Suzanna Werner. It couldn't really have happened at a worse time.

It was caused by a phone call to the house Ronaldo had rented for his Brazilian entourage just outside Paris. One of Suzanna's friends had seen an article in the Rio daily paper *Odia* headlined NUMBER ONE IN FOOTBALL, NUMBER 13 AT TENNIS. It was subheaded: 'Moments of relaxation, two kisses, 15 minutes of conversation and a problem with Suzanna Werner.'

The story centred around Ronaldo's visit to watch the tennis at the Paris Open. The problem was that all his attention seemed to be focussed on 16-year-old blonde Russian player Anna Kournikova, a striking-looking girl who actually bore quite a resemblance to Suzanna Werner.

What infuriated Suzanna was that photos accompanying the article clearly showed Ronaldo kissing Anna on the cheek and then watching a men's match while sitting alongside her and her parents. And it wasn't as if Ronaldo thought nobody had spotted him; the 17,000 crowd spent more time watching him and Anna than the action on court.

In his defence, Ronaldo had originally gone to watch

the tennis with Brazilian team-mates Denilson, Roberto Carlos and Leonardo, but they were nowhere to be seen once he had settled down next to Anna Kournikova. Later it emerged that Denilson and Roberto Carlos had both mentioned how pretty they thought Anna was and Ronaldo had taken up their challenge to talk to her.

After a long conversation, Anna and her family left the stadium, but not before Ronaldo had been twice obliged to stand up to acknowledge the applause of the crowd. Ronaldo even told one journalist, 'I love tennis very much. It is my favourite sport after football. I have a very good backhand.'

Eventually, three security men had to escort Ronaldo — wearing a beige T-shirt with his own R-9 insignia — out of the stadium because there were so many fans trying to get his autograph. One of them said, 'I'd love to take him home with me. He's so cute.'

Ronaldo must have greatly regretted that incident because it infuriated Suzanna Werner and the couple ended up having a row on the phone. Ronaldo's room-mate Roberto Carlos confirmed that the cracks in their relationship were growing ever wider. 'They had some big problems,' he later told another member of the Brazilian squad.

CHAPTER 20

Spiritual Healing

Little has been mentioned about the great influence of black magic — *macumba* — and spiritualism on the Brazilian squad at France '98. Numerous players and technical staff believed fervently in *macumba*. These footballers were convinced that it wasn't just good football that was going to bring the World Cup back to Brazil.

There is nothing unusual about superstitions; taking certain kicks only with the right foot and leaning at a particular angle while running were just two examples. Not even reciting from the Bible just before a free kick seemed too excessive. Each to his own. However, much more bizarre than that, at least three of the team were actually taking voodoo artefacts on the field with them. And these same players had set up virtual shrines in their hotel rooms.

Ronaldo knew all about such things from his childhood but while he had a healthy respect for the opinions of witch doctors and voodoo priests, he stuck more to the

Catholic view of things. Just before the World Cup, he and his mother had even managed a brief audience with the Pope in the Vatican during which he produced his number nine shirt and persuaded the elderly Pontiff to give it a brief blessing.

Ronaldo actually believed that when he walked out on the field for Brazil he would have extra scoring powers thanks to the Pope's blessing. It was also the reason why he would never agree to swap his shirt throughout the tournament.

In contrast, Ronaldo's room-mate Roberto Carlos was one of those players who practised *macumba*. His background was steeped in the occult and he carried various items with him wherever he went. He also believed in signs from above and talked to Ronaldo about these beliefs just before the side's opener against Scotland. To an impressionable, gentle soul like Ronaldo, it was very bewitching. Roberto Carlos would go on about the spirits being angry or happy and why Ronaldo should be careful not to do certain things in case they invoked the wrath of the voodoo gods.

'Roberto Carlos was heavily involved in *macumba*. He was a country boy made good but he never forgot his roots and voodoo was an important part of all that,' one former team-mate explained.

As TV Globo journalist Pedro Bial explained, 'At this level of sport the spiritual side of the players is almost as important as the physical. That's why Roberto Carlos and his superstitions caused a few problems with Ronaldo.'

Junior Baiano, playing at the World Cup for the first time, even sought out his aunt, a voodoo priestess, before leaving Brazil to ensure that she gave him a satisfactory send-off. Ominously, he was told by his aunt that he should be careful because 'things may not go well in the squad'. Baiano later told one team-mate that he had only sought out the help of a voodoo priestess because he had already noticed bad things happening inside the Brazilian squad in the months leading up to the World Cup. He did not elaborate.

No less superstitious was Goncalves who carried with him to France a vast assortment of religious artefacts including a picture of our Lady of Apaicida which he hung on the wall of his hotel room the moment he checked in. He admitted he always put his right foot first on the field of play when running on to the pitch.

In the dressing room, at least half the side would get down on their knees and pray. One coach, Paulo Paixao always took all his religious knick-knacks out of his bag and laid them on the floor of the dressing room before every game. A picture of Jesus Christ and two prayer books were some of the bulkier items.

Goalkeeper Taffarel, Cesar Sampaio and Giovanni all seemed quite normal in comparison. They proudly told all the other players they were 'Jesus athletes'. Taffarel explained, 'I always pray that God will give this team emotional balance.'

He'd had an appalling experience on the flight over from Brazil because he believed that light turbulence represented some sign of disapproval from God.

Then there was Edmundo, The Animal. In the months preceding the tournament, he had regularly attended a spiritual centre. One of his closest friends helpfully explained, 'Edmundo is being protected by the spirits and this explains the way he plays. He also regularly goes to an evangelical church.' There was no explanation as to why he'd lashed out at the Argentinian keeper during Brazil's recent 1–0 defeat at the Maracana.

On the surface, Ronaldo remained a committed Catholic but in Brazil — unlike any other country in the world — such beliefs were often subsumed by an obsession with *macumba*. And Ronaldo wasn't afraid to acknowledge his debt to God. 'I've done so well at football because it's thanks to God. God chose me. God chose me for a happy, healthy and cheerful life.'

In the middle of all this came some bad news for Brazil — and especially Ronaldo. Romario had not recovered from the injury he'd picked up at Flamengo a month earlier. He was going to be returning home. The final decision was actually made by Ronaldo's mentor, Zico, who said afterwards it was the most difficult decision he had ever made.

Journalist Pedro Bial remains convinced to this day that it was Romario's departure just before the finals that sent Ronaldo into a tailspin. 'The pressure on Ronaldo doubled the moment Romario left.'

The Brazilian squad at France '98 sometimes suffered because of the sheer size of the group of backroom staff and so-called technicians whose sole aim was to help Brazil retain the trophy.

Brazilian journalists were bemused by the fact that one or two of these supposed soccer experts were actually close friends of the coach and the board of the CBF.

As TV Globo's Bial explained, 'A lot of people seemed to be just along for the ride. It cheapened Brazil and made a lot of people not take them seriously.'

Coach Zagallo put a brave face on the news of Romario's departure. In some ways, he was quite relieved because his relationship with the outspoken Romario had always been edgy to say the least.

But what concerned Zagallo was that all the expectations of 160 million Brazilians would now be focused on Ronaldo, not yet 22 years of age. Zagallo was already well aware of the way that pressure could have a detrimental effect on his star player. Now there would be no hiding place for Ronaldo ...

* * *

In the run up to the World Cup, many over-indulged Ronaldo to the point where he must have started to wonder where reality ended and all-out adulation took over.

And there were rumblings of discontent from some quarters about the fantastic wealth he appeared to be amassing following his moves to Barcelona then on to Inter Milan. Affection for Ronaldo in his home country was undoubted, even down to the Brazilian diminutive version of his name, Ronaldinho, because there had been another Ronaldo, the defender Ronaldo Guir, in the 1996 Olympic squad. The little one was the darling of the squad, especially after the departure of Romario.

But all the sentiment could not disguise the demands that Ronaldo's precocity brought him in the weeks before France '98 kicked off. The fact remained that he was the bread-winner for a large, poverty-stricken family, as well as a veritable army of agents, managers, bodyguards and assistants.

And many were already starting to refute the comparisons to Pelé. As one *Sunday Times* journalist wrote on the eve of the tournament, 'There are no signs that Ronaldo will be able, as Pelé was, to make you see the sport in a new light. In one respect, though, the Inter striker has had to carry a great burden which his great predecessor was spared in his youth.'

The facts of the matter were that half the footballing world presumed, even expected, that Brazil could not cope without Ronaldo in France. When it came to scoring goals, Brazil no longer had the resources it once enjoyed. The barren years between 1974 and 1994, when the World Cup fell into the hands of other nations, could be blamed entirely on this lack of a truly world-class striker. So much was expected of Ronaldo because his obvious gift was so scarce.

Many already believed that soccer was unashamedly exploiting Ronaldo long before he arrived at France '98. It was assumed that his reluctance to participate fully for long stretches in games was part of his inimitable style, but the reality was that he'd had virtually no break from soccer for the previous three years, apart from when he had been injured.

Ronaldo was completely indispensable. Experienced soccer watchers had already noticed that his play had not exactly been punctuated by decorative flourishes over the previous ten to twelve months. Increasingly, he seemed to choose the shortest route to goal, making him more reminiscent of a so-called old-fashioned centre-forward like Alan Shearer.

Few observers had forgotten the Inter v. AC Milan derby of March 1998 when Ronaldo made just three or four blinding, menacing runs and ended up helping Inter to a conclusive 3–0 victory. The same could be said of Inter's victory in the UEFA Cup final against Lazio.

But the regularity with which he'd found the net had made the world feverishly expectant of Ronaldo. In hundreds of thousands of words of newsprint and countless TV profiles, no one seemed in doubt that France '98 would be Ronaldo's World Cup. He tried not to show the pressure and actually bottled it up, to the point where he felt at times like the most repressed footballer in the world.

A week before Brazil's opening game with Scotland, the players were transported across Paris in the rush hour to take part in the opening ceremony of a Nike sports park. The CBF informed journalists that the players would grant interviews at the opening so this was taken as a way of forcing them to cover this very commercial event. Many saw it as a clumsy attempt by Nike to exploit the Brazilian team's mega-status within the World Cup.

Nike were so upset by the negative coverage — especially from the Brazilian press — that their representatives did not go out of their way to help journalists at subsequent training sessions. As one reporter said, 'It was all so different from USA '94 when the then sponsors, Umbro, actually provided two staff members to help journalists grab interviews in the chaos that usually ensued after every training session.'

Despite the cracks appearing behind the scenes, Ronaldo certainly appeared to believe that France '98 would be the highlight of his career to date. In the opening match against Scotland he would find himself being marked by one of those very same defenders Zagallo had warned him about; a 33-year-old tough guy who'd spent most of his career languishing in England's lower league divisions. To the expectant public at large Ronaldo looked as if he was set for an easy afternoon.

But Ronaldo genuinely feared the hard men of the Scottish side, especially his man marker, Colin Calderwood of Spurs. The Brazilian coach had given his team a stern warning about the spirit and physical toughness of the Scots — the fire in their bellies. One thing he didn't tell his squad was Calderwood's nickname — Edward Scissorlegs — a reference to his ability to chop attackers down.

As injured Scottish captain Gary McAllister, of Coventry City, said just before France '98 kicked off: 'If you go near him, you know something is going to hurt you, whether it be an arm or whatever. You'll come away all sore because he is so sharp and bony.'

The truth was that the opening game of the World Cup threatened to be awe-inspiring for many members of both sides, because the pressure was going to be very different from any other match either side had ever experienced before.

As Calderwood himself said just hours before the opening match kicked off, 'I have not tried to think about how I will play against Ronaldo. I watch Italian football on television and when teams have done well against Ronaldo it has not been because one defender has got the better of him. He can always beat you for pace so you have to get him to hit it three or four yards further away than he wants, so that a covering defender can intercept.

'You must have the discipline not to bring him down because Brazil are looking for those free kicks on the edge of the penalty area. With Ronaldo, you also need to stay alert. He goes through long spells in which he doesn't do very much and then he scores in the last 10 or 15 minutes.'

The message from Calderwood and many others was that they had Ronaldo in their sights — he was a marked man and any notion that he might stroll through the tournament, scoring and making numerous goals, might not prove to be as likely as many had once thought.

The game against Scotland should have presented few problems for Ronaldo and his team-mates, but with the eyes of the world watching the game, there was an added dimension that really shook Ronaldo in the hours just before the big kick off.

In the team hotel, Ronaldo tried to take a siesta but he was too nervous. Then he burst into tears and started shaking with fear. One Brazilian journalist at France '98 said, 'He was distraught. One team-mate told me that no one dared tell the coaching staff or medics. They just presumed he was a bit nervous and left it at that.'

In Brazil, a rather bizarre — yet perfectly understandable — tradition had developed. Before a game, many of the players would empty their bowels and bladder. It all went back to 1970 World Cup legend Rivellino who insisted on going to the toilet just before the team went out. He explained many years later, 'We would say, "Let's throw away the fear."' His other main superstition, always taking the field with the right foot, was copied by one or two of the 1998 side.

Ronaldo was so stressed before the Scotland game he did not manage to empty his bowels and bladder just before the match — as he had done before every game he had played in for the previous four years.

'Ronaldo was convinced that effected his form in the game against Scotland,' said Brazilian TV reporter Pedro Bial, who later explained, 'Everyone was talking about Ronaldo and how he was going to destroy the Scots single-handedly. He reacted by crying and shaking.'

After their fortunate 2–1 victory, even Ronaldo admitted, 'We weren't our best against Scotland but what mattered was winning. The Scots marked me closely for the

90 minutes, but fairly. I have never felt as many eyes on me as that game — and I liked it. Whenever I touched the ball, everyone seemed to go quiet. It was a magical evening. Unforgettable.'

After the press conference one journalist commented, 'Ronaldo looked terrified. He looks like a nervous wreck. God knows what he'll be like if Brazil get to the final.'

The day after Brazil's opening victory over Scotland, Ronaldo ignored coach Zagallo's advice not to see girlfriends or wives and arranged to meet up with Suzanna.

The couple met at the house rented for his family near Paris. Suzanna was still irritated by what had happened with that 16-year-old Russian tennis star but she knew that Ronaldo needed her. He seemed even more tense than before the Scotland game and he'd been so nervous about breaking Zagallo's curfew that he'd asked a crew from Brazil's TV Globo to film an 'at home' segment at the house so he had the perfect excuse. Much against his better judgement, Zagallo had agreed to allow Ronaldo to spend one night at the house. They were many grumblings from the other squad members who understandably felt that Ronaldo was getting preferential treatment.

Once inside Ronaldo's temporary home, the TV crew and journalist Pedro Bial soon realised that the young lovers had had yet another tiff.

'It was obvious they'd had another of their arguments,' explained Bial. 'He was even wearing a T-shirt with the words, 'Don't look at me, my girlfriend is jealous.'

'Suzanna was so embarrassed by that T-shirt she tried to divert our attention by grabbing Ronaldo's hands and showing off her engagement ring.'

While Ronaldo was undoubtedly happy to be at the house with his girlfriend and mother, he soon found himself being manipulated emotionally by his girlfriend. Instead of relaxing and thinking about Brazil's next game, he had to play peace-maker and try to ensure that their relationship did not collapse.

Brazil's next game against Morocco featured Ronaldo's first goal of the tournament. He sounded very relieved in a press conference immediately after that match, which Brazil won comfortably 3–0.

'That was the most important goal of my life because it was my first goal in the World Cup. I was mad with joy, like a prisoner being set free. We enjoyed ourselves against Morocco. We regained our old confidence. When things are going well, it's as if we are on fire. We did not want that game to end. That's when I really started enjoying playing alongside Rivaldo. I thought we made a great double act.'

But what Ronaldo did not mention until some days after the Morocco game was the seriousness of an injury he had picked up. He was under strict orders from Zagallo not to explain it fully under any circumstances. But he couldn't resist commenting on the foul that caused it.

'It was incredible. The referee didn't even show him a yellow card. I needed special treatment to try to heal the damage to my thigh. I don't understand referees. First they say one thing about dangerous tackling, then they behave in a totally different manner. It was as if the Moroccans were out to get us, they were dangerous.'

That incident freaked out Ronaldo because his knee had already been hurting from that injury back in March 1996 which had flared up again while he was at Barcelona. Now he had a thigh problem as well. And the tense dramas which were about to unfold wouldn't help his situation much either. But Ronaldo knew that he would have to play on through the pain.

Soon after that victory over Morocco, members of the 500-strong Brazilian press corps began hearing rumours that Ronaldo had more problems with Suzanna Werner.

Then Suzanna and Sonia had arranged a lunch at the house he had rented at Pontault Combault, near Paris. But Ronaldo did not show up.

Suzanna's earlier thoughts about the importance of

being faithful in a relationship were at the back of his mind. 'This is something that has been questioned by many young people. It is so difficult today. I don't believe much in faithfulness especially from men,' she said just before dating Ronaldo.

One Rio paper, *Odia*, claimed that Ronaldo's absence from the Paris luncheon was because he was so tired he had slept until 2.00pm and had forgotten to join Suzanna and his mother for lunch. But on that same day, Suzanna flew off to Milan to continue filming without having seen Ronaldo. Rumours of a break-up then gathered pace. *Odia* insisted, 'Ronaldo is being emotionally hurt.' Meanwhile, Mario Zagallo re-issued his warning to all his squad to keep away from their wives and girlfriends because he wanted no distractions from the important games to come.

At first, the rumours seemed to have come from nowhere. Ronaldo was in a state of confusion. He was simply too young, emotionally, to cope.

CHAPTER 21

The Suzanna Factor

On 21 June — the day before Brazil's final group match against Norway — Ronaldo heard rumours involving his fiancée Suzanna and TV Globo anchorman Pedro Bial, her colleague for the duration of the World Cup. Suzanna had been offered the job of 'roving reporter' by TV Globo for the duration of the World Cup tournament. Ronaldo suspected that the stories were being deliberately circulated to try to destabilise his form and ruin Brazil's chances of getting to the final. It later transpired that Bial was very happily married and that there was no foundation in the rumours.

There was also talk of Ronaldo having pain-killing injections in his knee so he could keep playing. If true, it would have been very risky because treatment drugs are usually taken orally because of the risk of damage by a needle.

Then one source inside the Brazilian training camp even suggested that captain Dunga was so unhappy about how the team were performing on and off the field that he had almost walked out on the side just before the Norway clash. Suddenly, Brazil's problems seemed to be mounting.

Ronaldo even called a press conference to try and dispel the gossip. He told a packed room full of journalists: 'The story that I had a knee injection before the last match is nothing but a joke, in really bad taste.

'I think it is cheap and really low and probably set up in order to try to knock me off my stride. OK, it is true that my knee has had a few twinges but nothing serious and it will not affect my performance.

'I'm doing training along with everybody else and in addition I've had massage and I am using lots of ice. The ultrasound equipment in the hotel has obviously helped, too.'

Then he tackled the rumours about Suzanna's alleged romance.

'The "news" about me and my girlfriend is another bad joke which is meant to break my concentration. I'm still wearing my ring. I'm used to people trying to break my concentration and I have learned to turn away from bad jokes and rumours.

'Of course it hurts me that some people want to lash out at me but what I do off the field has nothing to do with football news. I'm a professional and, when it comes down to a World Cup, that is what I focus on.

'Unfortunately, some people are not interested in the World Cup and every time I do something, anything, they turn it around and it becomes a bad taste story. All the players support me — we support each other. I get really fed up when the focus of winning the World Cup gets interrupted by a nonsensical story.'

Ronaldo's statement was significant as he had been obliged to talk openly because of the rash of rumours about him and other Brazilian team-members. But there were underlying problems inside the Brazilian squad despite their powerful display against the Moroccans in which they became the first team to qualify for the second round.

Dunga's alleged walk-out threat had come after a furious on-field row with Bebeto. And Ronaldo was even forced to refer to room-mate Roberto Carlos and some comments he was supposed to have made.

He told journalists, 'Roberto Carlos has said that Dunga probably wouldn't have tried to come head to head with the likes of Junior Baiano, because of his size, or Edmundo, because of his reputation.

'But Dunga has a big responsibility as the captain and everything he does we know is because he is doing his best for the team.'

Behind the scenes, Ronaldo was furious with Roberto Carlos for stirring up trouble within the team and he pledged to confront him when they talked in their room.

To make matters even worse, coach Zagallo found himself on the receiving end of some heavy criticism of his defenders from the Norwegian coach Egil Olsen before their match.

Zagallo snapped, 'I wouldn't lower myself to retaliating to his verbal attack. Whatever he says is up to him. If he wants to waste time talking about us Brazilians then it is up to him. At a World Cup there is so much to do in preparing mentally and physically and I wouldn't waste my time on Olsen.

'When we lost to Norway last summer we were very jet-lagged and the preparation for this match compared to that one is like night and day.'

Intriguingly, Roberto Carlos became much more vocal during this stage of France '98 and he also got in a few words about Norway.

'I think Olsen is talking a lot of nonsense. At this level, I am surprised that he has taken the time to deliberately offend Mr Zagallo. Olsen should respect Zagallo and on Tuesday night I will be looking for revenge — any campaign to put us off our stride will have the opposite effect. I consider myself to be one of the best wing-backs in the world and you don't get here without believing that you can overcome everything.'

The Norway match itself held a lot of painful memories for Ronaldo because of the earlier friendly, a 4–2 defeat in Oslo in May 1997. He was one of six players who'd survived from that side.

'It was a terrible pitch but they played quite well. I'm sure their coach is worried now, which is why he's trying to play down the comments he made before.'

Norway needed a win against Brazil to guarantee their progression ahead of Scotland after drawing their first two games.

As it happened, the Norwegians turned the World Cup on its head by defeating the Brazilians 2–1 on 23 June. Brazil — and especially Ronaldo — gave a poor account of themselves although it was pointed out that they had already qualified on top of their group for the second round.

Ronaldo was indignant about the result and said almost defiantly afterwards, 'Brazil are not only Ronaldo. I have to help the team but the team must also help me. With Brazil I have had to play in a different way to the manner I play with Inter, where I am used to receiving the ball differently. With Brazil I accept I must sacrifice for the team, running and moving around a great deal. But just as I do that for the team so the rest of the team must do that for me.'

It was an outspoken attack on his own team-mates and did not exactly do the Brazilian spirits much good. Ronaldo's nerves were shattered. He'd virtually limped through the game afraid to do anything too energetic in case his injury problems worsened. Zagallo was well aware of the problems but his attitude was that a half-fit Ronaldo was better than any other fully fit striker he had available.

Those who had not encountered Ronaldo in the flesh before France '98 were under the clear impression that he was a smiling, happy, carefree character. But within two weeks of the World Cup kick off, he was hiding a heavy heart and constant inner turmoil.

The main problem, besides his injuries, was Suzanna Werner. The couple had had another blazing row on the eve of Brazil's second-round game against Chile and he was left feeling resentment, self-doubt and an aching heart — all the usual symptoms of lovesickness.

During a meeting with Zagallo, Ronaldo was so tense he lost his temper and stormed out when Zagallo had tried to sort out Ronaldo's problems.

Ronaldo even admitted to one confidant that he was so distressed by Suzanna that he expected to be pulled out of the Brazil team for the Chile game. He finally admitted, 'Suzanna and I did break up, but only for two days. We're young and I'm under a lot of pressure. Suzanna has her own life and she has to do her own thing sometimes, which means our paths don't always cross when I want them to.

'My last day off I spent cooped up alone and miserable in the hotel while Suzanna was working. I wasn't happy but can I do? Life is like that sometimes.'

Ronaldo later insisted to friends that part of the problem was that he couldn't handle Suzanna working within the world of football with Brazil's TV Globo. Whether it was connected to her close working relationship with handsome commentator Pedro Bial it was impossible to say.

Rumours about that friendship were re-ignited when an Argentinian newspaper published an article headlined RONALDO HAS RECONCILIATION WITH SUZANNA.

According to the paper, 'Pedro Bial is making the Brazilian selectors very unhappy. Although there now has been a reconciliation between Ronaldo and Suzanna, Bial has become the third party in this dispute. He is older than both their ages combined.'

The paper went on to describe ex-war correspondent Pedro as 'a charmer who has had a number of attractive women in the past' and then proceeded to inform its readers of his background.

Then the article claimed that Bial had 'taken Suzanna under his wing to show her what to do' in her job as a part-time presenter for Globo TV at the World Cup 'and they have become very good friends'.

The article went on to say, 'It didn't take long for the relationship to reach Ronaldo's ears and it is now the only thing being talked about by the rest of the Brazilian squad. It has also been noted that Ronaldo gets very few visits from his fiancée and has to sleep at the team hotel leaving her alone in Paris.

'In Paris, there also happens to be Pedro Bial. He is like her shadow. There are many versions of what is really happening.'

The article was packed with innuendo but little substance. Many who read it saw it as a thinly-veiled attempt by soccer neighbours Argentina to try to demoralise the Brazilian team in their battle to regain the World Cup.

The story also pointed out that being engaged to Ronaldo had greatly helped Suzanna's career as an actress, including a leading part in a big-budget Italian movie. According to the paper, 'Ronaldo is not Suzanna's first true love but she is his and she has said that any man who treats her badly is a rat.'

The problem was that Ronaldo and Suzanna's problems were all too apparent so the suggestion that a third party might be involved soon gathered momentum, whether or not it was actually true.

As Pedro Bial later recalled in an interview in Rio in August 1998, 'The gossip was extremely harmful to me as well as Ronaldo. I am married to a young wife and we've just had a child. All this talk of me and Suzanna was professionally and personally very damaging.'

The gossip about Bial and Suzanna was taken so seriously in football-mad Brazil that Bial's elderly mother back in Rio had to be given police protection because of death threats inspired by the rumours.

Bial added, 'Both Suzanna and I were embarrassed by the rumours. She was particularly worried that it made her look as if she was just promoting herself to the detriment of Ronaldo.'

Bial confirmed that there was a small period of time when Ronaldo did stop wearing his engagement ring — although he continued to insist it was nothing to do with the allegations made against him. Ronaldo later claimed, 'I took my ring off because I hurt my hand in training. I was afraid my finger might swell and I wouldn't be able to get the ring off.' But he then conceded, 'Even if we did have a disagreement, it would be normal, as we are courting.'

'Look, they certainly fight a lot. But they're young and in love and very Latin,' said Bial.

As Ruth de Aquino, editor of the biggest circulation newspaper in Rio, *Odia*, explained, 'Suzanna and Ronaldo's relationship had changed fundamentally over the previous two years. When they first started going out together no one could believe she would date such an ugly guy.

'She was a cute, ambitious young actress with serious plans to work abroad. No one thought they could possibly fall in love. Then, all of a sudden, she goes out to Europe to join him.

'Suzanna is always the one talking about getting married. Things have changed between them. Ronaldo has more confidence and his persona has changed. Today he can pick any woman he wants. He is no longer seen as an ugly man. Ronaldo is now the sexual animal.

'You see, Suzanna is the first real girlfriend in Ronaldo's life. All the others were not serious. Suzanna and Ronaldo were encouraged to get together even though her parents were horrified to begin with.

'You have to remember that her background is conservative, middle class. Getting engaged to a footballer is not exactly encouraged. That's why many suspected Suzanna's motives when she first started dating Ronaldo.'

And in France, Ronaldo soon found himself with a new

set of admirers. The Parisian gay community chose him as one of their sexiest men following the publication in *Paris Match* of him in tight black trousers and no shirt looking like Rodin's thinker.

But that award wasn't likely to be much consolation for Ronaldo.

*　　　*　　　*

Before the match against Chile, Ronaldo actually told one friend he would either score a couple of goals or he'd hit the bar and the post and be taken off at half-time. That was a measure of how insecure he felt. As his mother had believed all along, he was still emotionally a youthful teenager. Why should he understand how to respond to these pressures?

In fact, Ronaldo scored twice against Chile in their 4–2 win, the first from the penalty spot. But even so he insisted in public he could do better. He felt he should have been involved in more of the open play and, once again, he was punishing himself unnecessarily.

'I can't just sit there and expect the ball to come to me because that makes me easy prey for defenders. None of us can relax until we get to the final, lift the cup and take it back to Brazil.'

But Ronaldo did later sound more relieved after the game against Chile.

'It was a brilliant victory. We were on top of our game again. It didn't matter how the opposition tried to upset us, that was the evening I realised how good we were and how it seemed we possessed all the qualities needed to win the World Cup. I also scored two goals, though I must admit I was nervous before the penalty. After the game, I kept my shirt to give to Inter president Massimo Moratti. Do you know he had come to watch me, rather than go to see Italy play?'

The day after Brazil's victory, Ronaldo agreed to give a

one-to-one interview to TV Globo reporter Pedro Bial despite rumours of his friendship with Suzanna Werner at France '98. Before doing their on-screen interview, the two men discussed the matter in detail. Bial says today that Ronaldo did not believe the rumours. 'He was just angry that people were making up stories. He had no problem with me at all.'

In Rio in August 1998, Pedro Bial recalled that 'awkward' meeting.

'Ronaldo kept referring to the pressure on him but insisted he could cope. It was as if he was answering his own fears rather than the questions I was putting to him.'

To make matters worse for Ronaldo he was also caught up in the middle of his mother's continued war of words with his father Nelio.

'It was not very relaxed for Ronaldo. They were often in conflict and Ronaldo's father, Nelio, had to stay in a hotel a long way from the house Ronaldo was renting for his mother and Suzanna. I felt sorry for Ronaldo. You could see the strain of it all on his face,' added Pedro Bial.

Ironically, Ronaldo had spent upwards of £200,000 flying various family and friends over from Rio and then accommodating them in rented houses and hotels in the centre of Paris. Now they were proving such a diversion that there was a very real danger that his game on the field would be affected.

To understand the pressure to which the Brazilian football team is exposed — the hopes and dreams of 160 million Brazilians rest on the squad's shoulders — one has only to look back to the legendary 1970 World Cup-winning side. Just as there was in the build up to 1998, an air of expectancy seemed to follow that team's every move.

When they won 4–1 in the final against Italy in Mexico City, one of their star players, Rivellino, fainted. As he later explained, 'I fainted with relief. I don't remember anything. All I remember is being in the dressing room. I also knew what would have happened if we had not won.'

The emotion was that charged. The importance was undeniable. The pressure for Brazil at World Cup time was second to none.

Following the game against Chile, Ronaldo became even more convinced that he needed to improve his work rate significantly in every game if he was truly to deserve the title of the world's best player.

'It is a special gift I have from God and our common aim in this squad is to take the World Cup back to Brazil. For that reason, I'm desperate to improve and score more goals for Brazil,' he told one journalist earnestly after it had been suggested that his work rate was not up to scratch.

During the second half of the World Cup campaign in France, Ronaldo became noticeably more irritable — and he was taking all criticism as a personal insult. In the past, he'd usually managed to shield himself emotionally, but the torrent of articles in newspapers and magazines were upsetting him. He hated reading about himself but he felt obliged to seek out such articles. It was almost as if he was punishing himself because he felt he had not been performing as well as the Brazilian nation had expected.

After years of never allowing anger to get the better of him — repressing his true feelings on a whole range of subjects — Ronaldo may well have been better off letting rip rather than bottling everything up. Becoming slowly more angry and frustrated in silence meant that he tended to experience more tension than someone like Romario, who told the world everything he was thinking.

And in the middle of all this chaos, Ronaldo had a strong urge just to go home to Rio. The problems with Suzanna and his injury worries sparked a bout of homesickness, especially since he was staying in the team hotel well away from his family in their rented house. He hadn't had a chance to return to Rio since Inter had ended their season.

At France '98, Ronaldo even spoke to Martins and Pitta

about a possible move back to Brazil from Inter. They pointed out in no uncertain terms that this was impossible. They also told Ronaldo to concentrate on the World Cup — nothing else mattered. But their well-founded advice simply made Ronaldo feel more dispirited. As a result, he would sing the praises of his homeland at every opportunity.

'Brazil is everything and football in Brazil is so much more than you can imagine. That's the important job I have here,' he said, following the Chile game. 'I want to make my country proud.'

When Ronaldo was asked by one reporter about a possible return to Rio — playing for Flamengo — he insisted that he could not talk publicly about such a move because he and the rest of the Brazilian squad only had one aim, that of keeping the World Cup. But, privately, he pointed out to one close friend, 'Flamengo is the dearest club of all and once Flamengo always Flamengo. There is something special, something mystic about it — if you were a *Flamegista*, then you would understand.' Inter Milan didn't seem to fit into the equation.

Back in Rio, gossip of Ronaldo's potential return to Rio interrupted the tidal wave of World Cup chatter. It was claimed that a furniture magnate called Kleiber Leite was behind the plan. He had pulled off a similar coup when he had brought Romario back to Flamengo from Spain a year earlier.

The club itself was convinced it could recoup an expected $100 million outlay by filling the Maracana Stadium with 120,000 crowds each and every week.

Then Flamengo vice-president Michel Assef insisted in Rio that he was tabling the bid. 'We are going through with this deal,' he told one Rio newspaper. 'We were approached by a businessman who told us that a bank was interested in Ronaldo's transfer.'

Ronaldo's agent, Pitta, told the paper, 'But I don't think it's possible. He is happy where he is and, besides, he has a four-year contract with Inter Milan.'

The paper also claimed that Banco Opportunity, a Brazilian bank and asset management company, would help finance Ronaldo's transfer.

But as one observer pointed out just after Brazil's game against Chile, 'All this speculation leaves Ronaldo with his head, heart and future in a spin just at the time when he needs to be thinking of nothing but that little golden trophy.'

And then there was Suzanna. She had the power to make or break the form of the world's most famous footballer.

In Rio, rumours of Ronaldo's problems with Suzanna had reached fever pitch. From Italy, where Suzanna had snatched two days to complete some film work, she even publicly denied that her engagement to Ronaldo was over. 'The end of our affair is all rumours and now is not the right moment to make up stories about us. Ronaldo at this time has to have a cool head and eye also.'

Suzanna completely ignored reports that Ronaldo had removed his engagement ring. 'The other day I played a film role without my ring because my character does not use it.'

That comment was an unintentional dig at Ronaldo by Suzanna because during one of their many arguments he had thrown a jealous fit because of a steamy bedroom scene she had to act out for her role in that feature film being made in Italy.

'I just can't stand the thought of her kissing another man, let alone being in bed with one, even though it's only for the cameras,' he told one friend.

Ronaldo's problems weighed heavily as Brazil careered towards yet another World Cup Final.

On 26 June, Ronaldo's former Barcelona coach Bobby Robson, working as a World Cup pundit for British television, persuaded his erstwhile protégé to agree to an exclusive TV interview. Ronaldo agreed to the interview on the understanding that he would only be questioned by Robson.

It was a strange scenario; Robson grabbed Ronaldo at the Brazilian training camp and had the look of an excited cub reporter as he breathlessly threw a handful of questions at his former star. Ronaldo looked like a rabbit caught in a car's headlights. The content was meaningless but there was a blank expression on Ronaldo's face throughout.

One journalist explained, 'He just didn't seem to be on the same planet as the rest of us but we all just presumed that was what he was like normally.'

On 2 July 1998, Ronaldo admitted in public for the first time that he had been suffering from pain in his left knee but insisted to journalists that it would not keep him out of the quarter-final clash with Denmark.

Ronaldo told one reporter, 'It's a slight pain. It hurts when I strain, when I sprint or when I stop suddenly. I can take the pain. During a game, I'm so concentrated that I forget it hurts.'

Only a few days earlier, the Brazilian team doctor had let slip that he believed Ronaldo was overweight. In fact, that was simply an excuse to cover the fact that Ronaldo had been struggling with his injured leg ever since the game against Morocco.

In the background, CBF president Ricardo Teixeira was following events very closely. During his regular meetings with Nike, they had a running joke about Ronaldo *not* playing. It was playful banter but beneath the lighthearted chat was a very serious message that no one could deny. If Ronaldo was unfit to play, it would be a marketing disaster for the company.

Of course, they could not expect to influence selection of the Brazilian side but that didn't mean they weren't very concerned whenever there were rumours about Ronaldo's fitness. And it is worth remembering that Nike were everywhere; every shirt worn on the field or off seemed to feature the company's tick logo and their executives swarmed around the team's training sessions like besuited guards of honour.

The pressure they exerted was enormous.

CHAPTER 22

Rabbit in the Headlights

After a few close shaves, Brazil secured a 3–2 victory over Denmark. But Zagallo abandoned his normal principle of intervening only at crucial moments and stood on the very limits of the officially allocated squad area shouting, yelling and swearing at his team and officials. His frustration was apparent for the whole world to see — he was clearly extremely uneasy.

In the stands, thousands of Brazilians booed the coach whose negative tactics, they believed, were responsible for their side's struggle for victory. The Brazilian press had already dubbed Zagallo 'the 200-year-old coach' and claimed that it was unhealthy for Zagallo still to be clinging to the head coaching job.

On the touchline, Zagallo became increasingly hunched and the tracksuit top he was wearing hung loosely on his once powerful torso as some of the little strength he had left was expended in verbal abuse and dramatic gestures towards his players.

Afterwards, Zagallo had the good grace to admit the irony that one of the opposition's so-called 'beautiful' players was the primary cause of the veteran coach's mental and physical distress.

'That is what is tiring for me — the tension of a wonderful player like Brian Laudrup being given the space to display his talent,' said Zagallo.

After beating Denmark to qualify for the semi-finals, Zagallo broke down in tears when he telephoned his family and needed medication in order to combat the stress which threatened his 66-year-old heart.

The man who had started France '98 looking vital, bright-eyed and prepared for anything, suddenly appeared frail, stooped and old. Back in Brazil, nobody seemed grateful that Zagallo had cleverly replaced the supposedly irreplaceable Romario with the rejuvenated veteran, Bebeto, and was still winning games. After three goals and two assists, the use of Bebeto seemed like the signature of a maestro to many non-Brazilians.

As Scottish manager Craig Brown told one colleague after Brazil's victory over Denmark, 'If they boo a coach like Mario Zagallo, what chance do the rest of us have?'

On the surface, Ronaldo seemed a little more relaxed. 'I found it a lot easier making the assists than having to score the goals. It didn't matter that I didn't score. I always knew that the top-scoring award mattered nothing by comparison with trying to win the World Cup.

'Of course, I knew after the quarter-finals that Batistuta and Vieri were out of the running, but it was more important to me that Argentina and Italy, two powerful teams, had been eliminated. I must say about Denmark that they were a remarkable team in the full sense of the word. One of the best in the world.'

Despite the problems simmering just beneath the surface, most of those watching France '98 had an innate sense of wonderment about Ronaldo and that tended to cloud what was really happening to him.

In the *Daily Mirror*, soccer writer Mark McGuinness insisted after Ronaldo's performances against Scotland and Morocco that he was still destined to be the biggest star at the tournament.

McGuinness wrote, 'Anyone who has witnessed Brazil's opening two games can have no doubts that we are witnessing the coming of age of the game's most sublime talent.

'South America's finest produce startling individuals. But every once in a while, they come up with a player who is just that little bit ... well, extra special. Ronaldo is their golden child.

'Quite simply, he floats like a butterfly and stings like a bee. His strength and balance are incredible and knocking him off his feet has proved an impossible task so far.'

However, in the same glowing article, Ronaldo was quoted as at least conceding that life was not easy in Italy for the most famous footballing face in the world.

'It is difficult to live a normal life under these circumstances. In Italy, this is much more difficult because of the way the country feels about soccer and lives soccer — much more than anywhere else.'

At the back of Ronaldo's mind there was a feeling that escaping the bright lights of Italy and Europe might be the only answer to his inner turmoil.

He'd never forgotten how much he enjoyed visiting the USA during the '94 World Cup and on a couple of other trips during the previous two years. He loved America at the time because no one knew or recognised him.

Ronaldo might own a silver Ferrari, a beautiful apartment in Milan and numerous other properties in Europe and Brazil, but he started to feel he would happily swap it all for a life of peace and complete contentment.

And every now and again the façade of super-confidence in himself and Brazil would slip. In one unguarded moment following the Denmark game he was even reluctant to predict Brazil's victory at France '98. 'We have the best players. But to have the best players and to win is not the same thing — we have to prove it.'

Before the semi-final match against Holland, Dutch coach Guus Hiddink criticised Brazil for a 'lack of organisation' in their play.

Typically, Zagallo replied, 'Let's look back to 1958. I won a World Cup that year, and here I am 40 years later, competing for a fifth title.

'As a player I changed the way left-wingers play, although I didn't get the credit for it. I was already a coach on the field. Then when I became a real coach, I was also criticised for being too innovative. I have a lot of respect for Holland, but I don't need to take lessons from another coach or another school of football.'

By a strange twist of irony, only French coach Aimé Jacquet had been the recipient of so much wounding scepticism from fans and journalists alike throughout the tournament.

Brazil held their nerve against the dangerous Dutch in a penalty shoot-out to reach a record sixth World Cup final. Philip Cocu and Ronald De Boer missed the crucial spot kicks to leave Brazilian keeper Claudio Taffarel as the hero and Ronaldo even admitted he was grateful for the victory.

Mario Zagallo ran on to the pitch with tears in his eyes after Taffarel had saved Ronald De Boer's penalty. Once again his health looked decidedly worrying.

'Sudden-death play-offs are always unpleasant,' Zagallo said, 'but at least we succeeded. It is a terrible stage to go out of the competition.'

Both sides had chances to win but either horrendous misses or brilliant tackles kept the score at 1–1 throughout the golden goal period, in which the first team to score wins the match.

The hero that day, Taffarel, put the victory down to divine intervention. 'It was not me making those saves, it was God.'

Brazil's hard-won success over Holland seemed to drain their resources in a similar way to Argentina's exhaustion following their titan battle with England in the second round.

Certainly, Ronaldo found himself closely marked by Frank De Boer who refused to succumb, even when reeling before the speed and power which Ronaldo exhibited to reasonable effect as the game rolled into extra-time.

Three times Ronaldo comprehensively eluded De Boer. Once he scored, once he was chased down by Edgar Davids — another heroic standard-bearer for Holland — and was pressurised to fire inches wide.

On the final occasion, De Boer himself regained ground to make a desperate clearance with a boot thrust between Ronaldo's legs as the World's Best Player accelerated into a shooting opportunity.

The last of these incidents came in the additional half-hour allowed for a golden goal, and the galvanising effect on Ronaldo of that opportunity was clear. He kept probing the Dutch defence, almost as if his life depended on it. Single-handedly he took on the opposition defence over and over again.

And more often than not, he was trying to create goals for others as well as himself. To observers, it seemed as if he had forgotten the somewhat selfish obsession with beating Juste Fontaine's toll of 13 goals at the Finals and, instead, devoted himself to others.

The problem was that when Brazil finally clinched victory under the most strenuous of circumstances, Ronaldo was completely and utterly shattered. His injured left knee was in agony. In some ways, he had matured in thought and deed on that fateful day against Holland.

The ease with which Brazil had come through the opening group phase had lulled him into thinking it was going to be a comfortable ride. Now Ronaldo found himself at the centre of an anguished drama in which many of his own countrymen were predicting disaster, despite the fact that Brazil had reached their fifth World Cup final.

At a press conference following the game, Ronaldo was muted. 'The most difficult moment for me came after Kluivert's equaliser. We knew we would have to dig deep to prove we were the better team. Similarly, our happiest moment was the sensation after we won the penalty shoot-out. Taffarel was fantastic. Holland would have beaten anyone else that night. We really did think after that game that we could beat anybody.' But did he really believe those last few words?

Ronaldo may have been having his own problems at France '98 but girlfriend Suzanna Werner seemed to be going from strength to strength.

In early July she was hailed by the world's press as the face of France '98, even though she was only one of the players' girlfriends. Her job with TV Globo had given her access to a perfect position in the stands for every match. And match camera crews seemed to delight in cutting to smiling, blonde Suzanna at least three times during every game. Whenever play became a little boring, billions of viewers across the world would get a glimpse of Suzanna, wearing eye-catching low-cut tops and plenty of make-up.

Down on the field of play, Ronaldo felt a great deal of insecurity about Suzanna, despite his apparent trust of Pedro Bial. She would only sit a few feet from the handsome TV commentator, who was falsely alleged to be having a relationship with her.

A couple of days before the final against France, the Brazilians deliberately leaked a story to the world's press claiming that Ronaldo had been declared fit for the most important match of his life.

They admitted that he had pulled out of training after just 30 minutes on 9 July, but actually that it was purely a precautionary measure following a 'slight ankle strain'.

Instead of full training, Ronaldo jogged casually round the Brazilian's training pitch half-a-dozen times before returning to the gym for some weight training, which he had been supposed to do every day since that operation on his right knee two years before.

Brazilian team doctor Lidio Toledo even assured newsmen that Ronaldo would carry out some more training that afternoon to ensure that he was not having any further injury problems. In fact, Ronaldo's fitness — both mental and physical — was causing great concern to Brazilian coach Zagallo and his backroom staff.

'Ronaldo seemed in a daze. He barely said a word to anyone and it was clear that something was troubling him but no one knew how to react to it,' one member of the squad told me seven weeks later in Rio. 'I suppose we all just tried to ignore it in the hope it would all blow over. The truth was that none of us wanted to face up to the prospect of there being a problem with Ronaldo.'

And another squad member said in an interview in Rio in August 1998, 'I heard that Ronaldo was very unhappy. We knew there was something wrong but no one would actually talk about it.'

Meanwhile, Zagallo put on his bravest face for the waiting media. 'One hundred and sixty million people will be chanting for Brazil this Sunday,' he told a packed press conference. Zagallo looked distinctly sombre, but no one dared ask why.

'We will not let this opportunity go away,' he continued. 'It is in our hands, it is a dream final — a dream cup. We respect France but we have no fear. We have been in five World Cup finals and this Sunday will be France's first.'

In truth, there wasn't much else Zagallo could say. He was extremely worried, not only about Ronaldo but also about at least three other team members who seemed distracted and lacking vital ambition.

Significantly, not everyone was convinced that Brazil were such a great team. Holland's Jaap Stam saw the cracks begin to appear during his team's semi-final clash with Brazil. He insisted, 'Frankly, Brazil are no longer the best team in the world. There are many others who are at least on the same level and that includes Holland. France are as strong and even better in some areas. But they do not have a goalscorer like Ronaldo.'

Stam's words rang like a warning siren to the ears of many in the Brazilian team camp. If Ronaldo wasn't happy, how on earth would they cope?

And for Ronaldo there was no hiding place. Because so few people had any idea of the behind-the-scenes turmoil, he was still being exposed to dozens of requests for media interviews and having to avoid them like the plague.

Many fans and members of the press seemed to expect him to be a poet, a philosopher, even a politician. The truth was that Ronaldo was a commodity and a cultural phenomenon, as well as being an extremely talented footballer. He was also in dire need of break from the beautiful game.

In some ways, he remained the mummy's boy who liked nothing more than her homemade treats, words of support and an early night. Ronaldo longed to go back to the house the family were renting near Paris, cuddle up next to Suzanna and forget about football. But Zagallo had already admonished him for sneaking out after some of the previous World Cup games. This time there would be no escape.

The five-day countdown to the final against France seemed interminable to Ronaldo because he knew only too well that unless Brazil won the World Cup for a fifth time then he would get much of the blame. He was having trouble sleeping and his unease was disturbing room-mate Roberto Carlos. There was a growing tension between the two men. Roberto Carlos, with his black magic practices and superstitions, had drained Ronaldo earlier in the tournament; now it was the other way round. Ronaldo was having a detrimental effect on Roberto Carlos because he seemed so depressed all the time. He hardly spoke and was lacking in energy during the day because he wasn't sleeping properly at night. Roberto Carlos had even got into the annoying habit of waking Ronaldo up every time he talked in his sleep.

Roberto Carlos had also irritated Ronaldo by going on and on about how much he had hated being at Inter Milan before his move to Spain. It didn't exactly help things between the two men.

Team-mate Leonardo — probably the most eloquent of all the Brazilian players on show at France '98 — summed it up perfectly when he said, 'The demands on Ronaldo, the expectations, are something crazy.'

Leonardo refused to elaborate because he knew, along with many of his team-mates, that Ronaldo was not coping very well.

The pain in Ronaldo's left knee was getting worse after every match and even Brazilian trainer Claudio Delgado let slip to one journalist that what Ronaldo needed more than anything was rest. Inside the Brazilian camp, there was very real concern, but what could they do? The World Cup final was about to be played and they would certainly not be resting their best player just because he seemed a bit down and had a minor injury he'd managed to carry through much of the tournament. Any physical discomfort could be sorted out with the right treatment.

That 'treatment' meant Ronaldo being fed a round-the-clock cocktail of anti-inflammatories, combined with other drugs. These included local anaesthetics Lidocaine and Xylocaine, which are well known sometimes to cause a number of side-effects, including convulsions and seizures. The anti-inflammatory drugs were Voltaren and Cataflam which could be both taken by pill or injection. While not against FIFA rules, some of the drugs were considered extremely powerful, and if large enough doses were administered, they could have an adverse effect on the player.

Doctor Michael Turner, who sits on the British Olympic Association's medical council in London, said in September 1998 that the key issue was whether any of the drugs were injected. He explained, 'There is always a huge temptation in sport to stick a needle in someone before a big game. It's often a case of patch them up and send them out.

'The key point is whether Ronaldo took these drugs by injection. It seems likely, because otherwise you wouldn't need the pain-killers (anaesthetics). The only need for those anaesthetics would be if you're sticking a needle into an area that is already inflamed. If Ronaldo had been taking the anti-inflammatories in pill form, there would have been no need for the Lidocaine.'

At one stage, a couple of Ronaldo's team-mates even suggested he should take some herbal medicine and one of them tried to persuade the team doctor to rub tree bark into his injured knee. Desperate measures for desperate times.

Off the field, Ronaldo had to brace himself and literally run the gauntlet of television cameras and pressmen whenever he ventured outside the stadium, training ground or hotel. Ronaldo became so paranoid that he even told one team-mate that he was convinced that if he didn't speak to the Brazilian media they'd just make up a slur story about him.

Even Zagallo pleaded with the press, 'Leave him alone. The boy has it hard enough. No other footballer has gone the way he is going.'

Life back on the streets of Bento Ribeiro must have seemed easy compared to this. Ronaldo was the axis of the football planet with virtually nowhere to turn. His innocence had long since been stripped from him, to be replaced with a robot-like existence, in thrall to Nike and the men in suits.

In short, he was extremely vulnerable.

As *Mail on Sunday* soccer pundit Michael Calvin explained just before the final, 'The corporate culture cannot comprehend football's resonance, its social status. He is a one-man marketing campaign.'

And the rumours had a jading effect on Ronaldo. Over the previous month, he'd been accused of being overweight, homesick, lovesick, an egomaniac, aloof from his team-mates, and jealous of players like Rivaldo who was being hailed as the true star of the Brazilian side.

Rivaldo leapt to the defence of his compatriot. 'My relationship with him is the best possible. There are no problems between us.'

Back in Rio, the pressure was mounting by the hour. Many regarded Ronaldo as their property and they believed they were owed a good return for their 'investment' in the former street kid. Objectivity was impossible on the streets of Copacabana because, as Ronaldo himself admitted, 'In Brazil it is victory or exile. There is nothing in between.'

Zagallo could see where it was all heading but he was powerless to do anything — he'd seen it all before. 'The trouble is that football has changed in every sense since 1970. There is no space to add fantasy to the game, so we will never see that kind of football again. No one allows us to play any more.'

Behind the scenes, Zagallo was also growing increasingly worried by Ronaldo's continued reliance on coaching assistant Zico, his Brazilian footballing hero. On a number of occasions, Zagallo actually had to talk to Ronaldo through Zico, whom many believed had been appointed to the squad purely to look after their golden striker.

Other senior players like Cesar Sampaio and Dunga also played occasional paternal roles. After all, it was Sampaio who found Ronaldo weeping as he read that magazine article which predicted his career would end up like Maradona's. It seemed that the pure and simple talent of the man and the sheer thrill of watching him play had almost been forgotten.

The hunt for greatness, the biggest football obsession of them all, was a merciless search. The game may need gods now more than ever before, but that quest was deadening the heart and soul of Ronaldo.

The World Cup was supposed to throw up that one great god, that one ruling deity, to give a sense of hierarchy to the tournament. The pressure had been building on Ronaldo from the day he moved to Barcelona two years earlier.

He had not been allowed to arrive gradually. His talent had been trumpeted before it was fully matured, exaggerated and lauded before it had been properly tested. The danger was that when the ultimate test came, the reality would not match up to that dream.

Certainly he had created many goals during Brazil's route to the final but it had become clear that he was not a Maradona in the true sense; he could not control matches to the point of utter domination.

And then there was the factor of Brazilian pride. After the semi-final against Holland in Marseilles, Pelé tried to insist that Ronaldo was the man of the match, but that was sadly inaccurate.

Before the Finals, Ronaldo had been living in a cocoon that was supposed to protect him from his own celebrity. He still listened to music, surfed the Internet for hours and spent a great deal of time with Suzanna.

Just before the final against France, Ronaldo insisted that he still had his feet firmly on the ground. 'I know who I am and where I have come from, and I am not going to change. I really missed my childhood.

'One minute I was playing for São Cristovao in the Brazilian second division, watching the stars on television, and the next minute I was one of the stars. I had to grow up very quickly. It was not long ago that I was a child, but I have had to live away from my family since I was 15. Don't forget, I went to Holland when I was 17.'

It was almost as if Ronaldo was trying to make excuses. He knew what people were saying behind his back and it hurt. But he also knew that much of it was true.

'Scoring goals is everything to me,' he added. 'It is my passion and my life. Nothing gives me greater pleasure. My football is about imagination and intuition, about those moments that have people on their feet applauding. On the pitch I am bold. Everything I do on the pitch, I do with the same aim, scoring the next goal.'

The beautiful game, it seemed, took many prisoners.

The Brazilian captain, Dunga, summed it all up when he told one reporter, 'When you are Brazilian, it is not enough simply to put on your jersey and wait to see what happens. We must build the most beautiful football possible from our humility, our perseverance and our determination.'

In the dressing room before the semi-final clash with Holland, Dunga had called all his team-mates together and led them in prayer for a successful conclusion to their mission.

'We are very mindful of God,' said Dunga. 'We always pray for protection so that nobody gets hurt and that we win. We have lots of faith. We have this superior force in our lives and we take it on the field of play.'

During many of Brazil's previous World Cup campaigns, the squad had, as they progressed towards the final, joined in the *batucada*, the small but enthusiastic contingent of fans who'd made the expensive and arduous journey from Brazil to congregate outside their hotel.

That exuberant, samba-driven support had become synonymous with Brazil's attitude towards the game. As 1970 captain Carlos Alberto says today, 'We danced with the supporters. It was good for our spirits and it was our way of saying thank you for their support.'

But the *batucada* were not welcome on the day following the game against Holland when the entire

Brazilian squad held their own barbecue at their hotel headquarters. The press and public were banned from the event so a gathering of cameraman and fans were forced to watch the entire proceedings from 50 feet away on a public road.

'It was a sad indictment of how Brazil had changed. In the past, they knew they needed those fans. Now they were surrounded by Nike personnel, training staff and CBF officials, completely cut off from the real world,' said TV Globo's Pedro Bial.

Bial found himself watching the barbecue along with the fans and witnessed some extraordinary scenes involving Edmundo 'The Animal'. Bial explained, 'Edmundo got incredibly drunk and it was clear that he was berating certain members of the CBF. It was actually quite embarrassing to watch.'

Inside the camp, there were already rumours spreading about Ronaldo being injured in some way. The other players were nervous because they — along with Nike and half the world — believed that without Ronaldo they might well lose the World Cup.

In comparison, opponents France's problems seemed trivial. There had been non-stop controversy about the lack of support for the home team from the Stade de France crowd. Almost all of Aimé Jacquet's players and the coach himself had made it crystal clear they were deeply upset by the fan's apparent disenchantment.

The French team resented the fact that so many genuine supporters had been edged out of the new stadium to make way for tens of thousands of corporate guests from around the globe. Some of those VIPs were even selling their prized tickets for astronomical sums on the black market.

An estimated 300,000 fans had spilled on to the Champs Elysée after the home team's 2–1 semi-final victory over Croatia had taken them to the World Cup final for the first time.

French goalkeeper Fabien Barthez had even wanted the semi-final to be played elsewhere. He said, 'If we'd played in Lens the whole stadium would have been behind us.'

If their supporters were their only problem, then France had nothing to worry about.

CHAPTER 23

The Drugs Situation

Two days before the final against France, Mario Zagallo aimed a bizarre outburst at a group of journalists, which seemed to pre-empt the problems which became so apparent on the big day itself.

'My fear has been that they will never let us win in Europe,' Zagallo insisted. 'In Brazil, there is a deep suspicion that outside influences, such as bad refereeing decisions, and other factors beyond the control of the players, will stop us.

'I remember the same worry surrounded the team in 1966 when the best of Brazil's footballing generation, which included the great Pelé, were kicked out of the tournament in England on the field of play.'

Zagallo was actually well aware that his team were not in the right frame of mind and his apprehension was enhanced by the prospect of a super-charged confrontation with the host nation, played out amid a highly partisan atmosphere at the Stade de France.

Zagallo was particularly disturbed by the fact that a Moroccan referee was going to be in charge of the final. He was convinced that massive pressure would be heaped upon Said Belqola by a French nation which had not enjoyed so much unity since Napoleon marauded through Europe.

Zagallo always carried an icon of the Portuguese Saint Antonio with him everywhere. He kissed it regularly during all his side's matches. He knew he'd need every ounce of spiritual help to overcome France.

Meanwhile, more rumours of Ronaldo's injury problems began leaking from the Brazilian camp. Sources claimed that Ronaldo had been told that he should not play for at least 30 days after the final and an operation on that troublesome left knee had not been ruled out.

The CBF and its president, Ricardo Teixeira, were furious about the rumours surrounding Ronaldo's injury problems and immediately leaked an interview with their star striker which they hoped would balance the situation.

In it, Ronaldo was quoted as saying, 'If I keep going like this until I'm the same age as our captain Dunga — 34 — then I will have five World Cup winner's medals. I can see it's all opening up in front of me to enter the history books.

'It's just that I've got so used to scoring goals against the world's greatest defenders. I can only get better at it each time.'

Of his opponent for the big confrontation in the Stade de France, Marcel Desailly, Ronaldo was quoted as saying, 'Desailly has proved how good he is. I don't think he has made one mistake so far, it will be interesting on Sunday.

'I can't say for sure that we're going to win but I simply cannot imagine anything to the contrary.'

'We are a squad united in purpose, but containing players of great personality.'

But what Ronaldo had not mentioned was Edmundo clashing with Giovanni in training; the incident between

Bebeto and Dunga, when the captain harangued the striker for not tackling back, which occurred in the middle of a match; his lack of confidence; the problems surrounding his room-mate Roberto Carlos; and the non-stop pressure-cooker environment.

Ronaldo's words that day had been hastily assembled and issued through Teixeira and his CBF underlings. In reality, Ronaldo and the rest of the team were far from confident.

The day before the World Cup final, Inter coach Gigi Simoni rang Ronaldo to wish him luck for the big match and to ask him when he would be returning to Milan. Simoni later recalled that Ronaldo sounded happy enough and said he was looking forward to the final. In fact, that call had a hugely detrimental effect on Ronaldo because the last thing he wanted to think about was the following season in Italy.

Inside the Brazilian training camp, assistant medic Dr Joaquim Da Mata continued discreetly to supply powerful pain-killers and anti-inflammatories to Ronaldo. Among those drugs was Volaren, which was taken orally. He insisted that it had never been injected into Ronaldo's knee.

Both Da Mata and chief medic Lidio Toledo had strict orders to keep Ronaldo playing. Da Mata insisted that Ronaldo never played with pain, but before a number of matches he was visibly wincing when bending his knee for pre-match team photos.

'He has pain between matches and we give him a pill,' said Da Mata. He insisted the pain-killers would not cause any detrimental problems to the player's health or his ability to play.

O Globo newspaper in Rio claimed that Ronaldo *was* given pain-killing injections, one as late as several hours before the final itself. The drug used on that occasion was Xilocaine, a cortisone mixed with an anaesthetic. An unnamed member of the team squad told them the story and they insisted it was true.

Squad member Goncalves, a veteran defender who sat on the bench after losing his place to Junior Baiano put the entire drug treatment scenario into perspective.

'It's normal to play through pain. Absolutely normal. Think about it. There you are, you've worked years to get to the World Cup, you have made this huge investment, and you're not going to blow it because of pain you can play with.

'Many of the biggest stars play with pain because they have so much to lose if they don't. You are always an injury away from losing the business deal of your life.

'Look, what I'm telling you is the reality in the game now.'

The day before the final — Saturday, 11 July 1998 — Ronaldo sneaked out of the Brazilian team's hotel to see Suzanna Werner at the house she was sharing with his mother on the outskirts of Paris. He swore room-mate Roberto Carlos to secrecy.

Slipping out of the back entrance of the hotel, wearing a baseball cap and dark glasses he hailed a taxi without being spotted by anyone.

At the house, Ronaldo collapsed in Suzanna's arms and said he didn't care about all the gossip concerning her, he just needed her so badly. For at least three hours, he wept as he blurted out how scared he was of letting everyone down. The pressure was getting to him. Suzanna tried to console him but she was so shocked by his condition that she found it difficult to respond calmly and she eventually burst into tears as well.

By the time Ronaldo's mother returned from a shopping trip, Ronaldo had already slipped back to the team hotel.

That same day — after completing Brazil's final training session before the final — Ronaldo agreed to give another interview to TV Globo's Pedro Bial despite the unfounded rumours about Bial's relationship with Suzanna.

Bial takes up the story.

'Ronaldo walked over to a corner of the training pitch and we set the cameras up. He seemed relaxed.'

Before starting the interview, Bial and Ronaldo once again talked extensively about the rumours concerning him and Suzanna.

'He accepted what I told him and there was no problem between us.'

Ronaldo even repeated what he had told Bial earlier. 'I know that others are trying to make problems for me. They are trying to put me off my game.'

Ronaldo never actually revealed who 'they' were. But Bial felt that Ronaldo seemed distracted, although he insists there were absolutely no clues about what was really going on behind the scenes.

A few hours later, as Ronaldo was about to go to bed, there was also an emotional phone call from Suzanna.

A friend of Suzanna's called Marcello Ferriera explained.

'Suzanna said she felt she was neglected because her fiancée was totally focussed on the World Cup.

'She complained that all he thought about was football and the pressure on him to perform was enormous.

'Ronaldo's emotions were in a mess and his body just couldn't cope with any more stress. He had another huge tearful row with Suzanna on the phone. But it was more than that. It deeply affected Ronaldo psychologically. All his mental energy was devoted to the final against France and the slightest thing would upset that balance.'

According to 'close friend' Marcello, Suzanna had been devastated when she realised how much she had upset Ronaldo on the eve of the most important football match of his life.

In fact, there was an element of panic running through the entire Brazilian training camp because some of the team members had heard rumours that Ronaldo was 'ill'. They took this to mean he was injured. To a certain extent, they were entirely correct.

The two team medics, Toledo and Da Mata, were trying every drug they knew to treat Ronaldo's injured knee and they had noticed that the player himself did not seem at all happy about it.

'Ronaldo was often shaking with fear during those days before the final. He seemed extremely nervous, even compared with normal,' one squad member told me in Rio five weeks later. 'We actually began to wonder if his condition had been caused by all the drugs they were giving him for his injuries. He seemed so weird, almost in a daze.'

To make matters worse, CBF president Teixeira and Nike officials were anxiously circling demanding updates on the player's condition. Nerves were frayed.

Back in Rio, giant pictures of Ronaldo smiled down as usual from the advertising billboards in which the soccer star mimicked the pose of the landmark statue of Christ that looked down on Rio from the surrounding mountainside. The night before the 1998 World Cup final, Ronaldo finally fell asleep at about one in the morning. He had a restless night, tossing and turning, and making strange, incomprehensible comments in his sleep.

Finally, at 11.30am, Ronaldo awoke with a start. He looked up and realised the big day had arrived ... but would it bring victory or heartbreak?

CHAPTER 24

Countdown to Disaster

Sunday, 12 July 1998, Paris, France

The day began for Ronaldo and his team-mates at their hotel with a midday lunch of macaroni with tomato sauce and an apple for dessert. But the rest of the day turned out to be anything but ordinary ...

12.10pm: At the training pitch behind their hotel, Ronaldo's knee was once again causing problems so he received extra physiotherapy. Officially, team coaches insisted that it was no worse than in the three matches since the injury had been sustained against Morocco.

1.00pm: The entire team retired to their rooms at the Château de Grande Romain hotel for a siesta, either sleeping or relaxing before the big game against France. Roberto Carlos helped Ronaldo shave his head with a special razor. Then they watched TV and lay down on their beds in Room 209. Ronaldo turned on to his side and fell asleep.

2.00pm: Roberto Carlos was listening to his Walkman when, he later claimed, he was disturbed by the muffled sound of Ronaldo having some kind of fit. Ronaldo turned pale, began sweating profusely and then suffered convulsions, with his arms flexed and hands misshapen by the nervous tension. Screaming, Roberto Carlos called for help.

Edmundo and Bebeto were the first players to hear the cries for help. Carlos later changed his story and claimed he found Ronaldo in the bathroom lying on the tiled floor. He was having difficulty breathing and seemed to be almost swallowing his tongue. Cesar Sampaio and Leonardo also dashed to the room and Sampaio released Ronaldo's tongue He woke up from his fit and seemed to think he'd had a nightmare. He knew he'd been in the habit of talking in his sleep because Roberto Carlos had complained about it in the past.

Then other Brazilian players, woken by the disturbance, came to their compatriot's aid. Within seconds desperation took over. Roberto Carlos and Rivaldo started sobbing. Bebeto said he didn't know what to do.

Minutes later, team medics Toledo and Da Mata arrived on the scene. Toledo cleaned saliva from Ronaldo's mouth and he started breathing normally once more. Leonardo requested medication for Ronaldo but the doctors hesitated because Ronaldo would not then pass any anti-doping examination. Leonardo became quite angry with the doctors because he felt they were not doing enough.

The manager of the converted château, Paul Chevalier, had no doubts that Ronaldo had suffered a genuine fit of some kind.

'There was general alarm, with yells and shouts which woke up all the players, who were in the middle of their siesta. For a time, we heard people saying, "He's dead, dead, dead."

'It created a terrible atmosphere around the team which was clearly demonstrated later on the pitch.'

2.15pm: Ronaldo insisted to doctors that he was fine. He went back to sleep but that nap lasted just 15 minutes at which point he was woken for further medical tests.

2.45pm: Ronaldo got out of bed and took a bath before speaking to Roberto Carlos and Da Mata. They cracked a joke to try to help him relax. Doctors had already agreed to monitor Ronaldo for any further danger signs.

3.30pm: Mario Zagallo and his aides then had urgent talks with medical staff on whether Ronaldo should play. CBF president Ricardo Teixeira was present, but said nothing when it was announced by Zagallo that Ronaldo should remain on the bench and Edmundo would take his place.

4.00pm: Under pressure from Teixeira, Zagallo decided that Ronaldo should be taken for a complete check-up to the Clinic des Lilas, the medical centre laid on for 24-hour emergency treatment for World Cup participants. If he was cleared, then maybe he could play after all.

4.45pm: Ronaldo, Toledo and two bodyguards left the hotel to head for the clinic with Parisian police outriders escorting them through the traffic. The rest of the team finished their final preparations before departing for the Stade de France. In the coach on the way to the stadium, hardly a word was spoken because they were so shocked by what had happened to Ronaldo.

Hotel manager Chevalier said that when the Brazilians normally left for a match, there was a party atmosphere with singing and music, but this time there was a very different mood.

'When they left the hotel for the Stade de France, there was complete silence on the bus and we who knew them personally understood at that moment that there was no cohesion and they had lost the Cup,' Chevalier said.

5.55pm: Ronaldo's limo finally arrived at the clinic after battling through heavy traffic. He was ushered into a second-floor examination room for medical tests.

One nurse at the clinic said, 'When I saw him arrive I wondered what he was doing here. He looked happy and fit. I immediately thought he must have come to visit a patient, not for treatment.'

And clinic chief Philip Krief said, 'We could find no evidence at all that he had a fit.'

Ronaldo had arrived wearing shorts, a T-shirt and trainers. He even posed for a picture with some of the clinic staff and autographed a French soccer shirt.

Dr Krief added, 'When people have fits, their eyes widen and they dribble and lose their balance. The effects of these symptoms would still have been visible in Ronaldo when he was brought into the clinic, but they weren't there.

'Ronaldo had an hour-and-a-half of medical tests while he chatted to the staff and nurses and watched some football on the television.

'He had a full body scan and tests on his blood and mineral levels. After the tests we handed the results to the Brazilian doctor. We didn't make any kind of judgement about whether he should play or not. We simply gave them the results so they could make up their own minds. Our own records are confidential, but I can say that you don't walk out of a clinic the way Ronaldo did if you've had bad test results.

'We considered him to be physically fit.'

7.45pm: Tests on Ronaldo were completed and he was escorted back to the Stade de France by limousine. On his way out of the clinic, he stopped to pose for a photograph with the star-struck sons of clinic director Brigitte Elbaz.

Lidio Toledo later recalled, 'When he came out of the clinic at 7.45pm he was euphoric. He was boasting that all his tests were negative. Ronaldo told me as we left, "Doc, I've got to get ready for the match. It wouldn't be right not to play."'

Zagallo then submitted a signed team sheet showing Ronaldo's omission from the starting line-up. This was passed on to the relevant FIFA authorities and circulated to television networks around the world. The effect of this decision was earth-shattering — football fans and reporters worldwide could hardly believe that Zagallo would drop Ronaldo at this late stage. Speculation ran rife. One explanation, which seemed the most probable at the time, centred on Zagallo's wish to undermine the French team psychologically. Without Ronaldo to deal with, they might have had to reorganise their team structure only minutes before the final. Back in the Brazilian dressing room, Zagallo tried to bolster Brazilian spirits by reminding his players of how Brazil had won the 1962 World Cup despite missing the injured Pelé in the final.

8.10pm: Ronaldo arrived at the stadium. Zagallo then decided to reverse his earlier decision and play Ronaldo who started loosening up in the dressing room. Assistant coach Zico was so appalled by the decision he tried to dissuade Zagallo but his superior would not be swayed. CBF president Teixeira looked on, grim-faced throughout the proceedings.

8.15pm: Zagallo amended his original team sheet and, by way of explanation to the FIFA reps, said that Ronaldo's earlier omission was just a plot to trick the opposition. Under FIFA rules this should not have been allowed, because the team sheet had already been handed in an hour before the kick-off.

The one-hour rule had been strictly followed throughout

the tournament until the final. FIFA rules were supposed to only allow changes if a player was injured in the warm-up or taken ill. Ronaldo's case was the absolute opposite.

One referee, England's Paul Durkin, explained, 'In the game I refereed, this rule was strictly adhered to. I've heard of instances of team sheets being altered when a player has been injured in the pre-match warm-up but this wasn't the case here.'

FIFA, apparently ignoring their own rules, issued a statement in response. 'We were informed Ronaldo would be starting the match approximately 45 minutes before the kick-off. The names of the players are given for information purposes and the teams have the right to change the starting line-up right up to the kick-off.'

8.20pm: Ronaldo was very shaky once more. He seemed extraordinarily nervous. He was given a 'bluey' tablet by team doctor Lidio Toledo. It was a tranquillizer. Ronaldo took half of the pill immediately. Within minutes, he started to feel strange. His team-mates were completely unaware that Ronaldo had been given the drug. But they argued about Ronaldo's late inclusion. Zico, particularly, was against it.

8.45pm: In the dressing room, Dunga failed to huddle together with all his team-mates and lead them in prayer as he had done in all their previous World Cup '98 games. They also failed to go out for the warm-up on the pitch before the game.

8.55pm: Ronaldo was the last man out on to the field with the Brazilian team. As was traditional, he was holding — or rather, clutching — the hand of his team-mate. Suddenly, there was a surge of photographers trying to get a shot of Ronaldo. They almost crushed him in the chaos. Afterwards, many speculated as to why the French authorities allowed the paparazzi so close to the Brazilians.

8.57pm: Ronaldo winced as he crouched for a pre-match team photo. It was almost as if he was deliberately appearing to be in agony to cover up the dramas that had occurred earlier in the day.

The most important game of his life was about to begin.

CHAPTER 25

Let the Game Begin

9.00pm, 12 July 1998, World Cup Final, Stade de France, Paris

It was to prove a night of firsts; the first goal in open play since the 1986 final; the first time the hosts had played the Champions; the first time an audience of over two billion people had watched an event on television; and, most importantly, the first time France had ever won the tournament.

French jubilation and Brazilian despair were sealed in the following synopsis of the 90-minute match:

01.00: Stephane Guivarc'h's overhead kick sailed just over the bar but it was clear that France were going to prove a handful.

04.00: Guivarc'h was superbly played through by a Zidane 'nutmeg', but his first touch was poor and Junior Baiano easily blocked his run at goal.

07.00: Djorkaeff had a free header from a French free kick, but his effort was well over the bar.

21.00: A Roberto Carlos miss-hit cross almost caught French keeper Barthez off his line, but the ball went just over.

22.00: Ronaldo finally burst into life when he got the better of Thuram down the left and whipped a cross into the French penalty area which Barthez struggled to hold.

24.00: Leonardo's corner found Rivaldo unmarked but he headed right at Barthez.

27.00: Goal! A superbly taken Petit corner found Zidane rising above the static Brazilian defence to head home past Taffarel.

31.00: Ronaldo outpaced Thuram but keeper Barthez was quickly off his line to punch the ball clear, injuring Ronaldo in the process.

'If he had been in bad physical shape, he would never have withstood the collision he had with Bartez,' one of the doctors who examined Ronaldo earlier said.

40.00: A Leonardo free kick found Bebeto, but his header was no threat to Barthez.

'All the way through the first half, Zagallo agonised about bringing Ronaldo off, but he didn't have the courage,' Edmundo claimed later.

41.00: Karembeu's shot was deflected by Junior Baiano into the path of Petit who blasted well wide of the goal.

45.00: Thuram's superb long pass was missed by Junior Baiano but Guivarc'h hit it first time. His shot was easily saved by Taffarel.

45.00: Goal! Another corner, this time from the left, found Zidane unmarked once more.

His low, precise header made it 2–0. Brazil were in tatters.

56.00: A well worked Brazilian freekick found Ronaldo in

space but his point-blank shot was smothered by Barthez.

61.00: Barthez rushed way out of his area and was nowhere near the goal when Bebeto fired in a shot, which Desailly cleared for a corner.

64.00: An excellent long ball by Leboeuf forced Dunga into an error but Guivarc'h's shot from just six yards went well over.

68.00: Desailly was sent off for a reckless challenge on defender Cafu.

83.00: Dugarry was put through on goal by Zidane with only the keeper to beat, but he somehow blasted well wide.

90.00: Denilson hit the bar after good work by Edmundo.

90.00: Goal! Vieira played Petit into acres of space down the left flank and he slotted the ball past Taffarel.

* * *

The final whistle did not come a minute too early for the shattered nerves and spirits of the Brazilian team.

In the stand, Suzanna Werner pulled off the Brazilian flag which had been draped around her and buried her face in it, her shoulders shaking from the sobs. She'd seen the look on Ronaldo's face as he played that day and realised just how upset he was.

Across the world, many soccer pundits found themselves lost for words at Brazil's dismal performance. But most agreed the score should have been 5–0 or worse. Guivarc'h, weighed down by an expectant audience, missed three sitters and Dugarry another. Djorkaeff should have scored with a free header as well.

Mentally, Brazil had seemed barely involved at all. Cafu was the only effective player in the team, especially in the first half when he seemed to be given the ball over and over again and was just expected to run his heart out.

But most disturbing was Brazil's behaviour on the pitch, as three times they betrayed their country's reputation for decency. First, when the majestic Desailly fouled Carlos for his second yellow card, the Brazilian wing-back mimed a sending off by pointing to the dressing room. How strange it was to see a Brazilian resorting to play-acting.

Then Edmundo came on as a sub and almost immediately screamed at Baiano when the latter sportingly kicked the ball into touch while Lizarazu lay injured; and, completing this unholy trinity, when France repaid the compliment, Brazil failed to give the ball back from the resulting throw-in.

The final brought with it all the usual soccer inquests but many of the dramatic headlines in newspapers across the globe seemed to have swallowed the Brazilian excuses hook, line and sinker.

I NEARLY DIED screamed the back page of the *Daily Mail*. Ronaldo was quoted as saying, 'It was a tremendous scare. We lost the World Cup, but I won something else — my life.

'I don't remember properly, but I went to sleep and then it seems I had a fit for 30 or 40 seconds. I woke up then and my whole body was in pain.'

Brazilian team doctor Lidio Toledo told the newspaper he had 'come to the conclusion that it had to be a nervous fit'.

The *Mail* article referred to rumours about an epileptic fit and mental stress.

Ronaldo said after the final, 'I was suffering from something really strange which I have never felt before a game. I felt very bad — headache, nausea and stomach pains. There was so much pressure on me. It felt like the whole of Brazil was leaning on me.'

Even Zagallo admitted, 'It was a major psychological blow. All through the game, I kept wondering whether to take him off.'

And Ronaldo's Inter team-mate Youri Djorkaeff sensed what was happening when the two teams took to the field just before the kick-off. He said, 'I immediately noticed Ronaldo was not well and he told me so. I had told Ronaldo before the World Cup that we'd win it, but I don't like to see a friend sad and for this reason I did not joke with him.'

Then Ronaldo made a highly evocative statement to a select band of mainly Brazilian journalists. It was hardly reported outside his home country but it seemed to suggest that his problems did not end at the Stade de France on 12 July.

'I am finding there is so much hassle. I am expected to live up to being the supposed best player in the world. All Brazil is leaning on me in every match.'

So deep was Ronaldo's concern for his welfare and what happened he even referred to the word 'retirement' when pondering his predicament.

'Even though I have so many years already behind me, I cannot think about retiring because I am still too young. But perhaps only then will I lead a different life.

'For the moment, it is a life under pressure. I have not had a holiday for a year so I am going home to rest for a month, clear my head and think about nothing, especially not football, because it has all got to me.'

Listening to his words with some concern were his agents, Pitta and Martins. Retirement? That was out of the question. They had calculated that Ronaldo could earn upwards of $200 million over the following ten years and they were on a 10 per cent share of every penny.

After the game, Zagallo admitted that he should not have played Ronaldo but became so tetchy when asked what lay behind his decision that a press conference had to be abandoned. 'He played because he played. I'm trying to keep this conversation on a high level and you want to lower the level,' he snapped at the world's press.

Assistant manager Zico had clearly been in complete disagreement with Zagallo about playing Ronaldo.

'It's always a mistake to play somebody who's not 100 per cent fit. It was proved that even if he's the best in the world, he can't go on the field if he's not well.

'Ronaldo was sleepy, really groggy. He was in no condition to play. The medical department could have said no. If they had said, "Don't play him," Zagallo wouldn't have played him. At no time did the doctors want to say no.'

Assistant team medic Joaquim Da Mata felt that Zico was being unfair. 'It's a very big responsibility. You can't imagine. It was the most dramatic decision I have taken in my life. There were seven hours of drama, of doubt. I wouldn't wish this experience on my worst enemy. The decision was made by me and Lidio [Toledo] and was backed up by three French doctors who carried out tests at the clinic.'

One of those doctors, Dr Philip Krief, made a good point. 'In my opinion, it was not just Ronaldo who played badly against France, it was the whole Brazilian team. The fact everyone played badly simply raised questions about Ronaldo's condition that would never have been asked if Brazil had won the World Cup.'

After the game, the Brazilian squad returned to their hotel demoralised and depressed by their defeat. Many of the players wanted to fly home as quickly as possible. The victory celebrations for France made it even worse. It had seemed on the way back to the hotel that everyone in Paris was on the streets celebrating the home side's historic victory.

Roberto Carlos and a number of the other players remained convinced that part of Ronaldo's problems lay in his psychological state before the final. Roberto Carlos even believed that if Ronaldo had taken more interest in the spiritual side of things, he might not have had such a disastrous match. The two men sat up until the early hours talking about what had gone wrong at the Stade de France. But the more they spoke about it, the more distressed they both became.

Ronaldo wanted reassurance that Brazil's loss was not his fault. Roberto Carlos fully appreciated that but he found it difficult not to give the impression that part of the fault did indeed lie with Ronaldo. Ronaldo decided that in many ways he and Roberto Carlos were on different wavelengths.

By about 3.00am, Ronaldo was so fed up with talking to his room-mate that he called his mother and Suzanna and begged them to come to the hotel and get him. He knew he was still under curfew but he was past caring.

Eventually, Suzanna turned up alone in a hired limousine at approximately 5.00am, much to Ronaldo's relief. He did not even bother taking his bag.

Meanwhile, Roberto Carlos and at least four other Brazilian squad members — still unable to sleep — sat and talked further into the early morning. Eventually, five girls whom they'd called earlier turned up at the hotel just before dawn.

A Brazilian TV crew waiting in reception after covering the French festivities all night actually obtained footage of the girls arriving. But it was decided that no one should expose the players involved because, as one Brazilian journalist explained, 'We all felt sorry for the team. There was no point in making things even worse for them. Everybody knew about what happened but the press did nothing.'

Piecing together the statements and interviews given by all the relevant characters in the weeks following the match exposed a bizarre chain of events which lead many to believe that Brazil's defeat was verging on the inevitable.

The players and staff undoubtedly agreed on one

united story to tell the world about the biggest upset in World Cup history. As Bebeto and Roberto Carlos said to waiting pressmen after the game, 'One day, you'll know what really happened.'

Many of the players were deeply unhappy about not telling the entire truth to the media but they were told in no uncertain terms by CBF president Ricardo Teixeira that they would never play for Brazil again if they spoke out of turn. Edmundo found out a month later that Teixeira was nothing if not a man of his word.

Even the normally outspoken Roberto Carlos would only say of the 'fit', 'At that moment, I felt that my head was elsewhere. I was more concerned about the health of a friend.

'Today, I can say we lost the Cup at two o'clock on that Sunday afternoon, because until that moment the thought of losing the *penta* [fifth title] had not crossed our minds.'

Yet, what neither Ronaldo nor Dr Toledo admitted at the time to Zagallo was that his star striker had been given that 'bluey' tranquillizer just before he ran on to the Stade de France pitch.

If the coach had known about this, he might have refused to play Ronaldo.

Ronaldo's late inclusion caused a huge rift among the other team members despite later claims to the contrary. There was also the added element of Ricardo Teixeira who was in the dressing room before the match.

His presence was so distracting to the players that many later blamed that situation on why they refused to go out and warm up on the pitch. Zagallo cancelled the warm-up knowing full well that it would give the advantage to the French, but he had no choice.

Claims that Nike also entered the fray through Teixeira and one of their senior representatives at the final, sparked categorical denials from the sportswear giant. But there is no denying that they had a presence that evening as they had throughout Brazil's World Cup campaign.

Ronaldo's decision to take a tranquillizer just before the game has been heavily criticised by many experts. 'The pill would have slowed down his reaction time and co-ordination,' said Helio Ventura, a sports medicine specialist.

Then Brazilian defender Goncalves gave one of the most detailed accounts of what really happened at the hotel just before the final.

'I can remember exactly the terrible image that I saw at about 2.00pm,' he told one associate. 'Ronaldo was foaming at the mouth, struggling, breathing with a lot of difficulty and very pale. At one point he went purple. It lasted about two minutes. He started to breathe normally after about five minutes.'

There is no suggestion that Ronaldo would have failed a drugs test had he taken a cocktail of Lignocaine and cortisone to treat his injuries. Michael Verroken, head of the UK Sports Council's Anti-Doping Unit, said, 'It is permissible to use these drugs in controlled doses but the authorities would expect to be kept informed. Certainly, that's the system we used in Euro '96.'

But if Ronaldo had taken more than the prescribed limit of anti-inflammatories, though there is no evidence that he did, and then combined that with a tranquillizer, he would almost certainly have failed a drugs test.

However, in Brazil it is considered perfectly normal to take large doses of such drugs to overcome injury problems. As fellow player and Ronaldo's oldest friend, Calango, says, 'We have all taken the same drugs that Ronaldo took to recover from an injury. When you're injured, Cataflan is the stuff most players take. Everybody does it all the time.'

Then he added, 'I've played when I've felt completely knocked out by those drugs but that's the only way you can get through an injury. There is no other answer.'

One of the most disturbing aspects of Ronaldo's supposed fit was that it strongly suggested he suffered from some kind of epileptic disorder. Ronaldo angrily disputed such claims when they were made by team doctor Lidio Toledo.

But the version provided by room-mate Roberto Carlos clearly pointed in that direction. The point was that if Ronaldo was epileptic, the dangers to his health when placed in such a stressful environment were obvious. That could mean disaster for his career with Inter Milan.

If the official version was to be believed, the tests showed nothing whatsoever. But many in Brazil believed that this was not a satisfactory answer. Ronaldo owed it to himself and millions of others to find out the truth. If the rumours were untrue, then he had every right to feel angry, but if there had been some kind of cover-up then that was even more shameful.

The phone lines between Milan, Paris and Rio buzzed while medics, club presidents and journalists discussed the Ronaldo situation. At one stage, Inter Milan seriously considered suing FIFA, or Brazil, for allowing their prized property to risk his health.

Around this time, it was also claimed for the first time that a delegation acting on behalf of the Brazilian head of FIFA, Joao Havelange, the outgoing president, came with an unspoken mandate into the Brazilian dressing room before the kick-off. They were alleged to have told the Brazilians that Ronaldo would play 'whatever the consequences'. What role Havelange's son-in-law Ricardo Teixeira played in this scenario, in addition to Nike's role in the whole business, was still open to question.

Was it Teixeira's fault, or Havelange's? Should Zagallo not have stood firm against those footballing giants for the good of the team as Dunga urged him to? Or are they all puppets dancing to the tune of their paymaster? The straight answer to these questions had to be found, eventually.

Five hundred journalists from Brazil accompanied the team to France, yet not one of them seemed to have uncovered the truth about the biggest mystery of modern-day football.

CHAPTER 26

Casualties of War

Ronaldo must have deeply regretted his decision to fly home with the defeated Brazilian squad the moment their Varig MD-11 touched down in the nation's capital, Brasilia, on Tuesday, 14 July 1998. Any notion that he'd be left in peace to gather his thoughts and recover his health was ludicrously optimistic. First there was an audience with President Fernando Henrique Cardose followed by a tour of the city in a coach. Originally, the intention had been to use an open-topped vehicle, but following the defeat by the French, there were genuine fears for the safety of the players.

The whole country wanted to know what had happened before, during and after that fateful World Cup final defeat. But no one in the squad seemed prepared to talk about it, which simply added to the confusion and suspicion.

Arriving back in Rio later that same evening, Ronaldo

went straight to visit his mother in the suburb of Jacarepagua, to find 200 photographers camped outside her home.

At Sonia's house were Inter Milan owner Moretti, a private therapist, Inter doctor Givro Golti and a local neurosurgeon called Alex Tatano Barrois. They were there to examine their star player. Brazilian medic Lidio Toledo was allowed to observe.

It was only after the completion of these examinations that Ronaldo was encouraged to disappear on holiday. He was desperate to spend some time alone with Suzanna.

Later that same evening, Ronaldo headed for his luxurious condominium in nearby Barra de Tijuca to meet Suzanna but there were just as many paparazzi in attendance. When he tried to leave the apartment block with Suzanna, dozens of them chased him down the street until he managed to duck into a waiting limousine.

Being branded the man who had single-handedly lost the World Cup for Brazil was a gross distortion of Ronaldo's role in his country's downfall, but it must have felt like he was a wanted criminal in the weeks following France '98.

A couple of hours later at his father's home in Barra, he completely lost his cool and began screaming at the pressmen: 'What kind of life is this?' It was unusual to see Ronaldo actually lose his temper in public.

His older sister Ione explained, 'He just wanted to be in peace with his true friends.'

At another flat he owned in Barra, he agreed to meet his pursuers in an effort to get them off his back. Somewhat naïvely he even tried to persuade the waiting masses that stories about breakdowns and hysteria on the eve of the final were not true.

'I think there's been a big exaggeration in all this. I want more respect. I'm not a fugitive. I don't want to be chased every time I go to my mother's house ... I'm trying to lead a normal life, as far as possible ... I want peace and tranquillity. I don't want to be chased any more.'

Ronaldo insisted to the newsmen that he had no idea what had happened to him in the hours before the game. He also gave the clear impression that it was all in the past and didn't really matter.

'I can't explain what caused the attack,' he said. 'Only God knows what made me ill. In principle, I'm not doing any more tests. I'm fine. The tests proved that I've got no health problems.'

At that moment, Alexandre Martins appeared on the scene to assure the journalists, 'His state of health is perfect and he will not have these problems again. The tests have put a full stop to this.'

That first night back in Rio was so emotionally draining for Ronaldo that he insisted his agent and Suzanna leave the apartment so he could gather his thoughts and sleep alone.

Ronaldo had his best night's sleep in months. The following day, he returned to his mother's house and joined Suzanna, his family and friends for a steak at the Tourao Grillhouse in Barra. The following morning, Ronaldo told newsmen he was going to escape. 'We are going to travel and I am going to relax over the next few days.'

Shortly after speaking to the reporters, Ronaldo sped away from them in a blue Mercedes and headed for a nearby helicopter which was waiting to whisk him and Suzanna away to the exclusive resort of Angra dos Reis, on the coast south of the city.

Meanwhile, Dr Lidio Toledo continued to be hounded by the media whenever he ventured out of his home or office. Under constant pressure to provide a definitive diagnosis of the 'seizure' suffered by Ronaldo, Toledo seemed very uneasy about offering any further opinions.

And at one of his daily news briefings for the dozens of reporters camped outside his holiday home in Angra dos Reis, Ronaldo explained, 'I don't have any illness. It's nothing like epilepsy. I'm not going to have more tests. The tests were done in France and I am satisfied. Brazil lost to France because we played badly and they are using me as an excuse.'

He then repeated his pledge to go on holiday for at least a month and during that time he intended never to mention the word 'football'.

But in Brazil the witch-hunt continued. Allegations about Nike's involvement continued to circulate despite virtually daily denials from the sportswear giant.

And on the coaching front it seemed only a matter of days before Mario Zagallo was relieved of his post. Wanderlei Luxembourgo, manager of leading club Corinthians, was regarded as the most likely replacement, with Zico and captain Dunga retaining some kind of assistant coaching roles.

Half-way across the world, Italy's sports press were also growing increasingly obsessed with 'The Ronaldo Mystery'. Indeed, so intense was the scrutiny that Inter Milan, seeking to protect their enormous investment in the player, issued an official plea for sanity, criticising the 'many and misleading indiscretions concerning the player's state of health', which 'are of great damage to his person and his image'.

Throughout all this, former room-mate Roberto Carlos — still annoyed at Ronaldo for whatever reason — made another public statement about his compatriot. He told one group of journalists that Ronaldo had 'chickened out' on the eve of the final.

'He is as yellow as his shirt,' he snapped. As if to reiterate just how seriously their relationship had deteriorated, Roberto Carlos continued, 'Ronaldo was afraid. He became number-one player too quickly. He cried because he was afraid. He couldn't stand the pressure. It also looked to me as if had personal and sentimental problems.'

What an insult to Ronaldo. He was heartbroken when

he read of Roberto Carlos's comments. He was also bewildered. Those around him told him not to take any notice but Ronaldo remained a highly sensitive person. The insults hurt.

As for agents Martins and Pitta, their main priority was to get Ronaldo out of Rio and away from the limelight while they re-assessed the situation. At least $80 million rested on what happened over the following few weeks and they needed time to work out a new masterplan.

So Ronaldo, his father and Suzanna flew off to Las Vegas. But in Rio the controversy grew steadily by the day.

Then Roberto Carlos came out of his shell once more to say categorically that he thought Ronaldo had had an epileptic attack.

'I have no doubt that it was an epileptic attack because I have spoken to people who understand these things. 'I didn't want to say anything before the doctors but, in the room, I saw that Ronaldo was tense, holding in many problems.

'As soon as that happened, I thought it was an epileptic attack. But the doctors said it was a convulsion and I kept quiet. I know Ronaldo didn't deserve to go through all that.

'One day, Lidio Toledo will have to reveal what really happened to Ronaldo, because everywhere I go people talk about it; everyone asks me what happened.'

Brazilian team doctor Lidio Toledo was then hauled before a Rio medical review board and threatened by them that he might have his licence revoked if he failed to come up with a satisfactory diagnosis for Ronaldo's alleged 'fit'. Following Roberto Carlos's outburst, Toledo back-pedalled to the point where he completely reversed his original opinion that Ronaldo had been suffering from an attack of severe stress. Toledo informed the board that he believed an epileptic or neurological disorder was to blame.

'Stress was not the cause,' Toledo told reporters. Instead of clearing up the mystery of what really happened to Ronaldo, the issue was thrown into even more confusion.

Toledo did admit for the first time, however, that Ronaldo had taken anti-inflammatories for his injured leg, which could have caused convulsions in the weeks before the final. But he angrily denied having given the star any injections, following rumours that had been sweeping Rio since the final.

Perhaps justifiably, Ronaldo himself was gradually no longer being seen as the bad guy in the World Cup drama. Many Brazilians looked on him as an innocent young victim in the whole sorry saga.

In an unashamedly corny column in the *O Globo* newspaper, Brazilian novelist Roberto Drummond called Ronaldo a 'soccer Cinderella. They wanted to make you like Robocop, a goal-scoring and money-making machine,' Drummond wrote. 'Open your golden cage, caged bird, and sing your song of freedom again.'

In Rio in August 1998, another member of the Brazilian squad threw some more light on the role of CBF president Teixeira. He clearly stated that Teixeira came down from the stands at the Stade de France after the first team sheet had been submitted.

Teixeira was the man who had secured the £40 million Nike deal with Brazil's national side three years earlier. 'Teixeira was there and he was breathing down Zagallo's neck. Draw your own conclusions,' said the source.

Five weeks after the World Cup final, Teixeira suggested a fee should be paid to the CBF in return for an interview with a journalist researching the story of Ronaldo's apparent decline. Officials at the CBF referred all press inquiries to a sports writer in Rio who acted as an intermediary for those cash payments.

It was clear that whatever happened in that dressing room during those tense few minutes before the kick off, Ricardo Teixeira would remain very much in charge of Brazilian football.

Another possible, but distinctly outlandish, scenario was that some kind of gambling syndicate was behind an attempt to throw the match. It seemed highly unlikely, but in the past ten years there had been a number of bribery cases involving referees and teams who'd unfairly influenced Brazilian league matches.

As one Rio journalist pointed out, 'The Brazilian team did not go out to play. They might have been demoralised about Ronaldo. On the other hand, they might just as likely have decided amongst themselves not to compete to win the match. It does leave the question open.'

In Rio throughout August 1998, there were numerous rumours that Brazilian government investigators were following up a number of tips from inside the Brazilian squad. At least two of those informants claimed that the team had all been given drugs without their knowledge, or that of anyone connected with the Brazilian squad.

In August, there was an air of expectancy in Rio. One player explained, 'What really happened has to be revealed to the world one day. It's only a matter of time.'

Over in Italy, Ronaldo's other bosses at Inter Milan were still furious about what they saw as a stupid decision to play Ronaldo when he was clearly not fit.

Club owner Massimo Moratti said, 'The Brazilian Federation acted in an absurd manner. It was a serious mistake to play Ronaldo in those conditions. Even though he expressed a desire to play, I think someone should have looked at him more as a person than as a player. In general, he handles everything in an intelligent and balanced manner. This time, evidently, he wasn't able to.'

One of Ronaldo's closest friends inside the Brazilian squad, Leonardo, had his own views of what happened and why.

'What do you think? That the boss of Nike calls up on his mobile phone from New York and says, "Play Ronaldo, that's an order!"

'So you think there's a hot-line between Nike and our dressing room? Or Teixeira calls up Nike for instructions?

Or maybe I pick up my mobile and call Nike for my orders?'

The truth was that all these people were in the dressing room and, of course, Ronaldo wanted to declare himself fit.

'It's just a job,' says Leonardo. 'Sure, Nike wanted Ronaldo to play, and the football federation, and everyone else. It's the system, it's the economics, it's the pressure of the game today, and it's hard on the people who play. But it's not that hard.'

A few days after the final, Edmundo, back in Rio, lashed out at Zagallo over his handling of Ronaldo during the final. He also revealed for the first time some of the chaotic scenes that occurred in the Brazilian dressing room shortly before kick-off.

'There were furious arguments and clashes between the coach and players,' Edmundo said. 'Ronaldo felt he had let everyone down by not playing but all it did was cause complete turmoil in the dressing room.

'All the way through the first half, Zagallo agonised about bringing Ronaldo off but he didn't have the courage.'

Fiercely self-critical Edmundo even admitted, 'I should have been more prepared and I think I will be lucky if I get another game for the national team. I should have been mentally prepared to get over anything before a World Cup final.

'The whole country cannot rely on the well-being of one individual and I should have been ready to prove myself. I let down myself, my team-mates, Ronaldo and everyone back home in Brazil.'

But maybe it was Zagallo who came the closest to summing up the situation as far as Ronaldo was concerned.

'It's too much publicity. Because of this, he spends a lot of time away from his family. Most of the time, he just speaks to his parents on the phone. If he was my son, I'd know what to do.

'The problem is that even when he has a rest, a day off, everybody invades his privacy. The truth is that he is alone.

Imagine what is in the head of this boy who goes back to his mansion in Milan every day and has nobody to talk to.'

Also, nothing could detract from the fact that many in Brazil believed that Nike had been given too much influence over the national team and its internal affairs.

The one element that most chose to ignore in the inquests following the World Cup final was that Brazil played extremely poorly and actually did very well even getting to the final. France should also be credited with a performance worthy of Champions. Brazil may have been under par, but the French startegy, commitment and teamwork earned them a well-deserved win. And perhaps Brazil were simply not good enough to win the tournament.

It was worth remembering that Brazil had performed dismally during the previous 15 months including that 4–2 defeat against Norway, draws with Jamaica and Guatemala and a 2–1 defeat by Norway in the first round of France '98.

Meanwhile, Nike in Italy issued a corporate statement to convince the world that they played no part in Brazil's demise.

'With regard to rumours circulating about presumed pressures Nike put on the Brazilian national soccer team so that Ronaldo would play, Nike wants to emphasise that the report of such involvement is absolutely false.

'What is true is that the game was the most important moment of Ronaldo's career. To play the final of a World Cup is the dream of any player, Ronaldo included.

'Ronaldo and Zagallo decided together to crown this dream which the Brazilian player probably deserved. In all of this, Nike did not interfere in any way. And besides, why should it have?'

On 28 July 1998, Ricardo Teixeira and his CBF associates sacked Zagallo and his entire backroom staff. Zagallo, whose record had included 107 wins and only 12 defeats, would only say, 'The saga will only end when the new coach is named next month.'

The move had been widely anticipated since losing the World Cup final. Teixeira pledged to change the set-up from top to bottom but he would, naturally, be staying on to oversee the birth of the new Brazil.

'The management staff's work during the World Cup was excellent. But now we are going to build a new team that will begin working with their minds set on the 2002 World Cup,' he said.

Teixeira was rumoured to have been set on sacking Zagallo even before the final.

The 'Old Wolf' showed great dignity, even at the end of his career. 'I'm not walking away distraught. I've been with the team for five World Cup Finals, with four victories and one runners-up place. I'm very proud.'

Looking back on the final itself, Zagallo said of the chaotic scenes in the Brazil dressing room before the game, 'The players had been upset that the first team sheet did not carry Ronaldo's name. Everybody was very down and the team played to less than their full potential.

'It was a traumatic shock, and knowing he was not fit to play made us inhibited and inward-looking. It was a major psychological blow.

'I was wondering all the time if I should keep Ronaldo on the pitch or take him off. I didn't think he was fit, but Ronaldo told me he was.'

Significantly, Zico further conceded in the weeks following France '98 that his relationship with Zagallo had not always been ideal.

'I did the best I could but, in truth, my job was never well-defined,' he said. 'I could have participated more ... Zagallo didn't want me helping on the pitch to avoid giving the impression that I was training the team. But I'm sure that I could have helped more if I had been on the pitch.'

Zico reckoned his worst moment came before the actual Finals when he was blamed by many in the Brazilian media for axing the injured Romario ten days before the tournament kicked off.

'It was my worst moment in the Cup. I was alone, exposed and only had the support of Sandra [his wife]. I felt so bad that the thought of throwing it all in passed through my head. I came out as the villain in the story but this was an injustice ... time proved I was right.'

But there was one player not in the slightest bit sad to see the back of Zagallo. Edmundo spent most of his stay in France denying he was sulking at not being played ahead of Bebeto.

'While the current manager was there, I knew it wouldn't work for me. I hope that he is never my manager again. I wasn't born yesterday. If we get a coach who likes me ...'

Then there was Ronaldo. He had genuinely wanted to win the World Cup with Brazil above everything else; the money, fame, popularity, awards.

A few days after the disastrous final, he talked to a Brazilian journalist about the tournament and the aftermath. Ronaldo made some extremely open admissions.

'We were a squad united in purpose, but containing players of great personality. Nothing serious happened. Edmundo went a little far, clashing with Giovanni in training. But then he realised this was not the way to try to win a place in the team. The incident between Bebeto and Dunga (when the captain harangued the striker for not tackling back) occurred only because everything was becoming tense in the heat of the match.'

Despite the heartbreak of the final, Ronaldo still insisted that Brazil 'were a team of rare quality. We had older, experienced players but the younger players also had a great deal of experience and everyone was determined to do their best, to do everything possible to win the World Cup. Veterans like Dunga, Bebeto and Aldair have a teenager's enthusiasm for the game. It infects everyone, just like the way Zagallo had won over all the players with his passion for football.'

Meanwhile, the hysteria which followed Ronaldo's World Cup final disaster reached such epidemic proportions in Rio that one well-known commentator even went so far as to claim that the player's health could have been affected by the constant use of his three mobile phones.

In early August 1998, Edmundo re-entered the fray over Brazil's dismal performance by claiming the CBF and Nike had conspired to force Ronaldo to play.

'The Nike business is true,' said Edmundo in an interview published in Rio. 'There's a contract that says Ronaldo must play every game for the full 90 minutes.'

Nike reacted furiously by insisting that it would be 'madness' to interfere in such a situation. However, it was once again pointed out that of the 22 players in the Brazil World Cup squad, 11 were under personal contract to Nike.

Edmundo insisted that Teixeira was behind the Nike takeover of the team. Teixeira reacted two days later by pledging to never allow Edmundo to play for Brazil again — a small measure of the president's power inside Brazilian football.

The nightmare in Paris was about to spark an even bigger battle.

CHAPTER 27

Sex, Lies and Pharmaceuticals

In the *favelas* of Rio, fireworks are set off to light up the clear, dark evening skies when drug dealers want to tell their customers that new supplies have arrived. The only other time you see them is when Brazil win an important football match.

The sparks certainly started flying again as the subject of drugs and football merged on the arrival of Ronaldo back in his home town. Rio was about to provide the key to the pharmaceutical cocktail which may well have contributed to Ronaldo's downfall in the World Cup final.

Significant clues about Ronaldo's drug dosage during the World Cup treatment of his injured leg were revealed during enquiries in Rio in August 1998. Many believe the alleged fit was brought on by too many doses of such medication.

Ronaldo also admitted in Brazil's daily newspaper *Zero Hora* to taking drugs for stomach pains throughout the tournament. And speaking on Brazil's TV Globo channel he said, 'I had a knee problem during the World Cup and was taking an anti-inflammatory. I stopped taking it two days before the final as I was having physio and the knee improved.'

The drugs issue refused to disappear, particularly when enquiries were made into the post-match drugs tests that were supposed to have been carried out. 'There were no drugs tests,' one member of the Brazilian national squad revealed in Rio in August 1998. 'We were not surprised because we'd lost. What was the point? It wouldn't prove anything, would it?'

The drugs tests would have established the amounts of tranquillizer, anti-inflammatories and other drugs in Ronaldo's system.

We may never know the true answer.

* * *

Just after the World Cup, Ronaldo was proclaimed as the world's highest-paid footballer by the magazine *Business Age*. The publication reported that he had an annual income of £20.5 million. The next three players in the magazine's list of the world's 25 top-paid players — Denilson, Rivaldo and Roberto Carlos — were all Brazilian.

Soon after that announcement, a crooked Rio policeman called Romio Ronaldo Rangel, 32, decided to kidnap Ronaldo and his mother and hold them to ransom. Rangel was a military policeman from the 7th Battalion in the Rio suburb of Alcantura, near Jacarepagua. He had arranged the kidnap of a wealthy businessman's son earlier in the year and was suspected of having been involved in other kidnaps over the previous two years. Another crooked policeman called Ricardo Campos Lafayette, 31, was also involved.

First, Rangel and his accomplices checked out the house Ronaldo had bought his mother in the up-market residential complex of Jacarepagua, near the family's former home in Bento Ribeiro.

The house was surrounded by palm trees, lush vegetation and a high wall. And two armed security guards patrolled the grounds day and night to keep out unwelcome visitors.

But Rangel and his gang were confident they could overcome such obstacles and decided the snatch should take place just after Ronaldo's return from the World Cup.

Kidnapping had been a lucrative criminal activity in Rio for years and usually a policeman would work for the gang to provide them with inside knowledge of security precautions taken by such high-profile families. Few of the victims were actually killed, but the number of people found following ransom demands being paid didn't always add up so the investigating officers believed many such kidnaps were never revealed to the security forces.

Strangely, it later emerged that Ronaldo's stepfather had a vague link to Rangel, the man accused of the kidnap plan. This was solely because they'd worked together at the same police station some years earlier. Obviously, there was not the slightest suggestion that Sonia's husband was involved.

Rangel was arrested in Copacabana as he was about to set out for Sonia's home, according to Rio police. So, in the last week of July as the whole of Brazil tried to start forgiving and forgetting the disasters of France '98, the police contacted Sonia and Nelio to inform them of the kidnap plan and how they had foiled it.

It emerged that the gang were even planning to demand the release of another master criminal from jail in Rio as part of their deal to return their victims unharmed.

And, it seemed, even among the criminal gangs of Rio, the World Cup played a pivotal role in planning kidnaps; originally, the kidnappers had intended to snatch Sonia and Ronaldo immediately after the World Cup final, but the plan had been put on ice because of Brazil's defeat. During the following few days, the scheme came to light.

Meanwhile, an Italian magazine offered to pay $35,000

to the first person to get a photo of Ronaldo and Suzanna on their secret holiday following the World Cup. It sounded a lot less hassle than resorting to a kidnap.

In Las Vegas, Ronaldo, Suzanna and Nelio enjoyed four days of non-stop gambling and the luxury of not once being recognised during their stay.

Then they flew down to Cancun, Mexico, where the threesome continued to obey doctors' orders and avoid football at all costs.

As he swam with dolphins alongside Suzanna, Ronaldo looked like someone without a care in the world, a million miles from the heartache of the Stade de France.

As Ronaldo played a brief game of beach football at the exclusive holiday resort of Cancun Beach, in Quintana Roo, he did not even seem too bothered when a local photographer snapped away at him and Suzanna.

Back in Italy, an Inter Milan spokesperson was wheeled out to explain the actions of their star:

'Ronaldo needed time off and he's not expected back in Italy for training until August 20, although he may come back a few days earlier. He has spoken every day on the telephone to the club's president, Massimo Moratti.'

Inter had already accepted that their biggest ever investment would miss the club's opening Champions' League qualifying tie against Skonto Riga of Latvia. Ronaldo would also have the added bonus of sitting out the first two matches of Italy's Serie A season in September because he was serving a suspension following statements he had made about the refereeing of Inter's 1–0 defeat to champions Juventus in April.

On his return from Mexico in the second week of August 1998, Ronaldo was somewhat surprisingly voted the best player at France '98. It was an award which was greeted in Brazil with a lot of scepticism.

Ronaldo's former striking partner, Romario, condemned it as 'shameful'. He said, 'When they chose me in '94, we won the title. There were many other better players in France; Zidane, Petit, Davids, then Owen. Ronaldo comes about tenth on my list. Maybe not even that.'

Romario was particularly annoyed by what he considered to be a flagrant piece of favouritism towards his fellow Brazilian. 'People have to understand that the supporters are not stupid. They know what's happened here.'

Ronaldo himself insisted that his award was 'completely fair' and even cited the fact that the best player award was backed by Adidas, 'not Nike'. He told one Brazilian journalist, 'Getting through the first stage of the World Cup, I played very well. I know I wasn't good at the end but I am still the best player in the world.

'I would have picked myself. Zidane was good but he was thrown out for three games after getting sent off. I played all seven games and scored four goals. I think I could have done better. The problem was in the last game I was strongly marked and for this reason they are questioning the award.'

When Ronaldo was asked to respond to Romario's criticism, he said, 'I'm not going to get into that because I am always giving everyone a chance, but I know that I have to start separating my real friends from my false friends.'

On the subject of Nike and their alleged role in the final, Ronaldo also hit back.

'It's just a company that supports me. I have Nike on my shirt and on my feet. I wear their uniform but I don't wear them on my shoulders. Nike doesn't interfere with my life or team selection.

'I asked to play. The medical examination showed nothing wrong with me. I did all I could. There was no pressure on me to do anything.'

What Ronaldo didn't say was that Martins and Pitta were the most significant influences in the drama. And they were still carefully mapping out a 'relaunch' for their product following the setbacks of France '98.

On the subject of Suzanna and when their much talked-about wedding might actually take place, Ronaldo had this to say: 'I am going to marry her but I don't know when. Not this year. I just ask our fans not to believe any of the crap they may have read about our romance.'

But he did partially allude to some problems about jealousy between the couple.

'I am very jealous, of course. I understand her profession as an actress but I just don't like to see her kissing other men.' The previous few weeks may have had a profound effect on Ronaldo, but he still couldn't shake off some of those adolescent attitudes.

As he spoke, Suzanna was purring away in the background having just been told that her feature film début in an Italian art house movie was being acclaimed by the producers and she'd been told she had 'a very big future as a serious actress'.

Unfortunately, Ronaldo had refused to see the film because he was upset at the prospect of seeing his beautiful blonde fiancée making love to another man up on the big screen.

Ronaldo also hit back at rumours that he might be about to return to Rio to play for Flamengo. He said, 'I will not be coming back to Brazil for a long time.

'The organisation of football in Europe is so much better. Sure, I miss Brazil. I miss the times when I lived alone in Bela Horizonte. I also miss the biscuit pudding that my mother used to make for me. It's really fabulous.'

He forget to mention that since departing for Europe three years earlier, Sonia had been flying backwards and forwards across the Atlantic to make sure, among other things, that he would be able to enjoy that very same pudding.

Rumours of Suzanna's friendship with TV Globo's Pedro Bial continued to reverberate around Rio even after the World Cup final. Many claimed that Ronaldo had been so heartbroken by the stories that his fit had been a nervous reaction to the situation.

Another friend of the couple in Rio told me, 'Ronaldo told Suzanna he wanted to start again and that's one of the reasons they took off for the holiday in the US and Mexico.' What the source failed to acknowledge was that half of Ronaldo's family went with him as well. So much for a quiet, get-away-from-it-all holiday for the two supposed lovebirds.

In Rio in August 1998, Pedro Bial continued to insist that he had had no involvement in Ronaldo's World Cup problems. But he had clear opinions about who might be held responsible.

'Ronaldo was constantly under pressure. His mobile phones were ringing all day long. If it wasn't his agents, it was his mother, father, girlfriend or club. His family were always asking for stupid things that he shouldn't have been bothered with.

'But Ronaldo was so patient with all these callers. He never lost his cool. In reality, he was bottling everything up and that's why he lost it on the big day. Ronaldo's the kind of person who needs a wall to punch at the end of every day just to get rid of all those frustrations.

'He was keeping everything inside himself. He never let anyone see the real Ronaldo. It was very unhealthy.'

Whatever did happen between Ronaldo and Suzanna Werner during the World Cup Finals, there can be no doubt that it had a profound effect on the world's most famous player. But according to Rio radio presenter Sergio Piumatti, the problems began long before the tournament.

He explained, 'For the past two years, Suzanna Werner had been perfectly content with her role as Ronaldo's trinket. She was famous because of who *he* was — she was the girlfriend of the world's greatest footballer, and not because of who *she* was, one undeniably attractive girl among many thousands you can see on the beach at Ipanema every day.

'It is true she appears in a soap opera on Brazilian TV

but she was anything but a household name until her sudden notoriety. Overnight in France, she started behaving how she thought a star should behave. Everywhere the paparazzi went, Suzanna went too. Ronaldo might have imagined she was going to France to soothe his furrowed brow, but Suzanna Werner clearly believed she was also there to further her television career.'

TV Globo's Bial perhaps best summed up the attitude of Brazil once the dust had settled on the Ronaldo affair.

'I think the Brazilians reaching the final was a big achievement, especially since Holland were probably the best team at the finals. We only had individual talent. It was not a great team.'

In Rio, Ronaldo kept to a promise made before the World Cup Finals to appear on an educational TV programme in the second week of August. Not surprisingly, there was no escape from the media spotlight and the many theories that circulated as to what had really happened on 12 July.

One of the most far-fetched was that a chef in the Paris hotel where the Brazilian squad were staying had deliberately poisoned Ronaldo's lunch on the day of the final. Even Ronaldo had a laugh about this one when tackled about it on the programme. 'We had a buffet lunch that day so I don't know how he could have known what food I was going to eat.'

During his TV appearance, Ronaldo talked in serious terms about a charitable foundation he intended to set up to build a football school for kids from the *favelas*. The foundation would be called R-9, the same name as the nightclub he was intending to open in Rio later that same week. It also happened to be the same name as the brand of clothes Ronaldo's agents intended to sell around the world throughout the year. Naturally, they were to be manufactured under the auspices of Nike.

As one fellow guest on that same TV programme observed, 'Ronaldo did not seem to be sure of what he was actually talking about and it was clear the foundation was a long way off actually happening.'

Ronaldo also kept a promise to visit the children's ward at a local cancer hospital where his presence was greatly appreciated by many of the patients. It was then that someone pointed out that children with cancer particularly adored Ronaldo because of his shaved hairstyle. 'It makes those kids feel as if they don't stand out so much,' said one nurse.

Behind the scenes in Rio, Pitta and Martins had decided the best way to deal with the continued furore over France 98 was to tackle it head on.

They told Ronaldo he would have to agree to numerous TV, radio and newspaper interviews to try to kill off all the rumours surrounding the final. The two agents also saw it as a perfect opportunity to 're-invent' their star client, and provide an enormous amount of free publicity for the new nightclub venture.

Ronaldo was even booked to appear live on the *Jo Soares Show* from São Paulo the following week. It was seen as a brave gamble by the player but his agents told Ronaldo it was a great opportunity to re-establish his image in the light of the disaster in Paris.

Corporate role-playing was the name of the game.

CHAPTER 28

Fallen Hero

Ronaldo's poor performance in the World Cup final also had a knock-on effect in regard to his standing as the best player on the globe. In Britain, many were suggesting that *wunderkind* Michael Owen was already as good as Ronaldo. Liverpool captain Paul Ince had no doubts, 'Michael is up there with him in my view.'

On the eve of a pre-season friendly against Inter Milan — who were without the absent Ronaldo — Ince also provided a fascinating insight into how he almost stayed at his old club after being told about Ronaldo's move to Italy some months before it actually happened.

President Massimo Moratti's masterplan had been for Ince to provide the midfield strength to put Ronaldo through for even more goals than he had scored in his first season with Inter. But then Ince opted for a move to Liverpool in the close season of 1997.

Massimo even got back in touch with Ince half-way

through the 1997–98 season and begged him to rejoin Inter so he could once more become the driving force in Inter's quest for the *Scudetto*, the Serie A title.

But Ince told Massimo that Michael Owen was just as exciting a prospect and he intended to stay on Merseyside.

'I loved everything about Inter; the club, the place and the president,' explained Ince. 'He tried his hardest to make me stay and it was such a great life out there that I was sorely tempted.

'The fans loved me. I had everything and there was no reason at all to return, other than the attraction of playing for Liverpool. Anyone else and I wouldn't have come back.'

Then Ince revealed how Massimo told him of his plans to buy Ronaldo months before he eventually signed in the summer of 1997.

'He told me he was going to buy him and I didn't doubt him for a moment. I have to admit that was a great temptation. I'd have loved to have played with him. But then I thought of Michael Owen.

'He might still have a long way to go, but that applies to Ronaldo as well.'

One of the saddest assessments of Ronaldo's World Cup performance came from his former Barcelona coach Bobby Robson. Just a few weeks after the disastrous final, Robson proclaimed, 'They are killing him. They are flogging the kid to death. He's played 80 matches in less than a year and no wonder his body has said enough is enough.

'I feel for the boy. I really do. Nobody can put up with the kind of pressure he's been under. Maybe what happened was only a matter of time. It was absurd, the poor lad couldn't take it all in. Presidents don't get followed by the media as much as him. Then on top of that, they ask him to play 80 matches. Ridiculous.

'Ronaldo is an amazing physical specimen and the fastest thing I've ever seen running with the ball. But eventually his body could not take it and that is what happened. He works so hard at his game but he looked dead beat in the final.'

Nilton Santos, a legendary member of the 1958 Brazilian World Cup-winning side alongside Pelé and Zagallo, had very firm opinions of what went wrong for Ronaldo.

'Stop looking for a conspiracy. It's much simpler than that. All you have to do is ask yourself this: Why did they let the kid play?'

'Pelé was kicked out of the World Cup in Chile and he never even got considered for the final,' argued Santos. 'Now a kid has a convulsion, and four hours later they send him out to play in the World Cup final.'

In the middle of August 1998, Corinthians chief Wanderlei Luxembourgo was officially confirmed as new coach to the Brazilian national team. He immediately enhanced the reputation of all good witch doctors in Brazil by stating that he would be bringing his own voodoo expert on to the training staff.

Witch doctor Roberio De Ogum, from São Paulo, based his activities on the spiritual guidance of the African god Ogum. He also happened to be extremely rich and successful, living in a penthouse in one of the city's most exclusive areas and driving a brand-new Audi. It seemed that even Brazil's élite rich had use for a good old-fashioned witch doctor.

When Luxembourgo was asked whether it was a good idea to have a witch doctor on the training squad, he replied, 'Well, look at it like this. Roberio is a good friend of my family and I believe very much in what he does. When I hear criticisms of my connections with him I see no problem. I will not stop using him.'

In Rio, radio stations delighted in playing the jingle made famous by Ronaldo's TV commercial for Nike, with the new words: '*El amarelou* ... he's yellow ... he did chicken out ...'

CBF president Ricardo Teixeira continued to flex his muscles and prove that he was the most powerful influence in Brazilian national football. Having coldly disposed of Mario Zagallo and his backroom boys, Teixeira announced to the Brazilian media that Edmundo 'would never' play for Brazil again after the outspoken player had publicly criticised Teixeira and Nike.

'It was bloody outrageous, a bit like the head of the FA telling journalists that Alan Shearer would never wear an English shirt ever again,' explained one London-based sports journalist.

* * *

If he was a legend on the pitch, Ronaldo was in danger of becoming all too human off it. Somehow his frail, gentle personality only added to his appeal and a climate of forgiveness for what had happened at France '98 gradually gathered momentum.

But for all the tens of millions of dollars he had already earned, he needed to be careful that he didn't make hasty business investments, like so many of his predecessors, even including Pelé.

So when Ronaldo continued his personal rehabilitation in the aftermath of the final by opening his own nightclub in Rio just five weeks after the disaster in France, some eyebrows were raised.

The three-storey club on Rua Denaniao Flores in the centre of the upmarket Rio suburb of Leblon was the brainchild of Pitta and Martins. They and Ronaldo decided to call it R-9 and it was intended to be the first in a whole series of R-9 projects.

The glass-fronted, three-tier façade was designed by a Dutch architect and a *Carioca* designer was responsible for the interior. The club was intended to hold 400 people with a restaurant on the ground floor, a discotheque on the middle floor and a VIP hospitality room above it.

But even before the club held three consecutive opening nights, residents in Leblon began lobbying to have the club closed because of the disruption caused by the traffic outside the premises. The problem was that Leblon was more used to romantic little restaurants and a handful of bars than a steamy nightclub which attracted a bizarre mix of people from the day it opened its doors.

Leblon was full of Rio's old money families and Ronaldo and his crew came from the opposite end of the social scale. It was not a comfortable mix.

On the night I attended, Ronaldo was dressed in black trousers and an Italian silk shirt. Suzanna was decked out in a revealing black dress with minute shoulder straps, a gold necklace and some expensive-looking diamond earrings.

Many of Ronaldo's footballing friends attended and some had words of advice for the young superstar. Former Brazilian coach Carlos Alberto Perreira offered this warning: 'I hope Ronaldo's agents will help him to make sure the business works. Ronaldo really has to stick to his football.'

Ronaldo's father Nelio posed happily for cameras and told him in front of dozens of journalists, 'Congratulations, my son. This is a really beautiful place.'

Ronaldo had a stock response for anyone asking the banal questions. 'I am young and I am sure my fans will like this place. I am sure that within two months R-9 will become an important place for young people in Brazil.'

In the flesh, a short interview with Ronaldo threw up few clues as to his real personality. His replies were courteous but lacking in depth, and his habit of breathing only through his mouth while talking gave the distinct impression of unease, which remained with him throughout.

On the floor below Ronaldo's VIP room at R-9, dozens of shapely *Carioca* women patrolled the dance floor looking for men. Some of them were dressed in brief, tight-fitting skirts or trousers. As one male guest at the opening that night said, 'Like all Rio clubs, this place will soon get crowded with poor *Carioca* women from the *favelas* looking for a man to stay the night with and pay for sex. Nothing changes. They may look beautiful but it's your wallet they are really interested in.'

Ronaldo spent much of the evening in the VIP suite on the club's top floor watching local team Vasco beat his old club Barcelona 2–0. During the live broadcast, hardly a word was uttered and Ronaldo's agents refused to let any members of the press in to see Ronaldo until after the game had finished.

Suzanna sat dutifully on his knee throughout the game and occasionally hugged Ronaldo.

At the opening that night, Edmundo sent along his personal assistant to try to placate Ronaldo following The Animal's outburst after the World Cup. But his representative was verbally abused by CBF chief Ricardo Teixeira who repeated his threat never to allow Edmundo to play for Brazil again.

After watching the game on television, Ronaldo took one mouthful of a 'Phenomeno' sandwich (named after him) and he clearly wasn't happy. 'The bread's really bad and there's not enough salmon or lettuce.' He sent it back.

Later that same night, Ronaldo proudly told anyone who would listen that half the profits from his nightclub would go towards developing the charity foundation that he hoped would be up and running by the year 2000.

Ronaldo's appearance at his nightclub opening was marked by the presence of more bodyguards than had ever been seen before on the neat and tidy streets of Leblon.

And although France '98 was probably the last thing Ronaldo wanted to talk about, the subject continued to haunt him. He'd even invented a new stock response.

'What happened in the past stays with us for ever,' he told one journalist who spent the following few minutes trying to analyse what Ronaldo had meant by this.

On each of R-9's three opening nights, Ronaldo's agents constantly hovered in the background, keeping an eye on their prized asset.

The week after his nightclub opening, Ronaldo found himself being grilled by chat show host Jo Soares. Soares cut a bizarre figure alongside the obviously nervous

Ronaldo. The introduction said a lot about the way that many in Brazil had viewed Ronaldo before France '98.

'Football players in Brazil are seen as cheeky, cocky people. Romario was a classic example, but Ronaldo was different. He was nice and that image was carefully nurtured.'

Said Rio journalist Denis Wright, 'He came over as very honest about his attitude towards Suzanna. Soares wasn't that tough on him at all.'

For the moment, it looked as if Ronaldo had been let off the hook.

In the middle of Ronaldo's well-publicised visit to Rio in mid-August, a bizarre story emerged about a bitter row between Mario Zagallo and his one-time golden boy Romario. Zagallo had decided to sue the player because he had allowed an obscene painting of his former coach to be hung at his bar/nightclub originally called Café de Gol in the upper-crust Rio suburb of Barra.

The painting featured Zagallo sitting on the toilet in full colour and the veteran accused Romario of trying to humiliate him.

'I have grandchildren and they would be highly offended by this,' Zagallo complained. 'I will not allow Romario to do this to me. He's trying to make me look bad.'

Romario refused to be drawn into commenting about the legal battle except to say the whole matter was in the hands of his lawyers.

One of the biggest problems facing Ronaldo was that with his fame and wealth increasing by the day, he was in real danger of becoming isolated from the normal world as most people know it.

A classic example was that whenever other Brazilian footballers wanted to call him up when he was in Rio, they had to book an appointment through his agents who would then interrogate the caller as to why they should be granted an audience.

One player explained, 'I tried to call Ronaldo for a game

of beach football and I ended up being grilled by his agents who thought I was trying to get him on to the beach so a load of photographers could take pictures of him. I didn't bother staying in touch with him after that.'

19 August 1998 came and went without Ronaldo marrying Suzanna as he had said he would six months earlier.

Ronaldo returned to Italy without Suzanna the following day because, apparently, their Chihuahua puppy called Sharon Stone was ill with an eye problem. It sounded so ludicrous, although it was true, but there were some who wondered if Suzanna and Ronaldo had had yet another bust-up. Time would tell.

Back in Milan, and about to start pre-season training with Inter, Ronaldo found that his Italian bosses had called a press conference at the club's downtown headquarters.

He felt a million miles away from the stress that surrounded the World Cup final, and it showed. 'I've just had the best and longest holiday of my life.'

Then Ronaldo discovered that another controversy was dogging some of his Italian colleagues. A doping probe had rocked Italian soccer that month and was threatening to overshadow the start of the new season on 13 September.

The investigation was looking into the use and alleged abuse of drugs, whether legal or illicit. It was expected that eventually there would be a reconsideration of the lists of officially banned substances and doping procedures.

'I've heard very little about it because I was on holiday and I didn't want to hear anything about football, but I think what emerges could be good for football,' Ronaldo told the press conference.

The scandal broke after one coach claimed that a number of big names had taken drugs to increase muscular power in their bodies. Amongst those initially questioned were Del Piero from Juventus and former Juve star Gianluca Vialli, both of whom insisted that had done nothing illegal, and their names were cleared.

Ronaldo insisted that he had never taken boosters of the amino acid Creatine, which was at the centre of the Italian allegations. Creatine occurs naturally in the body and plays a key role in muscle contraction. Its use is legal and some teams use it to aid players returning from injury. Other clubs in Italy refuse to use it and some coaches say it should be banned.

Some of the biggest names in Serie A were allegedly involved. Turin judge Raffaele Guarinallo even warned that Ronaldo might be one of a number of stars who could be called to give evidence.

The scandal was set to rumble on into 1999.

When Brazil's legendary 1970 World Cup-winners set off for the tournament, hopes were so high that one popular Rio football magazine wrote: 'If Brazil lose in Mexico, Pelé will come home a prince and not a king. If we win, Pelé will come home a demi-god — and Tostao will be his king.'

As it turned out, Ronaldo only just scraped in as a prince following the disasters of France '98.

In the weeks that followed the tournament, Ronaldo started to repair his image, and gradually the population of the biggest soccer-addicted nation on earth grew to forgive him.

But beneath the surface, Ronaldo felt a deep resentment towards the situation in Brazil. He found his fame hard to handle despite his outward calm. And it was with a small sense of relief that he finally travelled back to Inter to begin his training at the end of August 1998.

In early September 1998, Ronaldo's agents were alerted to the planned takeover of Manchester United by Rupert Murdoch. It was a significant development because the two businessmen knew that United manager Alex Ferguson had always been keen to sign their star client.

Now with Murdoch's Sky-TV backing, the world's most famous football team would undoubtedly be in a position to improve on Ronaldo's already extremely lucrative contract at Inter.

There was no suggestion that Ronaldo was likely to move from Italy but Pitta and Martins were masters at pre-empting the next step in their superstar's career and they had always insisted on an escape clause in Ronaldo's contracts for that very reason.

As a feeding frenzy developed between top English Premiership clubs and rumoured big business takeovers, it was also revealed that Inter had made a bold move for Newcastle's Alan Shearer in a bid to create a dream strike force for the Serie A.

However, newspaper reports of the alleged sale of Shearer to Inter were, in reality, rather wide of the mark for one good reason; Ronaldo and his agents had even managed to get a clause added to his Inter contract that stipulated he would have a say in any purchases of other big-name strikers.

And Ronaldo was not a great fan of Alan Shearer after the two of them had clashed during the Tournoi de France in the summer of 1997. Ronaldo's agents later claimed that Shearer had fouled Ronaldo in an ungentlemanly manner and they felt the Englishman was not all he was cracked up to be. On 9 September 1998, Ronaldo produced a lacklustre performance in Inter's 1–0 victory over Cesena in the Italy Cup.

Ronaldo's long-awaited 1998–99 début for Inter in the Champions' League came with Real Madrid on 16 September, 1998.

It was a very significant event because it was Ronaldo's first European match since the World Cup final and the eyes of the world were on him once more. Everyone in Italy was particularly intrigued to find out if he could rediscover his form following disappointment in France.

Before the game, Ronaldo's Brazilian room-mate Roberto Carlos — who played for Real — tried to make a peace offering following his outspoken comments about

Ronaldo being 'as yellow as the shirt he was wearing' after the final.

In a rather thinly-veiled public relations exercise, Roberto Carlos revealed in a press conference that Ronaldo's father had thanked him for saving his son's life before the World Cup final.

Roberto Carlos said, 'Ronaldo's father thanked me for saving his son. Because we were sharing a room, he knew I was the first one to be aware of the situation.'

It all seemed rather pointless since most of the damage had already been done.

The match itself proved ominous for both Ronaldo and his Inter team-mates. Not only did they lose 2–0, but Ronaldo was substituted on the 74th minute after what one can only describe as a lacklustre performance.

There were many in attendance that night who wondered if the world would ever see the Ronaldo of old again.

Ronaldo's first goal in the 1998–99 Serie A season was a penalty against Piacenza in Inter's 1–0 victory on 20 September. Once again, it was clear that Ronaldo was not fully fit.

That night, Ronaldo and his other Inter Brazilian team-mate Ze Elias held a joint 22nd birthday celebration in a Milan nightclub. A cake in the shape of a football stadium and dancing until 4.00am were the main features, and Suzanna Werner was nowhere to be seen.

Within a few days, Inter admitted that Ronaldo was having problems with the same knee that had been of such concern over the previous two years.

On Monday, 19 October 1998, further cracks began appearing in Ronaldo's once-shining career at Inter Milan, following their 5–3 thrashing by Lazio.

It looked as if, once again, Ronaldo would be off on his travels ...

CHAPTER 29

Rebirth of a Superstar

Over the next three years, Ronaldo's injury problems grew steadily worse. He ended the 1998-99 Italian season on a reasonable high with six goals in just six matches giving him a total of 15 goals in 26 matches.

But in October, 1999, his frustration showed when he was sent off for the first time in his career during a Milan derby game. In November, Ronaldo scored but then limped off during Inter's league game against Lecce. He then required surgery on his right knee which kept him out for five months.

A few months earlier, his personal life had also taken a serious downturn when models Viviane Brunieri and Nadia Valdez Franca revealed in Rio newspapers that they'd both slept with Ronaldo while he was still engaged to Suzanna. The couple split up almost immediately.

Then Ronaldo met and fell in love with beautiful blonde Brazilian soccer player Milene Domingues. Their relationship was quickly sealed when she found herself pregnant and on Christmas Day, 1999, Ronaldo married 22-year-old Milene at his mother's house in Rio. She was already famous in her own right as Brazil's 'Queen of the Keepy-up' because she held the world record for keeping a football in the air — an incredible 55,187 touches in nine hours and six minutes.

Wedding guests included two of Ronaldo's close friends from his days in the favella. The groom's suit and bride's dress were gifts from Italian designer Giorgio Armani and Ronaldo gave Milene a Jeep Cherokee four-wheel drive car, which she drove to the ceremony, as a present.

Agent Reinaldo Pitta and his financial director Aloisio Freitas were witnesses at the wedding.

Milene and Ronaldo had first met back in 1995 when Ronaldo saw her during a half-time show at a match in Italy but their relationship did not take off until after his split with Susanna. On April 6, 2000, the couple had a baby son called Ronald.

Today Ronaldo says that Milene is the most important person in his life, 'She is my blessing by God, my life's dream. I have found the right person.' Many believe that Milene quickly became a calming influence on Ronaldo as his injury crisis threatened to end his career. He was just six minutes into an appearance as a second half substitute in yet another comeback game against Lazio in the Italian Cup on April 12, 2000, when he crumpled to the ground as he weaved unchallenged towards the penalty area, having ruptured ligaments in the same knee.

The following day he flew to Paris for an examination but it wasn't until November that year Ronaldo was once again operated on. His doctor warned him not to expect to play again until the start of the 2001 season at the earliest.

Another knee operation followed in the summer of 2001. Ronaldo then made his return to Italian league action in November that year. It ended after just 14 minutes when he limped off with a recurrence of a thigh injury.

Ronaldo then suffered two other muscular injuries in quick sucession.

Although, tragically, in February 2001, Ronaldo's wife Milene had lost the second baby the couple were expecting, the strength of their relationship helped him through his darkest days of injury and personal struggle as doctors continued to question whether he should ever play football again. When, in early 2002, Milene signed for Italian women's football side Fiammo Monza, Ronaldo had to remain back in Rio recuperating from yet more surgery.

But all that enforced time off from playing football did enable Ronaldo to set up a charity, the Sao Christovao Foundation, which immediately began raising millions of dollars for deprived children. And many friends say that the ever shy superstar is happiest in the company of children. A lot of that is no doubt connected to his own father's absence from home plus the fact that he was plucked from the favella and whisked to Europe at the ludicrously young age of seventeen.

Then in February 2002, Ronaldo underwent a four-week fitness programme in Rio. A month later new Brazilian team boss Felipe 'Big Phil' Scolari decided to put his reputation on the line and persuaded Ronaldo to play for his country even though he'd only played fourteen times for Inter over the previous three seasons.

Scolari was immediately accused by Brazilian soccer fans of indulging a half-fit superstar in the mistaken belief that he could rescue a collapsing team. Brazil had only just scraped through the qualifying rounds of the World Cup and there was talk of a crisis in Brazilian soccer. Even Pele admitted, 'Ronaldo's playing at 60-70 per cent of his potential. He hesitates and worries about getting injured.' But there was another school of thought; if Ronaldo could get back into action he might improve the team's chances of performing well at the 2002 World Cup in Japan and Korea.

The bitter arguments and relentless attacks from critics at home and abroad took an enormous toll on Ronaldo and his team-mates as they prepared for the tournament. Ricardo Seyton, a Brazilian FA official since before the doomed 1998 campaign and a close friend of Ronaldo even revealed that after each warm-up game most of the players burst into floods of tears.

'Usually after a game, Brazilian players pray - but these guys cried.

They cried for five or ten minutes, nearly all of them before they started thanking God for each victory.' And Ronaldo found it difficult to turn those taps of tears off. It meant so much to him to be back in the side after all he had been through.

As Seyton later explained, 'They called Ronaldo half a player before the tournament began. They said Rivaldo had bugs in his knees. They even said that Scolari was a thug.' For the first time, Brazilian players did not share hotel rooms during Japan/Korea 2002. But that didn't stop Ronaldo and his team-mates from remaining bonded and besotted with that 18-carat gold trophy.

Ronaldo and the other players passed most evenings during the 2002 World Cup campaign playing bingo or in their games room, where the sqad congregated until turning in at 12:30 am. The golf mad Ronaldo gave other team-mates like Roberto Carlos lessons on a video simulator.

Coach Scolari even planned to improve the players' motivation by showing them televised footage before every match. The pictures were of Brazilian supporters in the streets at home celebrating when the team scored and weeping when they let a goal in.

And throughout Japan/Korea 2002, Brazilian club doctor Jose Luis Runco fought a battle of words with medical staff from Ronaldo's Inter Milan club over fitness and training schedules. Inter did not want Ronaldo to play in any of the World Cup matches. Former Brazilian coach Carlos Alberto Perreira added to the ongoing drama by telling newsmen he thought Ronaldo might not get through the 2002 tournament. He said, 'He is not the same

Ronaldo we knew but he can still make a difference and he is stronger mentally than people realise. All this time when he was injured, we thought he might not come back but he never gave up. He bore all the criticism, even in Italy. But he promised, "I will show you" and maybe he will.' Ronaldo's dream World Cup comeback story began unfolding in the 50th minute of Brazil's opening game against Turkey, when he stretched to force home his first goal in a competitive international since July 1999. A jolt of recognition went through the crowd. Brazil scraped home 2-1 and Ronaldo was starting his climb back to the top of his profession.

That was to be the start of four magical weeks in which he rescued his own footballing genius and showed numerous examples of his own sportsmanship. After the end of each Brazilian victory he deliberately sought out opposition players to offer his condolences. Not once throughout the 2002 tournament did he put pressure on the referee, let alone get booked.

When Brazil surged through to the final thanks to a brilliant sixth goal of the tournament from Ronaldo against those earlier group opponents Turkey, it looked like the dream comeback really had turned into a stunning reality.

But yet more was to come.

On the eve of the World Cup final with Germany, it looked as if their goalkeeper and captain Oliver Kahn was set to be made the player of the tournament.

'He's brilliant but I think I might still get the ball past him,' promised Ronaldo.

Ronaldo's team-mates remained astonished by his sheer power and acceleration despite the fact he was not even considered to be fully fit. That pace and wonderful ball control had turned him once more into a striker who terrifies the opposition and makes goals out of nothing.

The winner against Turkey in the semi-finals had been a classic example of that.

On the day before the 2002 World Cup Final, Ronaldo

stood on the training ground, a proud figure in a Brazil strip, juggling the ball on his head, performing the occasional drag-back and striking shots with cold precision into the back of the net.

Observers watching the maestro hard at work that swelteringly hot afternoon were struck by how happy Ronaldo seemed. He was beaming from ear to ear, brimming with quiet confidence. And the expression on his face delighted all who were watching him.

Ronaldo even told waiting pressmen that the nightmare of 1998 was now far from his mind in Korea and Japan. 'People keep asking me about '98 but I have forgotten about it because the players have given me tranquility,' explained Ronaldo. 'The other players don't make me feel like the 'saviour of the team' and that takes a lot of pressure from my shoulders.' Ronaldo continued, 'It is totally different to then, closer to what I found in '94. The only difference to now is that people were restraining their emotions more then. There was Dunga there, Romario there, who kept the group together in a tough way. This is the first time I have played for Brazil where everything is even between every player.'

Two brilliant goals in the second half by Ronaldo sealed Brazil's World Cup final victory against Germany in Yokohama, Japan, on June 30th, 2002. Ronaldo was weeping with exhaustion and relief when the final whistle went in Yokohama. He'd been withdrawn by coach Solari with a couple of minutes still to go.

As he hoisted the World Cup trophy up in the air for all his millions of fans to admire. 'I'm just so happy. After four years of waiting, the agony is over for me.' Once again he'd become a symbol of hope to millions of bare-foot kids from the Rio favella where he'd struggled to survive as a child. So it was only right that he should dedicate his goals to his beloved family who'd helped him in his roller coaster ride out of poverty.

Ronaldo also knew that it was specialist physio Nilton Petrone who'd helped rescue him from the desolation of that career-threatening knee surgery.

Now he was also winner of the prestigious Golden Boot as leading scorer at the Japan/Korea World Cup with eight goals. And his aggregate 12 World Cup goals equalled the number of Pele.

So it was fitting that within minutes of that superb victory over Germany, Pele - the most famous Brazilian of all - kissed and hugged Ronaldo as he collected his winner's medal. 'It's only just beginning to sink in what joy we've brought to millions of people back home in Brazil. It's for them that we are so happy.' That night, Ronaldo was the last player to step onto the singing, rocking team bus. Ten of the Brazil squad had even managed a conga to the vehicle thus avoiding a huge crowd of South American journalists desperate for a word from the all conquering hero Ronaldo.

But behind the smiles, Ronaldo privately admitted that even if Brazil had lost the 2002 final he would have emerged happy because he'd proved so spectacularly that he was back to full fitness after three years of injury crisis. 'It was more than I could dream to have the World Cup in my hands. But it's not about personal records. None of this would have happened without the other players. This group had so much fight.' And when asked if winning the World Cup was better than having sex, he smiled and said, 'Well, you only get a World Cup once every four years.' Milene's response was not sought on this delicate matter.

Meanwhile coach Felipe 'Big Phil' Scolari rejoiced in the rebirth of his number one striker. 'I feel the joy of the Brazilian people. We've worked hard and feel the merit of that word. We had one objective and achieved it.' Now Ronaldo knew for sure that the shadows which had darkened his life for the previous four years had finally been dispersed and that he could now get on with his real life once again. As he put it, 'I'm slowly realising just what happened. My happiness and my emotion are so great that it's difficult to understand. This victory, for our fifth world title, has crowned my recovery and the work of the whole team. More than anything it's a victory for the group. The whole team battled and ran and helped each other. No individual can beat what the group achieved.'

THE MAN WHO LOST THE WORLD THEN WON IT BACK AGAIN — read the headline in the Daily Mail and it perfectly summed up Ronaldo's career following that historic victory over Germany in the 2002 World Cup final.

Just four years earlier he'd been a broken man, virtually sleepwalking through the appalling defeat by France only to then be virtually dismissed as a spent force at just 21 years of age. But on the night of the 2002 final victory against Germany he was back on top of the world.

As it slowly sunk in that he'd just staged the most magnificent comeback in the history of football, Ronaldo Nazario da Lima sat down and wept once more.

His extraordinary triumph had come after a heartbreaking spell of disappointments. Now at the age of 25, his redemption was complete. On a personal front, he was content; happily married with a two-year-old son. 'All I can say is that every goal I score now is a victory. Every time I walk on to the pitch it is an honour, a joy. I have to say that the nightmare is over.'

As Brazil celebrated Ronaldo's astonishing return to form in the World Cup, the man himself revealed the reasons behind his bizarre haircut, which featured just a small, semi-circle at the front with the rest of his head shaved. He said that it was so his son could recognise him on the television. He'd kept a more normal short style until after the 2-1 quarter final victory over England. Then in a phone call home to Milene in Sao Paolo, she told him that little Ronald had been mistakenly kissing the TV image of his equally bald teammate Roberto Carlos.

'I couldn't believe it,' Ronaldo explained. 'Roberto Carlos is so ugly! Can you imagine that? I told Milene that this couldn't happen again. So that is why I had the crazy haircut.' As the reality of his revival dawned following that historical world cup triumph, Ronaldo paid tribute to the doctor who undoubtedly saved his career. Paris-based orthopaedic specialist Gerard Salliant performed two knee operations on Ronaldo in 2000 and 2001 .

Sallient was in Yokohama as the superstar's special guest. Before the game he met up with the specialist and told him, 'My biggest victory is that I can play again.' Salliant explained, 'It gives hope to everyone who is injured, even those who are not sportsmen, to see that by fighting you can make it .

It's fantastic and hugely satisfying. I am very moved.' Across the world, other soccer heroes were lining up to congratulate Ronaldo on his amazing comeback. Former England skipper Alan Shearer said, 'Ronaldo went through such an agonising time four years ago. He has bounced back in true champions style. He deserves everything he's got from the World Cup and boy has he proved that he is the best!' The Newcastle striker added, 'Weaker players than him might have gone off the boil, mentally, after those first half misses and gone back into their shell. But Ronaldo knew he would get his opportunity eventually.'

From seizure to sainthood, the odyssey was now complete. Ronald wept tears of undiluted relief at his own redemption and floods of happiness for his beloved Brazil. No one had managed more than seven goals in this World Cup for thirty-two years. Not since German legend Gerd Muller scored a phenomenal ten in 1970.

Ronaldo and his Brazilian teammates were cavalier but also secure. But they never once betrayed their true romantic roots even though they had built a solid platform on the way to this famous World Cup victory.

Big Phil Scolari had rescued not just Ronaldo, but the entire team from a seemingly doomed qualifying campaign by battening down the hatches tactically before liberating

Ronaldo, Ronaldinho and Rivaldo at the onset of the finals.

But it was Ronaldo's recovery that was the biggest achievement. And the fact that it was the first time Brazil had scored in open play in the World Cup since their famous victory in 1970 was all the more incredible.

When Brazil re-write history they do so by telling the familiar enchanting story. The name is Ronaldo. The colour is yellow. The game is still beautiful.

Suddenly, the world had got the kid they called The Phenomenon back in all his glory with all his strength and menace restored.

EPILOGUE

There's still a kite tied to the telephone wires that are strung precariously across the back yard of the house where Ronaldo spent his childhood. The battered, rusting hulk of an old Chevette automobile sits abandoned next to the crooked wall nearby. Down the track, a few more shacks have been hastily erected by the ever-expanding families that flock to the *favela* of Bento Ribeiro.

And there are still dozens of kids out every day playing football on the streets and in the dusty wasteland. Down at the station where Ronaldo often tried to avoid paying the train fare because he simply had no money, the main building is crumbling fast and covered in graffiti.

But the kids are still playing barefoot on the streets. Now scouts wander amongst the tumbledown shacks and alleyways looking for a new Ronaldo. There's a handful of kids that everyone talks of in glowing terms; there's Carlos Alberto, aged 11, who is said to be as quick as Ronaldo was at that age; and there's Renata, a tiny fox terrier of a boy who is top scorer for the local junior team.

These boys and many of their footballing friends all have one dream — to buy a house for their mothers. They talk in almost mythical terms about the riches and fame that they hope football will bring them.

During Japan/Korea 2002, the entire hillside slum where Ronaldo grew up was covered in yellow and green flags. The average salary in Bento Ribeiro hasn't gone up much since Ronaldo moved out almost fifteen years ago, but that didn't stop the 68 bars in Bento from doing a thriving business.

In many of those bars there are photos of their local boy-made-good. Tripe soup can be ordered for under a dollar and the local drink, Condentao, costs about the same for a litre bottle.

In the local juniors football team, there are four kids called Ronaldo. It's not clear if there will be many more.

Meanwhile, in those same *favelas*, the killing of the innocents continue. More than 40 bodies, classified 'unidentified', are buried in the local cemetery every day. Many are children. In the nearest morgue, 3,000 unidentified corpses were disposed of in 2001. The majority were street children.

In Rio, they reckon two kids are assassinated every day by rogue policemen hired by local businessmen to rid the city of its 'vermin' ... one of those 'vermin' could just as easily turn out to be the next Ronaldo.

ACKNOWLEDGEMENTS

I owe many individuals who have helped me make this book possible my deepest thanks. But without Piers Thompson and Fergus Clarkson, this book would never have been written.

Also, my heartfelt gratitude to everyone in the warm and welcoming country of Brazil, whose help and guidance while investigating Ronaldo's remarkable life story was unwavering. Top of the list was my good friend Denis Wright, who fearlessly pursued many angles and leads on my behalf. Others across Brazil and the rest of the world include: Ruth de Aquine, Suzana Blass, Vivianne, George, Pedro Bial, Calango, Javier Montero, Renata Fraga, Harold Emert, Vinicius, Filé, Dan Bloom, Pierre Blomfield, Jacques Mertin, Paulo Rodi, Jon Ryan, John Blake and the staff of *Odia* newspaper in Rio.

There are numerous others including executives from the CBF and Nike who have asked that their identities remain secret.

The following books were extremely informative: *High Noon — A Year at Barcelona* by Jeff King, published by Virgin Books; *The Beautiful Game* by Chris Taylor, published by Victor Gollancz; *Bobby Robson — My Autobiography*, published by Macmillan; *Hand of God* by Jimmy Burns, published by Bloomsbury; *Football Babylon* by Russ Williams, published by Virgin; *The Beautiful Team* by Garry Jenkins, published by Simon and Schuster; and *Perfect Pitch*, edited by Simon Koper, published by Headline.

FOOTBALLOGRAPHY

Ronaldo — The Transfers:
1990 São Cristovao — cost nothing
1993 Cruzeiro — $30,000
1994 PSV Eindhoven — $6 million
1996 FC Barcelona — $20 million
1997 Inter Milan — $30 million

Total transfers (to September 2002): $56,030,000

Ronaldo — Wages:
Cruzeiro — $5,000 per month
PSV Eindhoven — $1 million per season
FC Barcelona — $1.5 million per season
Inter Milan — $5.2 million per season

Clubs:
1990–91 Social Ramos Club (Rio): 12 matches/8 goals
1991–93 São Cristovao (Rio): 54 matches/36 goals
1993–94 Cruzeiro (Beloa Horizonte): 60 matches/58 goals
1994–96 PSV Eindhoven: 56 matches/55 goals
1996–97 FC Barcelona: 37 matches/34 goals
1997–2002 Inter Milan: 69 matches/34 goals

International appearances: 57 matches/42 goals

International début: 24.3.1994 v. Argentina (2–1)

Honours/Titles won:
1991 — Winner of COMMEBOL U-16 championship
1994 — Member of Brazil's World Cup squad which went on to win
1995 — Runner-up with Brazil in Copa America
1995 — Top scorer in the Dutch league
1996 — Winner of Dutch Cup with PSV Eindhoven
1996 — Bronze medallist with Brazil at the 1996 Olympic Football Tournament
1997 — Winner of European Cup Winners Cup, FC Barcelona
1997 — Winner with Brazil in Copa America
1998 — Winner of UEFA Cup with Inter Milan
1998 — Runner-up with Brazil at the World Cup '98
2002 — World Cup Winners Medal

BRAZIL'S 2002 WORLD CUP CAMPAIGN

GROUP C
Brazil 2 Turkey 1
China 0 Costa Rica 2
Brazil 4 China 0
Costa Rica 1 Turkey 1
Costa Rica 2 **Brazil** 5
Turkey 3 China 0

GROUP C - FINAL TABLE

	P	W	D	L	F	A	Pts
Brazil	3	3	0	0	11	3	9
Turkey	3	1	1	1	5	3	4
Costa Rica	3	1	1	1	5	6	4
China	3	0	0	3	0	9	0

SECOND ROUND
Germany 1 Paraguay 0
Demark 0 England 3
Sweden 1 Senegal 2
Mexico 0 USA 2
Japan 0 Turkey 1
Spain 1 Republic of Ireland 1 (Spain won 3-2 penalties)
Brazil 2 Belgium 0
S Korea 2 Italy 1

QUARTER FINALS
England 1 **Brazil** 2
Germany 1 USA 0
Senegal 0 Turkey 1
Spain 0 S.Korea 0 (S.Korea win 5-3 penalties)

SEMI FINALS
Germany 1 S.Korea 0
Brazil 1 Turkey 0

THIRD PLACES
Korea 2 Turkey 3

FINAL **Brazil** 2 Germany 0

THE AUTHOR

WENSLEY CLARKSON is an invesigative journalist, who has written numerous non-fiction books, screenplays and television documentaries. His books have sold more than a million copies in seventeen countries worldwide. He has been an avid football fan since the age of nine.

'A bird came across a great fire in the forest and saw a hummingbird flying back and forth. Each time the hummingbird filled its beak in the river then flew back to the fire dropping its beads of water on to the flames.

The other bird stopped the hummingbird and asked, "I have been watching you a long time. What are you doing? Do you think you can extinguish the fire, are you crazy?"

The hummingbird replied, "No, I'm just here doing my part."'

An old Brazilian folk tale